Inward

Fieldwork Encounters and Discoveries
A series edited by Robert Emerson and Jack Katz

Inward

Vipassana Meditation and the Embodiment of the Self

MICHAL PAGIS

The University of Chicago Press
Chicago and London

The University of Chicago Press, Chicago 60637
The University of Chicago Press, Ltd., London
© 2019 by The University of Chicago
Published 2019
Printed in the United States of America

28 27 26 25 24 23 22 21 20 19   1 2 3 4 5

ISBN-13: 978-0-226-63938-3 (cloth)
ISBN-13: 978-0-226-36187-1 (paper)
ISBN-13: 978-0-226-63941-3 (e-book)
DOI: https://doi.org/10.7208/chicago/9780226639413.001.0001

Library of Congress Cataloging-in-Publication Data
Names: Pagis, Michal, author.
Title: Inward : vipassana meditation and the embodiment of the self / Michal Pagis.
Other titles: Fieldwork encounters and discoveries.
Description: Chicago : The University of Chicago Press, 2019. | Series: Fieldwork
    encounters and discoveries
Identifiers: LCCN 2018055501 | ISBN 9780226639383 (cloth : alk. paper) |
    ISBN 9780226361871 (pbk. : alk. paper) | ISBN 9780226639413 (e-book)
Subjects: LCSH: Vipasyana (Buddhism) | Meditation—Buddhism—Social
    aspects. | Mind and body. | Self.
Classification: LCC BQ5630.V5 P325 2019 | DDC 294.3/4435—dc23
LC record available at https://lccn.loc.gov/2018055501

♾ This paper meets the requirements of ANSI/NISO Z39.48-1992
(Permanence of Paper).

Contents

Acknowledgments

My debt of thanks runs wide and deep. First and foremost, I would like to express my gratitude to the many participants in this study, who welcomed me into their homes and their hearts. No less, I wish to thank the teachers and volunteers at the Vipassana Meditation Foundation in Israel, Illinois, and Massachusetts, whose hospitality and loving-kindness extended not only to their students but also to this researcher.

My scholarly community has long been my emotional and intellectual refuge. The focused attention of Andrew Abbott, Andreas Glaeser, John Lucy, Steven Collins, Erika Summers-Effler, and Jack Katz contributed immeasurably to this project. Specifically, Andreas Glaeser prompted me to pursue this line of research and modeled what it is to be a teacher, a scholar, and a person; Andrew Abbott's endless flow of fresh ideas showed me what creativity and independent thinking are all about; and Jack Katz's invaluable comments on this manuscript helped me to hone my argument and contribution. Wendy Cadge, Stephan Bargheer, Iddo Tavory, Karin Nisenbaum, and Naama Kopelman all offered sage advice at different phases of this project.

My colleagues in the sociology department at Bar Ilan University in Israel were my support network while writing. Financial support from the Schnitzer Foundation at Bar-Ilan University helped with the last stages toward publication. A special thanks to Sara Tropper, who copyedited the manuscript, for her fine editorial flair.

My final and most profound thanks go to my family. Without my parents, Rina and Alex Pagis, my sisters, Dalit and Ifat, my beloved son, Aran—who has never known life without this project—and most of all my husband, Udi, this book would never have been written. I am forever grateful for their love.

Note on Terminology

A number of Buddhist words appear in the book, all introduced in Pali, the scriptural language of Theravada Buddhism from which vipassana meditation originated. *Vipassanā*, the most used Pali word in the text, is pronounced by teachers and practitioners as vih-pah-san'-ah. Other Pali words include *nibbāna, samādhi, satipaṭṭhāna, ānāpāna, sutta, dhamma, dukkha, anatta,* and *mettā.* Many of these words are spelled with diacritical marks, as above; however, for ease of reading I have omitted those marks. I use the Pali terms and not the Sanskrit ones, as these are the terms used in the vipassana retreats I studied (e.g., nibbana and not nirvana, dhamma and not dharma, sutta and not sutra).

Turning Inward

Interiority has come into its own. More and more people are looking inward, toward their minds and bodies. This gaze is oriented through different channels and practices, many of which are based on religious or spiritual traditions. *Inward* is about one such practice: vipassana, a Buddhist meditation of mindfulness that involves a nonjudgmental or detached observation of the body and mind.

The practice of vipassana and the microsociological world that surrounds it form the core of this book. Yet the reader will be taken far beyond vipassana itself. In my inquiry, vipassana is used as a window onto the complex relations between bodies, selves, and social worlds. Through examining the phenomenological reality of vipassana practitioners, their silent interactions in meditation centers, their heightened sensitivity to the body, and their attempts to transform themselves and their social lives by monitoring bodily sensations, I supply a sociological framework for the study of the place of embodied awareness in processes of self-making. Such a framework enhances our understanding of the connection between inner self-relations and self-other relations, and of the role of the visceral body in linking the two.

What does it mean to look inward? What do we find when we do so? This is a challenging question, because the notion of inwardness implies an inversion of the usual direction of attention in everyday life. Generally attention is focused on the world in which one acts, that is, the world outside oneself. On a personal level, this world might be the text I am writing, the game I am playing, or the conversation I am having with a friend. In the course of such daily action, I am tacitly aware of different aspects of the embodiment of the self—adjusting my fingers on the keyboard when misspelling a word, feeling a pain in my back and moving in order to relieve it, noticing anger rising up and trying to control my desire to shout. This awareness is kept at the background of action and behavior in the world, as my focused attention is set on interaction with other people and things.

As social beings, we interact in the world with an awareness of how others perceive us. Thus in everyday interaction one diverts attention to one's body, emotion, or behavior in order to adjust to, or influence, others' perceptions of us. While such awareness of the embodiment of the self is key for social interaction, it is mostly under wraps, kept at the background of awareness, a base from which one attends to the world. It is the world that is at the focal point of attention, not one's interiority.

The kind of inward looking that this book investigates turns such activity inside out. It puts interiority at the focal point of attention, as a subject of interest in and of itself. Such inward looking may have a goal or vision that is connected to action in the world—one might go to a psychotherapist and speak about one's emotions in order to be a better mother. Or one might practice yoga in order to modulate one's reactions to feeling frustrated or anxious over the course of the day. But the situated practice of looking inward is distinct from daily action and engagement. It entails a diversion of attention away from the world and toward the self. Moreover, when we so divert our attention, we start "finding things." I, for example, discover emotions, thoughts, and sensations that are new to me and that are now becoming a part of who I am. My inner sphere expands as a whole world of interiority is revealed.

It is the diversion of attention away from daily engagement, the break in the flow of daily life that takes place during the gaze inward, that makes it such a compelling case for sociological inquiry. If we take seriously the sociological insight that the self is always embedded in social relations and interactions, then we are confronted with the question: what kinds of social worlds and social relations emerge when people adopt practices that shift their focus inward, toward the invisible dimensions of our being?

The challenge that such inward-looking practices present to sociological inquiry has led to a concern among sociologists that the "subjective turn" that characterizes modern culture represents a dissolution of the social fabric, with people becoming antisocial, overly individualistic, and perhaps even narcissistic.[1] However, such notions ignore the growing institutionalization of inward looking in social spheres that are becoming a central part of our society. These spheres are weaving new social fabrics and even creating new communities.

This book offers a microsociological account of one such inward-looking practice, an account that reveals that the turn inward relies on the surrounding social interactive sphere and thus cannot be characterized as antisocial or solitary. The reader will learn that the turn inward calls for the cultivation of a new relation, a new dialectic, between self and other, between self and the social world. A society of inward-looking individuals requires particular social relations, particular modes of social interaction that supply the collective base from which individuals explore their own subjectivity.

Meditation offers an extreme case of the turn inward because, more than other introspective techniques, it involves a radical turn away from the world. This is because meditation is not language based. The turn to meditation, and with it other bodily based practices, shows a shift from the previously popular "talking cure" (e.g., psychoanalysis) to corporeal methods that turn toward interiority.

Theories on the social base of introspection tend to stress language. Language is a shared symbolic system that is by definition social. We learn our words from other people. Our conversations with others serve as the basis of our conversations with ourselves. Indeed language is a natural candidate for the production of self-reflection, since it has an easily accessible reflexive capacity. Through language one can speak about oneself with others, produce biographical narratives, and engage in inner dialogues. G. H. Mead went so far as to claim, "I know of no other form of behavior than the linguistic in which the individual is an object to himself, and so, as far as I can see, the individual is not a self in the reflexive sense unless he is an object to himself."[2]

The notion that language is the primary channel through which individuals explore themselves is evident in many self-reflective practices and techniques in contemporary Western culture. Foucault's inquiry into the power of self-verbalization, originating from the practice of confession and migrating into the consulting room, offers various examples.[3] The therapeutic discourse, which is based on the talking cure and with it on improving communication skills, rests on what Eva Illouz has dubbed the "textualization of subjectivity."[4] We talk about ourselves, we write in diaries, we write blogs, we go to therapists and life coaches, we engage in endless conversations about who we are.

Alongside practices that are based on verbalization of the self, however, other self-reflexive techniques have penetrated the contemporary culture of self-introspection. In the main, these techniques stem from societies that are suspicious of language as a medium for self-knowledge. They prefer a different medium for turning inward—the medium of the body. Yoga, meditation, healing, and alternative medicine are just a few examples of practices that turn to the body in order to produce self-knowledge, self-mastery, and self-grounding.

In contrast to practices of inward looking that rely on the inherent reflexive capacity of language and symbols, bodily based introspective tech-

niques rely on the reflexive capacity of the body. Such practices involve awareness of processes of meaning-making that are embedded within the somatic
level. Somatic or embodied meaning-making processes have received much
sociological attention in the past several decades.[5] Yet embodied semiotics is
usually understood as subconscious and habitual, captured by the notion of
"habitus," a dimension of self that is hidden from direct reflection.[6] Taking
a totally different tack, bodily based introspective techniques transform this
dimension of selfhood into an overt subject of awareness. These practices,
vipassana meditation among them, are cultural-specific ways that bring the
tacit "inner lining" of experience to the forefront of attention, rendering it a
subject of reflection and manipulation.

What is tacit about the inner lining of experience? Of course we routinely
attend to our bodies. But this attention is recruited to action in the world. My
interaction with you follows bodily cues and nonverbal responses and expressions. If I see you are having a difficult time listening, I might raise my voice
or change my tone. I search your response for indications regarding my "self,"
I attend to the "me" that is reflected back to me, adjusting my body accordingly. If you smile at me and I interpret this smile as a friendly gesture, I will
smile back. If you smile at me and I sense an attempt to humiliate me, I will
react in shame or anger.

Self-awareness in interaction requires a dialectic movement between self
and other, between attending to the external social world and attending to
the body as a base from which action takes place.[7] In this dialectic movement,
the inner lining of experience is tacit. I do not concentrate on my breath or
on the tension in my muscles. My breath, my muscle tension, and my heartbeat act as a base for my behavior and are available for reflection, but during
interaction are not the primary objects of attention.

Now, imagine starting to tilt this dialectic in a way that the body becomes
more central to my attention, while others and the social world turn into aids
or anchors from which I investigate my body. So when I feel my muscles contracting into a smile, instead of focusing on your response to my smile, I divert my attention to these muscles. Or when I touch you, instead of focusing
on how you feel, I shift my attention to how my hand feels while touching you.
Or when I talk to you, instead of focusing on your responses to my words, I
focus on the sound of my voice or the movement of my tongue.

This is not an easy task. As an experiment, try touching the end of this
book, or the end of tablet on which you are reading the electronic version
of this book, and feel it—it is most likely smooth and straight. Now try to
feel your finger touching the book or the tablet. This is quite complicated. As
Merleau-Ponty writes, "the moment perception comes my body effaces itself

before it and never does the perception grasp the body in the act of perceiving."[8] Instead of simply feeling the world, you are trying to feel yourself feeling the world. This requires attending to the inner lining of experience, which
normally serves as a background to our actions.

Such an inversion of the usual order of attention for prolonged and con-
densed periods does not jibe well with mundane social life. Vipassana meditation and other such inward-looking practices originated in relatively monastic spheres and were not designed to be practiced by the masses. To borrow
Weber's typology of religion, meditative practices represent a religious "flight"
from the world.[9] In Buddhist terms, vipassana tries to expose "ultimate
reality," a reality quite distinct from the conventional one. This is why meditative practices were traditionally done either in solitude or in the company
of other monks, and accompanied by renunciation, withdrawing from the
everyday social order and joining an alternative one.

Recent years have seen a growing attempt to integrate meditation into
conventional life. Long meditation retreats and daily practice of meditation
are becoming increasingly common, with individuals keen on cultivating the
ability to track the inner lining of experience, to feel themselves feeling the
world.

How can we account for such allocation of time and energy to this effort?
What do people find when they divert their attention to the inner lining of experience? What kind of alternative social order enables such process of cultivation? How do people utilize the practice of meditation and extend it to their
daily lives? What kind of tensions and resonances then emerge? And last,
what can the inversion of attention in vipassana meditation teach us about
relations between self-body-other in other contexts?

The Journey

Sitting at his office at a major American university, Peter, a professor of computer science, recalls what attracted him to vipassana.[10] Several years ago he
sought something that could help him, or as he puts it, provide answers to the
questions that he had about life. Having a Quaker father, he had encountered
meditation in the past: "I wasn't raised with that directly but that was present,
that was part of my secondhand experience, and I have gone to that a couple
of times." Yet he was not interested in religious belief or a religious community and felt quite remote from Christianity. He read some Buddhist texts and
tried learning meditation from books, but he found that "reading about it
doesn't do anything. . . . Even if you try it once then you have doubts — 'wow,
this doesn't look as amazing as they said it would be' — and then you don't do

it again." When he heard about a ten-day vipassana retreat from a friend, who
described the course as a "meditation boot camp," he decided to give it a try:
"The moment I heard this description I knew I really needed it, since it forces
you to try the teaching now. So other teachings pointed towards it, but without the structure to make it happen, it is extremely difficult, I think, for people
to get very far in it, to really understand it, to really confront it."

A chilly spring day several weeks hence finds me entering the meditation
hall at the vipassana meditation center in Illinois, near the city of Rockford.
The center used to be a small countryside farm, and the meditation hall was
originally a residential house, whose inner walls were torn down to create a
large open space. Besides the meditation hall, the center includes a kitchen
and dining hall, dorms for retreat participants, and dorms for the volunteer
staff and teachers, each facility located in a separate building and connected
by walking trails.

I remove my shoes at the entrance to the meditation hall, then slowly and
quietly take my seat on a small meditation cushion and mattress. The lights
are dim as I peer around at the unadorned white walls. Less than two feet away
other meditators sit on similar mattresses and cushions. The hall, which could
hold fifty people, is not full. I recognize Peter from afar, on the male side of
the hall, but conforming to the norm of silence, I do not gesture to him. A
moment later the meditation teacher enters and sits down on a higher seat at
the front of the hall. Facing the meditators and without a word, he presses a
button. The sound of recorded chanting begins, followed by the familiar voice
of the head teacher S. N. Goenka instructing me to concentrate on my breath.
I close my eyes and enter meditation.

A year later, on the other side of the Atlantic, I am again sitting, this time
in the comfortable living room of a house located in an upscale Israeli suburb,
interviewing Sharon, mother of two and successful self-employed graphic designer. I had met Sharon several months earlier at the Israeli vipassana meditation center in Hazeva, a small village in the desert. We shared a room at a
ten-day meditation retreat with two other students, yet we had exchanged not
a single word. In the meditation hall I could see Sharon in the row in front
of me, meditating silently. Our eyes would meet in the room while we waited
for the shower or in the dining hall as we stood in line for food, but all I knew
about her was her name and that this was her fourth meditation retreat. Only
on the last day, when the participants were allowed to speak, did we find ourselves in deep conversation.

Sharon offers me tea along with a retrospective of her encounter with
vipassana.[11] Three years ago, when she and her husband had been at a coffee

shop with friends, one friend, "who is totally not a spiritual person, a very material person, works in marketing, who was very stressed at that time," told them that he had decided to "do something for relaxation, to go to a ten-day silent vipassana retreat in the desert." This was the first time she had ever heard the word *vipassana*, but something about this ten-day silence attracted her, and she found herself saying, "You know what, that suits me too—I also want to go." The timing was perfect in terms of work, she recounts, and she felt lucky that a space suddenly opened up in the already-full registration. Sharon recalls that she had no sense of what awaited her: "When I got there, I realized I had no idea what I had gotten myself into. I did not know vipassana was a type of meditation; it was a complete surprise that you sit silently with yourself—and that is it." When she went to the first retreat, she did not think she would ever attend another, yet something in the experience captivated her. She tried meditating at home alone, but finding that her focus diminished with time, she decided to join a weekly group vipassana sitting. Family- and work-related pressures shot up over the year, and eventually she decided to return to the meditation center for another vipassana retreat.

Sharon and Peter are two among many vipassana practitioners I met during my fieldwork. For three years I conducted extensive participant observation in the two vipassana centers described above and in weekly vipassana groups in the vicinity of Chicago and Tel Aviv. Together with the Massachusetts vipassana center (visited briefly) and myself as an autoethnographical field site, these people and spaces form the backbone of this book. The fieldwork continued sporadically for another five years as I periodically contacted practitioners for informal follow-up conversations.

The choice for research in Israel and the United States stems from my own biography. In 2002, three years before I embarked on this research, I participated in a ten-day vipassana course in Israel, my home country, at the same meditation center where a few years later I met Sharon. I had long been interested in trying meditation, and a friend recommended vipassana. I had some background in yoga and tai chi, both of which are practiced in circles where meditation is highly regarded. This prior taste of vipassana sparked my sociological curiosity, mainly because I perceived a resonance between the meditative attitude and phenomenological/constructivist sociological perspectives. Yet at that time I had no intention of turning vipassana into an object of sociological investigation, and I continued to practice it sporadically without returning to meditation retreats.

Fast-forward three years: I was studying at the University of Chicago when the first vipassana meditation center opened near Chicago, using the teaching method I had learned in Israel—vipassana meditation as taught by S. N.

Goenka. This captured my attention, and I discovered meditation groups dotting the university campus, including a vipassana group. Mindfulness was on the rise, becoming a visible social phenomenon. No longer confined to alternative circles, it called out for sociological inquiry.

In Israel I saw that a similar process was taking place: meditation was entering the mainstream. At this point I felt the time was ripe for me to embark on this study.[12] Thereafter I traveled back and forth between the US and Israel, conducting fieldwork in both sites. These two locations, Israel and the United States, represent two non-Buddhist "Western" social contexts in which meditation practice in general, and vipassana in particular, has become extraordinarily popular.

Vipassana meditation, also known by the terms *insight* and *mindfulness*, involves silent and still, nonjudgmental observation of the body-mind phenomenon. In a nutshell, this means paying full attention to thoughts, feelings, and sensations without holding onto them or acting on them. In contrast to other meditations, vipassana does not require a mantra or an external object such as a candle or a picture to focus on. Instead it uses the universally accessible body and mind as objects of attention. Therefore one can practice some level of vipassana when engaged in other activities—when eating, driving, washing dishes, or even in conversation. Still, the main practice is compartmentalized into specific temporal and spatial frames, either in solitude or with others, usually in a sitting position. Some schools also teach vipassana while walking slowly.[13]

Vipassana has long been practiced in Southeast Asia in Theravada Buddhist countries (e.g., Burma, Thailand, Sri Lanka), penetrating the "West" only recently. The presence of nonmonastic vipassana meditation centers in both Buddhist and non-Buddhist locations is considered a modern phenomenon.[14] Traditionally vipassana has been practiced mainly by monks, but the twentieth century saw the emergence of Buddhist reformation movements that advocate meditation practice to the laity. The opening of vipassana to the laity eventually led to its exportation to the West.

Around the world, one finds different vipassana schools that follow slightly different versions of the practice.[15] Vipassana Meditation as Taught by S. N. Goenka has been at the forefront of pushing the popularization of vipassana meditation among non-Buddhists. This school emphasizes the tracking of bodily sensations through a technique called "body scan," which has won many practitioners in other vipassana and mindfulness schools.

Centers that follow Goenka's teachings—two hundred worldwide and eleven in the US—use almost identical teachings, with some variations oriented to Hindu and Buddhist audiences. Like other vipassana teaching schools, such as the popular Insight Meditation Society (IMS), the centers offer meditation retreats ranging from one to sixty days, conducted in almost complete silence, and besides vipassana, teach breathing meditation (*anapana*) and *metta* meditation (loving-kindness). This structure of teaching was imported from SouteEast Asia with some adaptations to a non-Buddhist Western audience.

When I began my research, I was planning to add a comparative view between Israel and the United States. Since the teachings in this specific vipassana school are standardized, I was interested to see what happens to this standardization when it encounters different audiences. I soon found out that the audience in the two locations is extremely similar. In fact, I realized that if I were to erase the language and specific cultural and social identifications, it would probably be impossible to differentiate between the Israeli and American interviews. In both locations I met doctoral students, lawyers, psychotherapists, financial advisers, teachers, and physicians—the full gamut of professions from the upper-middle socioeconomic class. Their religious identification also overlapped, as most neither self-identified as Buddhists nor considered themselves religious in any other tradition. (Self-definitions varied from secular to agnostic to atheist to spiritual.)

In addition, their motivations, goals, and interests seemed to reflect a distinctly global trend. Doron, age forty, an Israeli engineer, turned to vipassana after his divorce in the hopes of finding happiness, while Rachel, forty, an American graphic designer, began vipassana after she and her husband split up and her mother died. Jessica, fifty-two, an American who is employed by an NGO, was hoping that vipassana would help her manage her alcoholism. Dana, thirty, an Israeli scientist, tried TM for a while and then moved to vipassana to deal with her chronic depression. Tony, thirty-three, an Israeli financial adviser, sought out vipassana in the process of reevaluating his career choice, while Daniel, twenty-six, an American aspiring artist, began when his professional accomplishments seemed too distant from his professional dreams.

Doron, Rachel, and the other vipassana practitioners I met in Israel and the US shared with me life stories which, when juxtaposed, reveal joint patterns. I use the term *practitioners* as shorthand for a varied group of individuals connected by participation in at least one ten-day meditation retreat and some self-reported level of current practice. Some practice one or two hours a day, some only for fifteen minutes on the train or before nodding off to sleep. Some turn to meditation in moments of need (e.g., when feeling stressed) but do not practice regularly. Their level of practice and their visits to meditation centers fluctuate as they move along their life trajectory. These are a small fraction of the millions around the world who experiment with the practice of meditation, an estimated thirty million in the US (including but not limited to vipassana practice).[16] They are a part of a growing, visible phenomenon found among the upper-middle educated strata in postindustrial locations, in which people turn to the body in the hope of finding solutions to their daily, this-worldly concerns.

The Argument

I undertook this research piqued by the puzzles that emerged from the quasi-monastic, somewhat exotic, nonmundane nature of vipassana practice. I ended it with the realization that vipassana bears much resemblance to many other practices—including, among others, dieting, physical training, smoking and even the most mundane coffee breaks and bathing rituals—in which individuals turn their focused attention to the background embodiment of the self, to the part of our being that is tacit or invisible in ordinary social life. In this sense vipassana meditation is a collectively honored, institutionalized occasion for doing in an explicit and elaborated way what is a natural part of life.

To be human is to be social and corporeal at the same time. Thus when engaging with the world one needs to deal with two dimensions, or tracks of attention.[17] I need to attend both to my body in action and to the way the world and especially social others respond to my action. A common solution to this problem is to push the embodiment of the self to the background, to "turn it tacit." This does not mean that this embodiment is completely disregarded—in fact, everyday life is filled with moments in which I need to attend to the inner lining of experience: I do so every time I bite my tongue or miss a step. But these inversions of the direction of attention represent interferences with competent behavior, as I struggle to return to position and continue my action.[18]

I argue that alongside our daily mundane mode of attention, we find practices that encourage and invite people to relax their focus on the responses of others, to relax their focus on social engagement with the world. This is done through a prolonged and deliberate turn to the background embodiment of the self. While these practices have "solitary" and "private" dimensions, they are not asocial. In fact such practices are encouraged and incorporated by communities, institutions, and routines.

From a sociological point of view, we turn ourselves into objects by using reflections that are communicated to us from the gestures and responses of others.[19] Daily interaction requires constant attention to the way others see us, to our behavior as perceived by others. Since our selves are dependent on others, we project somewhat different selves depending on the social context—as a mother I respond to the way my son sees me, while as a professor I respond to the way my students see me. In everyday life, my friends, family, and colleagues portray a self for me, have expectations of my behavior, expectations to which I must respond or take into account.

In the context of meditation, I illustrate how vipassana represents a hard, concentrated effort, accomplished with the help of others, to stay away from the self as seen by others. This effort takes place in the meditation center, in weekly group meditation sittings, or in solitary daily practice at home. Yet the effort is not limited to the situated practice on the cushion. It tends to spill over into daily life, as practitioners turn to their inner lining as a way to manage the shocks and splits to the self as they move through social relations in their daily life.

For vipassana meditators, the practice supplies an experience of "embodied transcendence," as the body is what transcends all the situations we are in, all the social selves we produce.[20] When shifting attention to the inner lining of experience, when pushing the awareness of the self as viewed by others to the background, meditators find an affirmation of existence that is not dependent on relations or interactions with others. It provides a solution to the experiences of anxiety and rapture that characterize the life of my informants, and with it many others in the contemporary world.[21]

Vipassana is one way of achieving such embodied transcendence. For others it can be fasting, jogging, playing music, smoking, or sex. All these practices represent institutionalized spheres in which people turn their focused attention to what many sociologists assume to be as the dispositional, practical, nonreflective dimension of social life.[22] It is through this attention to the inner lining that people help each other to forget about others—to use the social group to decrease attention to the way others see them. It is through attending to the most conventional, mundane details of the background embodiment of the self that people discover the possibility of transcending social situatedness and social dependency.

Importantly, the process described in this book in the context of vipassana is but the tip of the iceberg, an extreme case of the intertwining between the private and the public, the visible and the invisible, the collective and the solitary. The social world in this sense supplies institutionalized practices that serve as a pause from the social game of active and engaged interaction. It supplies communities, routines, and rituals, some of which are considered religious, some secular, through which practitioners turn inward without stepping out of society, experience solitude without being isolated, and thus negotiate the tensions that arise from the dual nature of human beings. Through these practices people find ways to be both social and corporeal, ways to relax anxieties regarding what others see or think, a bodily based transcendence that enables a smooth transition between social relations.

Overview of Chapters

I have two main goals for the use that I make in the book of the rich ethnographic data I collected. The first is explaining the social world of vipassana practice and the appeal of this practice to contemporary postindustrial society. The second is using vipassana as a window for understanding the place of the body in processes of self-making, an understanding that can be generalized to other practices and social worlds.

The second chapter, "The Popularization of Meditation," introduces the historical and cultural context of this ethnographic study, illustrating how vipassana, a previously monastic practice, was transformed into a modern self-reflexive practice that concerns the phenomenology of the self. The chapter identifies four stages in the diffusion process of vipassana from its monastic context in Southeast Asia to the contemporary Western secular sphere. In each stage, meditation, and particularly vipassana, was carried by social, political, and economic changes, being a fraction of something much larger and significant. In the first stage, as a reaction to colonialism, Buddhist evangelistic movements moved vipassana from its traditional monastic sphere into that of the laity, a development that was picked up by Burmese politicians as a way to produce a new national and collective identity. Second, vipassana was a small slice of the exotic "Oriental" interests of intellectual and economic elites in the US and Europe, alongside esoteric societies and occult-oriented groups such as Theosophy. Third, in the sixties vipassana was imported to the West by middle-class European and American young adults as a part of their search for lifestyles that defied normative authority. Last, vipassana was picked up by parts of the intellectual stratum in the West—neuroscientists, psychiatrists, and university students who bridged science and meditation, moving meditation from Buddhism and counterculture to the mind/body health model. The chapter locates the specific school of meditation studied in this book within the much larger field of contemporary meditation practice, clarifying the ways in which the findings of this study can be generalized to other forms of meditation teaching.

The third chapter, "Collective Solitude," illustrates that diverting attention inward to the inner lining of experience is hardly an individualistic or asocial process. The phenomenology of selfhood this book tracks is produced through sharing an intersubjective space where self-other relations influence and enable the cultivation of self-to-self relations. This community, shaped by the conditions of the silent meditation center that I term "collective solitude," enables participants to entrust their interactive urge to still and silent others, to pause from direct and acknowledged social engagement. The chapter tracks a shift from interactions that require thinking about others and their reactions, such as performing a still body or feeling guilt about interfering with others, to interactions based on rhythmic and emotional synchronization and mutual attunement. As I will demonstrate, this silent community is an important foundation for the later solitary practice which takes place at home, in which meditators utilize sensory cues associated with group meditation to reconstruct a meditative environment. Paradoxically, meditation participants need others in order to forget about others. They utilize the group to put aside their social concerns and enter the meditative state.

The fourth chapter, "Meditation in Daily Life," tracks how practitioners use vipassana in ways that make it relevant to their lives and selves outside of the meditation center. It illustrates how the technique that originally helped monks to disconnect from the taken-for-granted reality of daily life is now helping individuals to *maintain* daily life, offering solutions to this-world concerns. The chapter opens with a description of the situated practice of vipassana as taught in meditation retreats, elaborating on the inversion in the direction of attention on which vipassana practice is based. The chapter then moves to the perceptions and accounts of practitioners as they try to generalize the experiences they encounter in the situated practice to their life outside of the meditation center in two contexts: first, in the relatively compartmentalized daily meditation sittings, and second, while acting and interacting in the world. In both contexts, meditators use vipassana to bridge the shocks and splits of the self as they move between social situations and relations—from work to home to driving to job interviews or romantic dates. Daily meditation sittings turn into spaces where one "cleans" or "processes" emotional situations or pauses from daily life and social judgments so as to return with "charged batteries." Brief moments of observing breath and sensations while acting in the world are used by practitioners to withhold their routine response to situations, or in their words, to "check" and "catch" themselves. Vipassana practitioners thus turn the body into a central medium for discovering, knowing, monitoring, and healing selves.

The fifth chapter, "Negotiating Intimate Relations," analyzes the ways meditators and their significant others negotiate intimate social relations. Building on Weber's theory of world-rejecting religions, the chapter tracks the "world-rejecting" and "otherworldly" traces that are embedded in the practice of vipassana. The chapter returns to the meditation center, illustrating how meditation retreats serve as unique social spaces for training in a specific mode of social interaction. In the meditation center, participants learn to be with others while decreasing the awareness of the self that is projected to them from the eyes of others, keeping such awareness tacit. They learn to disengage from the self that is outlined for them by their significant others and focus on the inner lining of experience. This meditative interaction mode tends to seep into everyday life and into different social circles, sometimes in resonance and sometime in tension with the anticipations of intimate others. While management of anger is considered a positive and useful use of vipassana, significant others also attribute to vipassana a level of social withdrawal, of reduced motivation for playing the social game. Significant others' perception of change is then picked up by meditators, who react to these judgments and evaluations. The chapter follows the perspectives and interpretations of both meditators and their significant others, and the tensions and debates that arise from conflicting demands and expectations.

The sixth chapter, "Becoming a Meditator," presents the life trajectories of vipassana practitioners and the life-course orientations they use to organize their biographies in relation to meditation practice. With the exportation of meditation to the "West" and as part of becoming a nonreligious practice, vipassana lost the traditional social institutional frame that organizes progress in meditation. Practitioners themselves now make sense of their practice and formulate answers that provide biographically based meaning and motivation. These answers are not rigid but change over time in conversation with the life of the practitioner. The chapter identifies three life-course orientations that together capture the way meditators integrate the practice into their biography. The first is meditation as a tool in departing from an unwanted past experience of self toward a more desirable experience of self. The second is meditation as a way to maintain a desirable self that was found to be fragile and difficult to sustain. The third is meditation as a way of life, a trajectory that characterizes serious meditators who were wholly taken by the practice. The chapter illustrates that in the two first trajectories, the question whether meditation "works" is central to the way meditators locate vipassana in their lives and find the impetus to continue to meditate. In the last trajectory of serious meditators, such "internal" commitment is externalized as social circles are recruited to strengthen it.

The seventh and concluding chapter, "Bodies, Selves, and Social Worlds," offers an interactionist and phenomenology-based analytical frame for the role of attention to the inner lining in everyday life. The chapter ties the previous chapters together and models the relation between self and social world that takes place in vipassana practice. It then extends the suggested frame and analyzes a variety of practices that are homologues to vipassana—that is, have an equivalent structure and pattern, though not necessary the same use and experience—beginning with the more extreme practices that dramatize the inversion of attention and gradually moving to the more familiar social world. The practices analyzed include embodied therapies such as biofeedback, tai chi, and yoga; body-cultivation techniques such as jogging, going to the gym, juicing, or dieting; preparations for public performances such as playing musical scales and training in ballet; deviant behaviors such as eating disorders, self-cutting, and taking drugs; and last, everyday life practices such as sex, smoking, and eating. The chapter ends with a discussion of religious practices that are based on attending to the inner lining, such as fasting, praying, singing, and pilgrimages, illustrating how the transcendence that religions focus on thematically is elicited corporeally by embodied religious practices, connecting abstract and spiritual ideas of salvation to the most mundane, personal bodily experience.

Through following practitioners of vipassana meditation, *Inward* sheds light on the role of the body in the production and maintenance of self while retaining a microsociological perspective on the self as connected and contextualized in social relations. Taking the reader on a journey into the world of modern meditation practice, the book draws on and extends the embodied-based approach to the study of subjectivity and offers a novel perspective on the study of the tacit dimension of social life.

The Popularization of Meditation

In 2005 the Dalai Lama delivered a speech at the annual meeting of the Society for Neuroscience (SFN) in Washington, DC. The largest scientific conference in the world, the SFN hosts more than thirty thousand participants each year. In that meeting, two thousand neuroscientists gathered to hear the Dalai Lama's presentation, "The Neuroscience of Meditation." Richard J. Davidson, professor of psychology and psychiatry in Madison, Wisconsin, director of the Laboratory for Affective Neuroscience, and named one of Time magazine's one hundred "most influential people," had suggested this specific speaker and this particular talk.

Apparently having a distinguished neuroscientist on your side does not prevent controversy. Prior to the conference, the president of the SFN had been deluged by correspondence from researchers opposing or supporting the invitation of the Dalai Lama. The former group opined that the SFN ought not to mix religion and science. The latter argued that meditation is not a religious practice but rather an important subject of neuroscientific inquiry. After a long debate, the SFN council approved the lecture. And thus it happened: the Dalai Lama stood in his orange robe before a rapt audience of thousands and spoke of the similarities between Buddhist contemplative techniques and neuroscience, the positive impact of meditation practice, and the benefits that can accrue from collaborative research.

To put this into context, imagine an SFN conference in which the pope is invited to speak about the benefits of prayer as a contemplative technique, pushing for collaboration between neuroscientists and Christian monks. Such a scenario hardly seems plausible. However, fifty or even thirty years ago the appearance of the Dalai Lama at an SFN conference had been equally unthinkable. His lecture, which linked meditation, a Buddhist spiritual practice, with neuroscience, arguably the epitome of secularism and materialism, is only a particularly dramatic example of the widespread penetration of meditation practice into everyday life. Everywhere teachers of various Buddhist meditations, such as vipassana, Zen, or Tibetan, are touting the benefits of meditation: inner peace, stress reduction, and improved interpersonal relationships.

Classical sociologists have claimed that we are moving into a secularist, science-based, society, one that is characterized by a "disenchantment of the world."[1] In the past fifty years, a growing number of sociologists of religion have rejected this secularization theory, noting that in fact religion has hardly disappeared from rational life.[2] Still, while religion is incontrovertibly alive and well in multiple public spheres, the frontiers of science have been considered a bastion of secularization. And so the public presence of the Dalai Lama at the SFN raised considerable controversy. Yet alongside this contestation we see a growing and simultaneous embrace of science and secularism, on the one hand, and practices and perspectives that originate in Buddhist traditions, on the other. Stripped of their authoritarian and law-based background, these practices retain an inward-looking and self-explorative dimension.

This chapter follows the process of diffusion of meditation at large and vipassana in particular from its traditional monastic home to its contemporary configuration as a modern, secular self-reflexive practice. It centers on four main historical stages, illustrating how in each stage vipassana meditation was swept along with broader social changes, a single element of a larger social movement. In each stage vipassana changed its role, audience, and agents, shifting from a monastic practice to the promotion of Burmese national identity to an esoteric spiritual movement to a counterculture practice to a science-based technique for self-exploration and psychotherapy.

Meditation is a self-cultivation practice that aims to transform the way one experiences both self and world. However, in different social and cultural contexts actors have used what they have perceived as the transformative power of meditation to advance different goals—religious, nationalistic, political, or resistance. In its process of diffusion, meditation was progressively disassociated from these broader social currents and frames of significance, gradually receiving an independent standing that converges around the self. Over time it became an instrument for coping with this-worldly problems, a sphere where one can embrace a fresh, somewhat otherworldly experience without needing to cross borders or enter foreign territory.

From Monasticism to Lay Meditation Practice

Our journey takes us back to the Theravada Buddhist countries of the twentieth century, where we will explore the transformations that took place in the practice of Buddhism as a whole.[3] Originating in ancient India, Theravada is considered the oldest form of Buddhism, more ancient than Mahayana Buddhism and Vajrayana Buddhism. Theravada Buddhism is practiced today in Southeast Asia, particularly in Burma, Laos, Thailand, Sri Lanka, and Cambodia, while Mahayana is mainly practiced in China and Japan, and Vajrayana Buddhism in Tibet. Each of these Buddhist traditions features somewhat different meditation practices.

A number of Buddhist-based meditation practices have become popular in the Western world, including Zen meditation (Mahayana), Tibetan meditation as taught in the Shambala school (Vajrayana), and vipassana meditation (Theravada). In Theravada Buddhism, vipassana is considered a central practice on the path toward enlightenment, a path traditionally reserved for those who chose to live a monastic life and engage in introspection, being "constantly mindful of body and mind in the present."[4] The following historical review focuses on vipassana meditation and its popularization in Theravada Buddhist locations, with an emphasis on Burma (present-day Myanmar).

Before the end of the nineteenth century, the places we know today as "Buddhist meditation centers" did not exist, in either Buddhist or non-Buddhist locations. In Buddhist regions one could learn to practice meditation by going to the monastery. Nonmonastic institutional spheres that propagate meditation to the laity are a modern phenomenon.[5] Even in Thailand and Burma, where there is a long history of temporarily ordaining boys for a short period, lay meditation practice was not common. From the beginning of the twentieth century onward, however, the practice of Buddhism began to shift, and with it the practice of vipassana meditation changed too. A hundred years ago it was rare to find laypeople practicing meditation, but in contemporary Burma and Thailand, millions of Buddhists spend days or even months in silent meditation centers.[6]

This transformation can be traced to the British occupation of Burma in 1885 and to the modernization and urbanization of Southeast Asia. In her historical study of the mass meditation movement in Burma, Ingrid Jordt shows that the teaching of meditation to the laity, which began in Burma and continued in other Theravada countries such as Thailand and Sri Lanka, was a response to colonialism. This propagation was advocated by different evangelistic Buddhist movements, whose success can be grasped only when one understands their connections to political spheres and the ways in which lay meditation practice enhanced national and religious identification following Burma's independence in 1947.[7]

The rise of lay meditation practice led to a blurring of the traditional distinction found in Buddhist societies between monks and laity. This distinction is central in Southeast Asia, and many scholars argue that Theravada Buddhism is split into two different religions—one for monks and another for householders.[8] According to the traditional folk ideal of Theravada Buddhism, it is monks who are expected to attain enlightenment. Householders are only supposed to support the monks on the path by giving donations.[9] This distinction between the role of the monk and the role of the householder safeguarded the authority and status of the monastic order. Not unlike other monastic traditions, such as those found in Christianity, the monks had access to knowledge and texts that laity did not (being illiterate), and with knowledge comes authority. [10] Perhaps more important in this case, the monks had access to certain spiritual exercises that were kept semi-secret from the laity. In traditional Buddhism, monks maintained that vipassana should be learned only after years of practicing *samadhi* (concentration). Establishing such high levels of concentration could take years of practice, usually in faraway forests and secluded caves. Thus vipassana practice was mostly limited to a small group of meditation virtuosi.

The new reformation movements that emerged in Southeast Asia around the beginning of the twentieth century challenged the distinction between monks and the laity. These movements claimed that everyone, regardless of his or her knowledge of Buddhist texts or experience in concentration training, can practice vipassana, gain insight into the real nature of reality, and progress on the path toward enlightenment.[11] As Erik Braun informs us, while the idea of starting meditation practice directly with vipassana can be found in the canonical and authoritative Theravada Buddhist texts, this style of practice was little known and of secondary importance. Moreover, meditation had never been promoted to a mass audience.[12] By advancing on this path, the new movements challenged the centrality of the study of Buddhist texts (an important part of monastic practice). Every believer now had access to mystical and spiritual experiences, confronting the "monopoly" of the monks over enlightenment.

Scholars and Buddhist leaders disagree over whether these movements indeed represent a break from "traditional Buddhism"—if such a system ever existed.[13] According to Jordt, the past two centuries have witnessed multiple Buddhist reformation movements, each involving a revival of meditation practice among both monks and the laity.[14] Such reformations always included what she calls a "purification" of the monastic community, shaking up the old power structures and refreshing them. In addition, contemporary Buddhist reform movements stress that according to the Buddhist scriptures Siddhartha Gautama (the Buddha) did not instruct those who sought salvation to become monks (although he did request some degree of renunciation).[15] Still, the influence and range of the new reformation movements are much wider in scope than those of previous ones. Thus we can say that the mass lay meditation movement does represent a rupture in the stronghold of monastic institutions over meditation practice.

The Buddhist shift bears intercultural resonance. Christianity, for example, experienced such a seismic movement with the rise of Protestantism, which led to "monasticism in this world." The Protestant Reformation stressed personal responsibility, direct access to God, and autonomy of religious practice. It accentuated engagement with worldly suffering and an egalitarian perspective as Protestant priests served the community, spending time with the dying and offering advice on personal problems.

The transformation of Buddhism in Southeast Asia shows similar characteristics, and some scholars have gone so far as to dub this transformation "Protestant Buddhism."[16] Enlightenment is no longer restricted to monks; every believer can progress on the path and have direct access to spiritual experiences. Monks have become more this-world-oriented, either through the teaching of meditation to the laity or through what is called in the literature "engaged Buddhism"—taking stands on social and political issues.[17] Moreover, lay followers have been given the status of meditation teachers, taking on important communal functions that were previously reserved for monks.

This transformation becomes obvious when we trace the lineage of teachers who practice vipassana. The notion of lineage, or chain of teachers, is used in contemporary meditation schools to legitimize persons and practices. In this context, lineage means a direct and personal relation between a mentor and a student in which specific techniques of meditation practice were passed on. Through lineage, meditation schools anchor their teaching in the "greater" past, accentuating the continuity of practice while often playing down changes that have been made to the teaching.

We can trace the lineage of vipassana meditation as taught by S. N. Goenka to the end of the nineteenth century, to the Burmese monk Ledi Sayadaw (1846–1923; *Sayadaw* denotes a royal teacher), a famous scholar and meditation master known for his reform perspectives who wrote texts oriented to a nonmonastic audience. Saya Thetgye, his close disciple, was a Burmese farmer who renounced his householder life at the age of thirty, after the death of his two children in a cholera epidemic. In 1914 Saya Thetgye was given permission by Ledi Sayadaw to teach meditation. In 1937 a government official by the name of U Ba Khin (who in 1948, with the end of the British colonial occupation, became the first accountant general of Burma) began his meditation training with Saya Thetgye. In 1952 U Ba Khin opened an international meditation center in Rangoon, where he taught both local and foreign students in Burmese and English.[18] S. N. Goenka, a Hindu businessman born in Burma, received his meditation training in this center from 1955 to 1969 and eventually became a teacher outside Burma.

This glance at the lineage is instructive. While the first teacher was a monk ordained in childhood (as were his teachers before him), the three teachers who followed began their adult life as householders, and neither U Ba Khin nor S. N. Goenka ever renounced family life. This line thus begins with a monk, follows with a renounced householder and then a Burmese government official, and ends with a non-Buddhist businessman. U Ba Khin worked as a government official and served as a meditation teacher simultaneously. For fourteen years S. N. Goenka kept up his business activities while deepening his meditation practice. Eventually he handed over the business to his sons and devoted his time to meditation teachings. Here we observe a modern shift in Buddhist countries: the emergence of lay meditation teachers who teach laypeople, women, and even foreigners. For the first time in the history of meditation teaching, a lineage of householders who practice and teach meditation was formed.[19]

Ledi Sayadaw is the key to this transformation. It was mainly his students who spread his teaching in Burma and beyond. In addition to the lineage traced above, another known lineage can be tracked from Ledi Sayadaw to Monyin Sayadaw to the famous meditation teacher Mahasi Sayadaw, whose teachings are followed by many meditation centers in Burma and Thailand. Although one can trace the lineages of Mahasi Sayadaw, S. N. Goenka, and other famous Vipassana teachers such as Pa Auk Sayadaw back to the same teacher (Ledi Sayadaw), these masters each produced slightly different versions of vipassana. For example, one finds differences with respect to concentration on the breath (abdomen or nose), time dedicated to concentration training, and attention given to each of the four objects of mindfulness (the body, bodily sensations, the mind, and objects of the mind). In the non-Buddhist world it is common to find meditation centers that adhere to one version of vipassana or teach a combination of several.

Cosmologically speaking, the mass meditation movement was inspired by an informal prophecy regarding the teachings of Siddhartha Gautama, known today as the Buddha, meaning the enlightened one. According to this prophecy, twenty-five hundred years from the day that Siddhartha Gautama reached enlightenment, his teachings would begin global circulation. Politically, this movement involved both monks and laity searching for ways to restore national pride and collective identity while resisting British occupation, which had dismantled the Buddhist kingdom and with it the traditional state-monk-laity social order.[20]

The synergy between the political and the cosmological is obvious in the teachings of Ledi Sayadaw, who as Jordt writes, in the face of British colonialism "exhorted his lay students to 'practice [that is, meditate] as though your heads are on fire.'"[21] Such resistance did not directly defy the British authority, as the British maintained the right of religious freedom. Moreover, even though some conservative reaction arose among certain monks, in general the vipassana revitalization movement received the support of both the Burmese political elite and the monastic religious elite.

The process of the revival of vipassana practice jumped scale with the founding of the new state in 1947. The same governmental elite that had gained its status during British colonialism sought to legitimate the new rule and strengthen national identity in a country that prior to the British occupation had been governed by kings whose rule was supported by the monastic community (the *sangha*). Lay meditation practice, which produced a link between the new government and charismatic meditation teachers, provided such legitimation. The first lay meditation center in Rangoon, established in 1947, was the fruit of a tripartite vision, that of Burma's first prime minister, U Nu; a wealthy Burmese donor, Sir U Thwin;[22] and the charismatic monk known for his experience in meditation practice, Mahasi Sayadaw. It was precisely this collaboration between the three elites—the governmental elite, the business elite, and the monastic elite—and their joint effort to produce a national-religious based identity, which catalyzed lay meditation practice.

This impetus was marked by a top-down introduction of meditation. U Nu required that his cabinet members meditate. U Ba Khin, for his part, founded the Vipassana Association of the Accountant General's Office, oriented specifically to the practice of employees of that office. Such associations were headed by laypeople belonging to the elite strata. While the first meditation courses were attended by educated elites, over time the popularity of the retreats filtered down to the other classes. When Spiro conducted research in Burma in 1960, only educated urban Burmese joined meditation courses; forty years later, Jordt reported that a visible share of the meditators came from the urban lower class or nearby villages.[23]

The interclass diffusion of meditation practice in Southeast Asia brings to mind Norbert Elias's account of the European "civilizing process" as certain behaviors that promote self-restraint spread from the elites to other classes.[24] In the case at hand, the elite group not only served as a model to be imitated by members of the middle and lower classes but also built and supported institutions that facilitated this downward diffusion—including open-access meditation centers, work time dedicated to meditation, and meditation courses in penal institutions. In India, yoga and later vipassana took similar trajectories.

For Gombrich and Obeyesekere, the spread of vipassana meditation represents a "laicization" of meditation: for the first time "meditation is seen as instrumental, a means to success in ordinary life."[25] Intriguing in itself, the notion of meditation laicization neglects the fact that meditation practice for the laity preserves important monastic elements. Stressing that meditation is taught in silent retreats that offer temporary renunciation of the world, Gustaaf Houtman suggests that instead of the laicization of meditation, we ought to study how lay meditation students became "monasticized."[26] According to Houtman, in Myanmar in 1990, the meditation center represented a monastery, the student was treated as a temporary monk, and the meditators aspired to nirvana. Likewise Joanna Cook shows that while Thai vipassana students do not refer to themselves as monks, the idea that members of the community should work toward enlightenment and concurrently improve their everyday lives is becoming mainstream in Thailand.[27]

In this historical and social stage, vipassana practice was not only about individual salvation but also about a social theory regarding a certain contract between state and society, about the role of the individual in the cosmic order, and with it about taking upon oneself the monastic role of both enacting and spreading the teachings of the Buddha. As Jordt has aptly put it, "Although individuals try to attend to their own personal salvation by striving to nirvana, they are simultaneously enacting broader social ideas about the arrangements of the state, the structure of cosmic time and their participation in a metahistorical project of *sasana* perpetuation."[28] In this sense the embodiment of meditation as a personal endeavor was part of a much broader religious-national movement, and every meditator embodies and enacts these broader political, historical, and cosmic transformations.

From "East" to "West": Early Encounters and the Sixties

As long as vipassana meditation was taught mainly in remote monasteries, it remained inaccessible to non-Buddhists, foreigners, and women. Indeed some monastic schools actively opposed the introduction of vipassana to non-Buddhists, asserting this meditation should be kept in its pure form behind the walls of the monastery. The reformation movements changed all that.

At the beginning of the twentieth century, Buddhist practice became more accessible to the West as part of a larger circulation of Eastern spiritual ideas and practices. The movement of vipassana from East to West can be tracked to diffuse movements that opposed orthodoxy and were crucial to the process that Colin Campbell has called "the Easternization of the West."[29] The spread of meditation received a powerful impetus from a singular nexus of reformation in Buddhist locations, and an American and European search for alternative ways of living and experiencing.

While for the Burmese vipassana practice was an enactment of national and cosmic social orders, it enacted something quite different on the other side of the world. Studies on the European and American encounter with Buddhism point to the turn of the twentieth century as a crucial period in which the educated and more affluent strata in Europe and the US began what was to be a lengthy preoccupation with "Eastern" thought.

The early fascination with Buddhism took different routes.[30] One was the elite and affluent class interest in aesthetic elements of Buddhism, especially Japanese culture and art. Another path, following the translation of Hindu and later of Buddhist texts into English at the beginning of the nineteenth century, involved academics and philosophers who had interest in Buddhist morality and ethics as a "religion of reason"[31] that represented the "antithesis of Western orthodoxies."[32] The third route, and the one most relevant to the story of meditation, comprised spiritual movements such as Theosophy, Anthroposophy, and New Thought. These esoteric societies were preoccupied with mysticism, magic, and the occult and found in Buddhism an attractive mystical religion.

The leaders of these spiritual groups were educated intellectuals, but their audience was rather diverse—from elite groups and artists in Hollywood to members of the less-educated upper class in rural areas.[33] These groups, and especially the Theosophical Society, were particularly drawn to Theravada Buddhism, alongside Hinduism and Japanese Buddhism. In fact Olcott and Blavatsky, who founded the Theosophical Society in 1875 in New York, are considered the first Westerners to officially convert to Buddhism, which they did while visiting Sri Lanka in 1880.[34] However, such conversion did not involve making any religious commitment. The Theosophical Society was eclectic, holding a panreligious perspective that drew on many different practices and sources.

For these groups, involvement with Buddhist and Hinduist ideas and practices signified an encounter with the exotic and the magical. It was the allure of an unfamiliar world, a world that had become available through colonialism. With the turn of the century such spiritual movements initiated the importation of Hindu practices such as yoga, viewed as mystical practices based on embodied wisdom, to Europe and the United States. Swami Vivekananda, a Hindu monk, introduced yoga to the West during a lecture circuit that he undertook at the end of the nineteenth century. These lectures were mainly oriented to members of esoteric groups. At just about the same time D. T. Suzuki, a well-known educated layman and Zen practitioner who was influenced by Theosophy, was busy doing likewise for Japanese Buddhism.[35]

These "esoteric Buddhists," as Thomas Tweed calls them, knew virtually nothing about the actual practice of vipassana.[36] The Pali texts that were translated into English were not meditation-oriented, and in fact the main text on which vipassana is based—the *Satipatthana Sutta*—was translated into English only in 1911. Since before the turn of the twentieth century vipassana was still a monastic practice reserved for the most devoted monks, it is likely that no participants in these spiritual groups ever met someone who practiced meditation.[37]

It was occultism and Theosophy that inspired the first Westerners to travel to Burma in search of meditative training. Such trips required massive effort and were limited to those who spoke foreign languages and could afford the travel. Allan Bennett (1872–1923), an analytical chemist from London who was a member of several esoteric societies, was one of the privileged few. While in his late twenties, he traveled to India to practice yoga, later continuing to Burma to take the name Ananda Metteyya and become one of the first Westerners to be ordained as a Theravada Buddhist monk. The German Anton Gueth (1878–1957) is another important figure. Gueth, who had extensive education in music and composition and great interest in philosophy and religion, was introduced to Buddhism in the context of a Theosophical lecture. In 1902 he traveled to Sri Lanka, paying for his journey by giving violin performances. From Sri Lanka he continued to Burma, where he was ordained as a monk and took the name Nyanatiloka. Nyanatiloka later became an important figure who taught vipassana to foreigners in Sri Lanka.[38]

The influence of these early encounters was limited. As Asaf Federman has informed us, despite the influential books on the practice of meditation that Metteyya wrote and published upon his return to England in 1908, his attempt to propagate vipassana in Britain was an overall failure. Federman links this lack of success to the interest of esoteric groups in meditation, which generated a negative association of magic and mysticism. In this line of thinking, meditation was rejected by elite philosophers and academics who at the time were interested in the more rational and ethical sides of Buddhism. Thus meditation remained marginal, mainly practiced by a handful of spiritual groups that evolved from Theosophy.[39] Still, this period laid the groundwork for the next stage. The early step of bringing Eastern religious ideas and practices to the West piqued people's curiosity. While meditation teachers and training centers were still scarce, books about meditation began to proliferate. In addition, yoga practice, which had become more available, set the stage for the later broad adoption of meditation.

Scholars of religion have drawn a straight line between early nineteenth-century esoteric spiritual groups, the emergence of the post-1960s New Age movement, and the more contemporary phenomenon that Courtney Bender has dubbed "the new metaphysics."[40] It is certainly true that the same interest in the antithesis of Western orthodoxies which motivated the early philosophers and spiritual mystics was reproduced by the counter-culture movement of the 1960s, albeit on a larger scale and with greater impact. However, while the aforementioned first step was mostly limited to the educated affluent elite and its preoccupation with the esoteric and exotic, the second step involved a decidedly middle-class audience from different sectors of both American and European society.

In brief, the Second World War led to the American baby boom. In both Europe and North America, higher education spread to the masses, and many middle-class young adults found themselves away from their families, leading a relatively independent life in college. By the end of the 1960s the US population included an unprecedented number of college-age persons. What we call the counterculture began mainly in the United States and England in this decade but had a strong resonance throughout Europe.

This historical stage is characterized not so much by an attraction to the magical as by an opposition to authority. The counterculture movement involved many different dimensions—political activism, sexual revolution, experiments with mind-altering substances, music, and art. All these were accompanied by a strong critique of the existing social and political order, which led to a search for alternative forms of living. The period was marked by a variety of oppositional stances: opposition to the Vietnam War and military force, opposition to traditional normative social arrangements (and experiments with various forms of communes), and resistance to traditional religious authority. These pushbacks represent the spirit of that period and are central to this stage of the diffusion of meditation.

Among the alternative lifestyle trajectories available to this era's young adults was the famed "journey to the East."[41] "The East" was already present beyond Southeast and Far East Asia through numerous books and some limited forms of practical training. The "journey" can thus serve as a metaphor for the adoption of different Eastern techniques, such as meditation and yoga, without actually travel abroad. However, the notion was not just metaphorical. Not unlike the previous century's interest in the East, which led to young-adult travelers to the East (on a very small scale), American and European young adults in the 1960s began exploring the world, and especially India, which was turning into a tourist center for self-exploration.

When these counterculture seekers entered "the East," they encountered a Buddhism that was at the peak of reformation—practice-based and not text-based, less connected to hierarchical religious institutions, and more open to foreigners. They found Buddhist monks who spoke English, a few even of Western origin, who could translate meditation into their language and worldview. For these seekers, Buddhism and meditation practice represented a novel lifestyle, worlds away from the hierarchical religious structure of their homeland, which could be used to confront the conservative way of living back in the US and in Europe.

The story of Barry Lapping, an American vipassana teacher and cofounder of the Vipassana Center at Shelburne Falls, Massachusetts, is illustrative. Barry was twenty-two years old and had just completed his BSc when he decided to leave the United States. These were the years of the Vietnam War, and though Barry was exempt from the draft, he thought the war was unjust and "had many thoughts regarding that way of life—all about material possessions and all." Being Jewish, he traveled to Israel and volunteered at a kibbutz: "In that period, communes were very popular in the US, and the kibbutz seemed to me like the ultimate commune—I imagined myself living in a kibbutz for the rest of my life. I was there for a few months and loved it—but then I was told, 'You are Jewish; you should join the army.'" Such a request represents the paradox of the kibbutz at that time, which supported a universal communal agenda alongside Zionist-nationalist ideology. Barry, who did not feel the national urge and was against the idea of military service, decided to move on. After reading a book about yoga, he decided to travel to India.

In the winter of 1970, Barry participated in a vipassana retreat taught by S. N. Goenka. Already then Goenka was known for his adaptation of vipassana teachings to non-Buddhist audiences, and the retreats were held in English. According to Barry, many participants were enthralled by the teachings and ended up participating in more retreats: "For a number of years I participated in course after course. Many of us lived together—we rented a house for six months for $60; it was very cheap. Every so often I returned to the United States to visit my parents."

Barry and his fellow meditators lived on very little in India; in fact, he financed a three-year stay in the country with the money he had received upon marking his bar mitzvah. This move itself merits a moment of discussion. The use of bar mitzvah gift money to study Buddhist meditation in India is a good example of the paradoxical transformations common to this period. Emily Sigalow studied the connections between Jews and Buddhism and found that among the participants in Barry's first retreat were Joseph Goldstein, Sharon Salzberg, Jacquelyn Schwartz, Wes Nisker, and Stephen Levine—all of whom are Jewish in origin and all of whom ended up playing pioneering roles in bringing vipassana to the United States. Other Jewish participants in this retreat included Surya Das (born Jeffrey Miller), now a known Tibetan Buddhist teacher; Ram Dass (born Richard Alpert), an American spiritual leader and author of the influential book *Be Here Now*; and Daniel Goleman, author of the 1995 best-seller *Emotional Intelligence*.[42]

Scholars offer different accounts of the attraction of Jews to Buddhism, including theological, cultural, and demographic reasons. In the 1960s, Jewish American young adults were usually well educated, belonged to relatively affluent families, and raised in secular homes. As Barry himself puts it, "This was a generation whose parents and grandparents went through horrible things in the Second World War and wanted their children to be educated and to succeed, to go to college. So there were many young Jews with higher education at that time who had thought about the uselessness of things that were going on but did not accept Jewish tradition either."

The Jewish-Buddhist linkage was also evident in Israel. The first prime minister of Israel, David Ben-Gurion, a fierce Zionist with no connection to the counterculture movement, was fascinated by both meditation and yoga. In fact, already in 1961 while serving as prime minster, Ben-Gurion traveled to Burma as a guest of the first Burmese prime minister, U Nu. During his stay at U Nu's house, Ben Gurion received meditation instructions each morning, while his secretary, Itzhak Navon, participated in a retreat delivered by U Ba Khin, the teacher of S. N. Goenka.[43] These intriguing connections circle back to the previous "Eastern" stage of popularization of vipassana as a tool in reaffirming Burmese national identity, as Ben-Gurion and U Nu were close friends, both tasked with building a new nation. It is no surprise, then, that Barry encountered yoga in Israel, nor that a generally positive attitude toward Eastern practices existed in 1960s Israel, a place that was not overtly influenced by the counterculture movement.

Counterculture travelers like Barry turned India into a search nexus for alternative ways of being. Hindu culture had always featured ideas of spiritual development, and yogis and gurus were an important part of the society. Due to the long period of British colonialism, India at the end of the 1960s was an easy destination compared to other counties in Southeast Asia. Most of the educated class spoke English, and transportation to and within the country was reasonably manageable. With the growing Western audience interested in practices such as yoga and meditation, yoga workshops and meditation retreats started opening up.

Celebrities, too, were important catalysts of this process. Enthralled by the Maharishi Mahesh Yogi, the Beatles traveled to India in 1968 to study Transcendental Meditation at his ashram. Around the same time that Goenka began teaching vipassana in India (1969), Chandra Mohan Jain, known today by the name Osho, began to promote himself as a spiritual guru, and in 1974 he established an ashram in Pune whose residents were primarily affluent Westerners. The Dalai Lama, who after being exiled in 1959 from Tibet established his new home in Dharamsala, India, also became a magnet for those interested in meditation teachings. Dipa Ma, another important meditation teacher, began teaching meditation in 1967 in Calcutta. Many of these meditation centers and ashrams were based on the social arrangement of the commune, thus serving as experiments in transforming traditional social structures.

This period brought a revival of Buddhist meditation practice in India. India is not a Buddhist country; indeed less than 1 percent of its population identifies as Buddhist. Nonetheless it is the mother country of Buddhism and the birthplace of Gautama the Buddha. In fact for seven centuries, between the third century BCE and the fourth century CE, India was predominantly Buddhist. From the fourth century CE onward, however, Buddhism declined and Hinduism increased. The Buddhist decline continued with the spread of Islam in India, and in fact for centuries, up until the beginning of the twentieth century, Buddhist practice was almost invisible in this large country.[44]

The twentieth century saw a return of Buddhist meditation practice in India. This shift has been attributed to the work of S. N. Goenka and his connections with the Hindu elite, alongside the influence of the Dalai Lama, who resided in India. Thus while the popularization of vipassana began in Burma, as mentioned above, it was in India, in a retreat conducted by Goenka himself, that the founders of the vipassana meditation centers in the US met.

The spread of these self-exploration techniques hinged on interaction with charismatic teachers, and indeed that period is known for producing gurus whose influence on the schools can still be felt. Goenka was one of various famous meditation and yoga teachers who traveled repeatedly from the East to the West. When Barry Lapping returned to the United States in 1975, he and other students of vipassana invited Goenka to give meditation courses there. Between 1975 and 1982 Goenka made yearly trips to the US and Europe to teach meditation. Monks such as Mahasi Sayadaw, the Thai forest monk Anjan Chan, and the Dalai Lama, as well as lay teachers such as Dipa Ma, also taught regularly in the US during this period. American and European teachers and students often returned to Asia to study with their masters.

Only in the 1990s, as meditation centers and schools became more institutionalized and local teachers gained authority and prestige, did the reliance on these charismatic leaders begin to dissipate. By now some schools have almost completely distanced themselves from the original "Eastern" teachers. In the case of vipassana as taught by Goenka, the connection to the master was kept: meditation centers in this school all use video and audiotapes of Goenka in their courses. However, the death of Goenka in 2013 might change this as time passes.

Following the above encounters, meditation centers were established in Europe and the United States. The San Francisco Zen Center had been founded already in 1959. In 1970 the first Shambhala meditation center in North America was established in Vermont. In 1975 the first vipassana meditation center was established in Massachusetts (Insight Meditation Society). Alongside these, as Wendy Cadge illustrates, immigration from Southeast Asia prompted the establishment of Buddhist temples, where vipassana was taught especially from the 1980s onward. While sociologists frequently view these two groups—the white Americans and the "cradle" Asian Buddhists—as distinct,[45] Cadge shows that the groups are connected by identifiable networks. Moreover, meditation teachers and monks traveling from Southeast Asia to the US frequently visited both Buddhist temples and American meditation centers.[46]

When importing meditation and Buddhist thought into their home countries, Western actors carefully culled fragments from a much larger cosmology and culture. Teachers in the East who adapted their meditation teaching to Western audiences had already begun this process. It was only when they taught students with a Buddhist background that they could assume a shared language regarding salvation and enlightenment. The adaptation process was further intensified when meditation centers were established in the US and Europe.

In this way the rich world of household Buddhism, meaning the non-monastic religious practice with its litany of beliefs, prayers, and rituals, was essentially left behind. That world includes, for example, the common practices of giving donations to monks as a way to improve one's karma, giving alms to the spirits of the ancestors, and rituals and prayers devoted to specific gods.[47] Belief in multiple gods and in general Buddhist cosmology was pushed to the background; as discussed in chapter 6, it is now seen as relevant to the practice of vipassana only when practitioners become serious meditators.

Although the counterculture introduced the idea of meditation to a broad audience, the first vipassana courses given in the West were very small. The first courses in the US were sporadic, some moved from one space to another, and some took place at the more institutionalized meditation venues—first at the Cambridge Insight Meditation Center and later also at the Dhamma Dharra Vipassana Meditation center in Shelburne Falls, Massachusetts, the first meditation center in the US to follow Goenka's tradition exclusively. Knowledge of the courses passed from one person to another, mainly through kin and friendship circles. It would take another thirty years for meditation to flourish on a global basis.[48]

To conclude, it is plausible that in the countercultural spirit of that time, to pracrice meditation meant to be a part of a significant broader social process. Defying authority and forging new social arrangements was the call of the day. This meant taking up new perspectives, in a bodily form, that challenged traditional religious structures. If postindependence Burmese meditated for their own salvation but at the same time enacted a wider process of state-society arrangements and cosmic order, the meditators of the 1960s and 1970s were busy exploring their own selves while opposing normative social arrangements and attempting to change the world.

The Mainstreaming of Meditation Practice

Ruth, age thirty-five, is a licensed psychotherapist who lives in the American Midwest. When we met in 2006, she was married and had one son. Ruth was raised as a Methodist and frequently went to church as a child. After her father's death in 2002 left her in emotional shambles, she started seeing a therapist. Yet, she says, "I was a terrible patient. I hardly spoke." The therapist suggested that she try meditation as a way to "manage [her]self." The idea of meditation was not foreign to her, as she had a close friend who worked in Richard Davidson's laboratory in Madison, Wisconsin, where brain imaging is conducted on meditation practitioners. Ruth tried learning meditation from books and tapes, but "that did not stick." She also tried yoga for a while, but that did not stick either. She then searched for a meditation course, but "I saw these meditation courses that cost about $1000 and I didn't think that was justified." Around the same time, her friend traveled to India and participated in a vipassana course offered free of charge. This is how Ruth ended up taking a vipassana course in Illinois.

In Ruth's story we see the process in which meditation moved from being a tool on the path to enlightenment to being a tool for people to deal with their daily lives. Here meditation is framed as a therapy that works hand in hand with Western psychological therapy. This framing is not limited to a small group of alternative therapists but is shared by licensed medical professionals who recommend meditation to their patients as a "self-management" tool, even though they themselves may have never practiced it. We also see how this framing is advocated in academic circles: Ruth's friend encountered meditation while working in a neuroscience brain-imaging laboratory in a prestigious university, a lab that studies the changes that take place in the brain during meditation practice.

Until the turn of the twenty-first century, vipassana was mainly practiced by those searching for an alternative lifestyle, as meditation practice still carried counterculture connotations. As the counterculture movement wound down, meditation appealed primarily to people in certain fringes of society, frequently referred to as "New Age." With growing public opposition to Transcendental Meditation, which was increasingly perceived as a cult, the public came to associate meditation with gurus, mysticism, and even brainwashing.[49]

The third millennium has brought a quantum leap for meditation practice. The audience for meditation has exploded as huge numbers of individuals seek a self-reflexive tool while maintaining a postindustrial lifestyle. Today meditation courses are viewed as normative alternatives to more institutionalized techniques of self-exploration (i.e., Western psychology). Meditation practice has shed its countercultural, mystical and New Age aura.[50]

Third-millennium vipassana practitioners are living in a world suffused with the sounds of meditation: books on the subject top best-seller lists, and meditation teachers are sought-after talk-show guests. Meditation is discussed in yoga classes, in university lectures, and by therapists and physicians. Many individuals have friends who meditate and invite them to weekly meditation sittings. Those who wish to try out meditation can go online and find elaborate websites with explanations of meditation centers and courses. A glance at popular magazines, from *Time* to *Fortune*, reveals the current fascination with meditation. "Scientists study it. Doctors recommend it. Millions of people—many of whom don't even own crystals—practice it every day," writes Joel Stein in a lengthy *Time* article dedicated to meditation practice.[51] Meditation has become a way to calm oneself, boost health, improve relations, increase self-awareness, and regain emotional balance. It is prescribed for chronic pain and high blood pressure. It is taught in hospital clinics, in high-tech companies, and in senior residences.[52] And in a move whose irony cannot be lost on former flower children and hippies, the military teaches meditation to soldiers as a stress-management technique.

Yet this development was not inevitable. For meditation to have turned into a ubiquitous self-reflexive practice, it had to undergo a process of delabeling from its counterculture connotations. This is not a trivial matter. How did it happen that meditation became available, both socially and culturally, to "people who do not own crystals"?

In order to answer this question, I distinguish between two groups of actors. The first consists of the leaders of meditation, the main promoters, the teachers, and the founders. The second is the audience and consumers, Ruth being one example. This distinction is important because these two groups do not necessary have the same motivations for practicing and promoting meditation. We can detect some countercultural orientation in the leaders' aspirations to change the world, but the audience and consumers seek out meditation mainly to improve their coping with this world rather than to make it a better place.

The leaders who actively worked to mainstream vipassana are privileged in terms of education, race, gender, economic status, and job, and more than a few are themselves products of the counterculture movement. Many of them began to practice meditation already in the 1960s, some even becoming meditation teachers. By the 1990s these individuals, who as young adults had searched for alternative ways of life, held prestigious positions in academic, business, and governmental circles.[53] This set of actors embraces science but at the same time was searching for certain kinds of experiences that science cannot provide.

Returning to the question with which I opened this chapter, I suggest that for these specific actors, prayer—be it Jewish, Christian, or Muslim—was not an attractive option, as it came burdened with the baggage of belief, rules, norms, and communal identity. But meditation had already been stripped of this "unnecessary" baggage when it was imported to the West. It held much less of a threat to the secular way of life. A look at a few of the figures who mainstreamed meditation is instructive here.

Richard J. Davidson is professor of psychology and psychiatry in Madison, Wisconsin. Born in 1951, Davidson is a baby boomer who spent the years of the counterculture movement as a student at New York University. In 1976, having just completed his PhD at Harvard, he published his first paper on the effect of meditation on the brain (together with Daniel Goleman, mentioned below).[54] Davidson frequently advocates meditation practice in different circles and gives lectures at Zen and Tibetan meditation retreats.

Jon Kabat-Zinn is a professor of medicine who founded the Stress Reduction Clinic and the Center for Mindfulness in Medicine, Health Care, and Society at the University of Massachusetts Medical School. Born in 1944 as Jon Kabat, he received his PhD in molecular biology from MIT in 1971. At the same time he was a student of Zen master Seung Sahn, and in 1973 he became a founding member of the Cambridge Zen Center. Kabat-Zinn has devoted his life to teaching mindfulness meditation, a fusion of vipassana and Zen meditation, turning it into a technique that is taught in clinical workshops for the treatment of depression, stress, and chronic pain.[55]

Other actors include Daniel Goleman, a well-known psychologist whose best-selling book *Emotional Intelligence* is based on insights derived from Buddhist meditation practice, and the Harvard graduate Adam Engle, who together with the philosopher and neuroscientist Francisco Varela (also a Harvard graduate) established the Mind and Life Institute, a US-based center for the study of the interface between science and Buddhism.[56]

Another actor from the medical sphere is Paul R. Fleischman, a well-known psychiatrist and a teacher of vipassana meditation in the tradition of S. N. Goenka. Fleischman presents a different perspective from that of Davidson and Kabat-Zinn, insisting on conserving the "spiritual" part of meditation practice side by side the "practical" therapeutic one. Thus he does not advocate scientific investigations of meditation practice. As he told me when we met: "Vipassana for me is a culture, not a science." That being said, Fleischman has written a great deal on the therapeutic power of vipassana, oriented both to a professional and to a public audience, promoting connections between vipassana and the fields of psychiatry and psychology. I met him in Israel when he was on a lecture tour, giving some talks oriented to the general public and others to a mental health audience.[57]

The prestigious positions held by these leaders and their normative, even conservative, way of life has enabled a large population to perceive them as role models. Compared to the counterculture stage, this stage produced a much larger joint category of possible adopters who share a similar culture and similar identity markers, able to adopt meditation as a part of a valued lifestyle. Moreover, their influence and power in academic networks enables them to push meditation practice in different institutional settings. Interestingly, while each of these actors may practice a different Buddhist meditation, the outcome is promotion of meditation practice generally and not a specific school of teachings. In fact, as will be discussed below, it is quite common for people to move from one school of meditation to another, experimenting with different meditation styles.[58]

In an extensive interview-based study on the contemplative movement in the United States, Jamie Kucinskas found that many leaders—scientists, psychiatrists, and even top business leaders—had a larger social vision for meditation practice. In order to spread meditation, however, they used what she calls unobtrusive tactics that would not threaten the secular character of the institutions where they worked. She illustrates how advocates of meditation "assimilate and blend into dominant institutions, beginning in esteemed organizations in each new field."[59] These leaders presented their meditation programs as secular solutions to the problems of each specific institution and thus got their program "in the door" without opposition.[60] For example, in the military, meditation was advocated as a tool to maintain performance in violent and stressful situations. Not surprisingly, army programs omitted any reference to Buddhist tenets of nonviolence.[61] After entering the institutions, these leaders hoped either that they could gradually expose practitioners to the values connected to Dharma or that the embodied practice of meditation in and of itself would lead to social change "from within."[62]

Among the extensive array of meditation practices, probably the most successful penetration into institutional spheres has been achieved by Kabat-Zinn's MBSR program (Mindfulness Based Stress Reduction), which is taught in psychological and medical clinics the world over, including US government–supported therapy for soldiers with PTSD. Other meditation schools followed this pattern as well. For example, between the years 2000 and 2010, vipassana courses taught in the tradition of Goenka were offered in prisons in India, Israel, Mongolia, New Zealand, Taiwan, Thailand, the UK, Myanmar, and the United States. In the US, these courses were offered at the W. E. Donaldson Correctional Facility, a level 6 maximum-security state prison in Bessemer, Alabama, and in the San Francisco jail. The courses mark a shift to the perception that meditation can be used as a rehabilitation tool not unlike other rehabilitation programs that are based on Western psychological logic. This utilization of meditation in institutionalized therapeutic contexts takes place in both Western and Eastern locations, including contemporary Burma and Thailand.

The scientific grounding of meditation practice facilitated this penetration into secular institutions. Since around 2000, we have witnessed an unprecedented growth in scientific studies on meditation practice. Researchers are investigating the changes the brain undergoes while meditating, the influence of meditation on vital signs such as blood pressure, and its impact on the management of stress or chronic pain. *Mindfulness* has become the most popular scientific term to denote the technique of nonjudgmental observation of body and mind (based on vipassana and Zen), and a look at scientific journals reveals a rise from 48 articles between 1966 and 2000 with mindfulness in the title, to 364 such articles in just two years, 2011–12.[63] While the first such scientific studies were conducted by scientists who actually practiced meditation (such as Davidson), interest in meditation as a psychological and health-related tool has gone beyond the community of practitioners, as researchers who are not necessary meditators join the scientific effort.

The scientific interest in meditation was spurred by a contemporary paradigm shift in psychology and psychiatry. Recent findings in neuroscience have led to a new understanding of the mind as deeply embodied.[64] These findings challenge Cartesian dualism, which separated the mind from the body and supported the superiority of the former over the latter. In the new paradigm, emotions are no longer thought to counter rationality, and feelings are considered central to any rational decision. It is therefore unsurprising that leading figures in psychiatry, psychology, and neuroscience have turned their attention to techniques that focus on the body-mind connection. The nondualistic approach of Buddhism has become relevant to neuroscientific attempts to understand the self.

The lecture of the Dalai Lama at the SFN yearly meeting is just one example of this burgeoning interest. During my fieldwork I participated in two scientific conferences that presented neuroscientists, psychologists, and meditation teachers side by side on the same panel. One panel ended in two minutes of collective meditation which the whole audience, consisting mainly of scientists and academics, was invited to join. These conferences were in no way exceptional, and the panelist choice and meditation activity were not regarded as strange. In fact such symposia have become quite common in academic circles. The organizers are leading scientists in top academic circles who do not identify as Buddhist and who promote meditation solely as a practical technique.[65]

The work of the above leaders remains critical to the recruitment of organizations and institutions that push the popularization of meditation. Today health services, and with them insurance companies, sponsor meditation lessons and meditation groups. Governmental institutions such as the prison system and the military give access to less-educated, lower-income, ethnically and racially diverse individuals who are outside the "natural" audience of meditation. Universities and research foundations offer funds and facilities to study meditation. Large companies sponsor meditation courses for their employees. Fitness centers, counseling centers, and therapy-based small businesses have all become agents in the diffusion process as they begin offering meditation among other techniques to improve the self. All these institutions act independently, without a central organization, in making meditation more available to a larger audience.

The outcome of this process constitutes a tipping point in the diffusion of meditation as a social practice. At this moment such diffusion is no longer dependent on direct interaction with the advocating agents. In the words of sociologists Strang and Mayer, once a social practice receives what they term "theoritization" and is framed through the use of a globally available model, "diffusion may still require direct contact, but in more modest amounts."[66]

The model of therapy and well-being permits a large number of people to relate to meditation even if they themselves have never meditated and have no direct contact with anyone who has. This state of diffusion has little to do with specific gurus or the charisma of particular meditation teachers. Today one need not know—or even have heard of—any famous meditation teacher in order to think that meditation is a legitimate healthy practice. Mass media and technology have been highly instrumental in this process. Newspaper articles announce that meditation is good for your mental health and is recommended by medical professionals. Blockbuster talk-show hosts such as Oprah Winfrey advertise the practice of meditation.[67] Moreover, applications that teach meditation, such as Headspace, are becoming more popular by the minute.[68] Meditation has become part of a normative lifestyle, together with jogging, dieting, and seeing a therapist.

At this stage of the diffusion, we are seeing a growing breach between the leaders of the movement and the recipients and institutions that adopt meditation. The leaders purposefully worked to secularize meditation and adapt it to the desires of a broad audience, catching a ride on the popularity of therapeutic discourse and its already existing infrastructure in many secular institutions. But these leaders, products of the counterculture period, still carry the spirit of the previous historical stage of meditation. For them, enacting meditation meant enacting the possibility of an alternative social world. Moreover, many of them hold stereological beliefs in the teachings of the Buddha which they share with the "Eastern" leaders of meditation (i.e., senior meditation teachers and monks). In fact, meditation teachers I met openly spoke of the "packaging" of meditation in ways adapted to the secular Western audience, a packaging they believe will be removed once people seriously enter the practice.

Government officials and prison psychologists, along with military and medical personnel, by contrast, treat meditation as another technique in the scientifically supported toolkit of mental health enhancement. The audience and recipients, in these institutions and among the general public, encounter meditation under this "secular" and "instrumentalized" framing.[69] And while a small fraction of practitioners may indeed become serious meditators, the large majority will not. Thus while the leaders who promoted meditation hope to change these institutions from within, at least in some cases we may be witnessing an institutional takeover.[70] These somewhat unintended outcomes raise debates between leaders, practitioners, and scholars on whether meditation, after being stripped of its religious background, still holds the logic and principles of Dharma (the teaching of the Buddha), and whether this new configuration of practice can lead to social transformation or, on the contrary, bolsters capitalist and neoliberal institutions and structures.[71]

Positioning This Study in the Contemporary Meditation Field

Peter, age thirty-three, a professor at a major American university, had long been interested in meditation: "I tried meditations in informal ways many times during the course of my life. I always lost concentration very quickly or sat for ten minutes, stared at a candle, and got bored, you know, or figured out my mind isn't built for it." In 1999, when Peter was twenty-seven years old, he heard about Shambhala from a friend and decided to give it a try. Shambhala is a Tibetan Buddhist tradition, and its secular version, called "Shambhala training," was imported to the US and Europe around the same time as vipassana. In most university towns and cities today, one can find Shambhala group sittings in a practitioner's home, free of charge and open to the public. Peter went to one of these meetings and for the first time in his life was able to meditate for a twenty-minute stretch. When he wanted to go again, he invited an acquaintance to join him. The new friend responded that she liked meditation and would love to come. When he asked about her meditation experience, she told him, "The only thing I ever did was the Buddhist boot camp—vipassana meditation." As Peter told me, he had never heard the word *vipassana* before, but "it got stuck in my mind that Buddhist boot camp sounded like something for me."

Contemporary meditation practice is part of a larger social field that includes a variety of practices. This field is, in fact, a crossroads where different traditions meet, with no specific charismatic leader or collective identity that unites them. Alternative body-based therapies such as shiatsu and acupuncture cross this junction, with their emphasis on the connection between mental and physical health. Contemporary yoga, tai chi, and aikido are further paths to ideas regarding bodily awareness. Different meditation practices, such as Zen, vipassana, TM, and Christian meditation also meet at these crossroads, and ideas and people circulate from one path to the other.

One can encounter these practices in a hospital clinic, in spirituality-related groups, or in a life-coaching session. The same people frequently visit these different spheres, and the agents of one sphere are often the agents of another. In her ethnographic research of seven spirituality-related groups in Massachusetts, Bender found that "zooming around" and exploring is quite common to participants in these groups.[72] Likewise, in my research I met yoga teachers who recommend that their students take a vipassana course, and it was common to meet tai chi or aikido teachers who recommend that their students take a Zen meditation course.[73]

Estimates of the number of Americans who practice meditation vary depending on the questions asked in surveys. According to the 2014 PEW religious landscape study, 40 percent of all respondents and 19 percent of self-defined atheists reported that they meditate at least once a week. The 2017 National Health Interview Survey found that 14.2 percent of respondents had "used meditation as treatment" in the previous twelve months, representing over thirty million people. Approximately half of those who reported using meditation specifically referred to mindfulness-related techniques such as vipassana, Mindfulness-Based Stress Reduction (MBSR), or Zen.[74]

To locate the specific school I studied in a much broader "meditation field," it is important to understand the different venues through which one can study vipassana or vipassana-based meditation. In the above diffusion story, we began in the monastery, moved through the meditation center, and ended in the hospital clinic and gym. All these venues of vipassana teaching— the monastery, the meditation center, and the hospital—exist side by side in both Eastern and Western locations.

If you have a Buddhist background, you might prefer to take meditation classes in a Buddhist temple, usually taught by a monk.[75] If you want to study meditation in order to deal with chronic pain or reduce blood pressure, your doctor might recommend an eight-week MBSR program in a hospital or at a community center. If you want to experiment with meditation for the first time, you may look into meditation classes at the nearest yoga or meditation center. And if you seek a more serious self-exploratory experience or have an interest in Buddhism, you may join a longer meditation retreat.

Among the different meditation teaching venues, this book focuses on people in the US and Israel who participated in at least one vipassana meditation retreat conducted in a meditation center that follows the teaching of S. N. Goenka. The following chapters thus shed light on a middle point in the journey from the monastery to the hospital, a point that preserves the structure of teaching created in the Southeast Asia mass meditation movement. The popular vipassana groups in the US that offer meditation retreats include the Insight Meditation Society (IMS) in Massachusetts and the Spirit Rock meditation center in California, both of which conduct beginners' courses of seven silent days, and under the organization Vipassana Meditation as Taught by S. N. Goenka there are eleven meditation centers around the US that conduct beginners' courses of ten silent days. In Israel vipassana retreats are offered by the Insight Foundation, which has connections to the American IMS, and

Vipassana Meditation as Taught by S. N. Goenka. The structure of the retreats in the different groups is quite similar—these are fully silent or semi-silent retreats in which people meditate for around ten hours a day (see chapter 3 for a full description of the meditation course).

In all these centers, either courses are offered free of charge or payment is requested based on income. Thus these meditation schools are not a part of the industry of meditation practice, and the teachers and organizers are not driven by a profit motive. Their main motivation is missionary in nature—to communicate the teaching of the Buddha as they understand it, accompanied by a strong belief that the spread of vipassana can better the lives of individuals and eventually produce a better society.

Among these schools, vipassana training in the tradition of S. N. Goenka is considered relatively conservative, as it seeks to preserve the structure of courses as practiced in Southeast Asia with relatively few modifications. These courses are a relatively demanding version of meditation training, as illustrated by the title "meditation boot camp." I use the term *relatively* because there are other more demanding meditation schools, along with less demanding ones.[76] Goenka's meditation training is based on sending new students to a full ten-day silent retreat. This training suits people who are willing to jump into a serious and demanding process of training and are seeking a transformative experience that, on the one hand, is radically different from their daily life yet, on the other, does not require forsaking or endangering their routines or lives (compared, for example, to experimentation with drugs or embarking on a long voyage to the East). This produces a self-selection criterion for the people who participated in this study. Thus caution is advised regarding generalizing the current findings to other vipassana teachings, especially those that are not retreat-based.[77]

At the centers I researched, the attempt to conserve the formal structure of the teaching is not accompanied by efforts to conserve the religious commitment that these meditation teachings hold in Southeast Asia. Like the meditation leaders described above, the Goenka meditation school enacts a strategic anchoring of meditation in the body-mind therapy field and not in the religious/spiritual field. For example, in contrast to teachers at the IMS, who tend to identify themselves as Buddhists, teachers in the Goenka school distance themselves from the notion of Buddhist or Buddhism, claiming Buddhism is a religion while vipassana is not. In addition, while Cadge found that, at least around 2002, many IMS members practiced vipassana with the belief that they would reach enlightenment, such stereological-based motivations are much less common in the Goenka school.[78]

Such distancing from religious connotations and anchoring in the body-mind therapy field is taken to its margins in the documentary *Doing Time Doing Vipassana*, frequently screened in lectures introducing Vipassana Meditation as Taught by S. N. Goenka. This movie follows a ten-day vipassana prison course conducted in India with the participation of non-Indian, mainly Western convicts. The movie tracks "success" stories of convicts who experienced strong self-transformation following the ten-day meditation course. The teachings of vipassana are presented as nonreligious and science-based, and the stories of the convicts are completely focused on self-discovery and self-healing.[79]

Still, despite the distancing from religious connotations, the teachings in this school are deeply connected to the teachings of the Buddha. Goenka himself was extremely well versed in Buddhist texts and was held in high esteem by other Buddhist teachers.[80] The *dhamma* (Pali for dharma, the teachings of the Buddha) in these teachings is not hidden from participants. On the contrary, vipassana practice is presented as the "pure" or "original" dhamma. To quote the school's website: "Vipassana, which means to see things as they really are, is one of India's most ancient techniques of meditation. It was rediscovered by Gautama Buddha more than 2500 years ago and was taught by him as a universal remedy for universal ills."[81] Such presentation ties contemporary vipassana practice directly to the Buddha, while underplaying 2500 years of transformation in the practice.[82]

The Buddhist origin is thus not hidden. In fact, it serves as a source of attraction and legitimation. Julia, whom I met at the Illinois meditation center, put it aptly:

> I knew it was a meditation course, and my friend recommended it as a very strong experience, so I wanted to try. But I did not know it was connected to the teachings of the Buddha—I had no knowledge of Buddhism or the Buddha or anything. I mean, I heard about Zen meditation in the past, but you know, there are so many kinds of meditations. So when I found out in the course that vipassana is a Buddhist meditation I was surprised. But I also found it reassuring—that so many people for so many years have practiced it, and it is not just something someone invented recently.

As noted above, the monastic, religious, and Eastern background still contributes to the allure of vipassana meditation, imbuing it with legitimacy and an aura of seriousness. The singular mix of the therapeutic and wellness framework, scientific legitimation, and anchoring in the mythical past of a respected tradition continues to attract people to the practice.

*

Our tour along the path through which vipassana turned into a globalized, readily available practice has revealed unplanned coordination between different social actors with various motivations and goals. Each of the historical stages featured different audiences and different agents of diffusion. In each stage, meditation "caught a ride" on the back of broader social movements. In each stage, to enact meditation meant to enact a social identity, but the social identities, and their significations, were in constant flux.

We began with evangelistic movements in Southeast Asia that resisted colonialism and launched a reformation that called for the participation of all members of the community, joining hands with politicians who used meditation as a way to create a stronger national identity. Continuing along, we met the enchantment with "the East" that emerged in the United States and western Europe around 1900 and set the stage for agents of the counterculture movement, who sought alternative experiences and self-exploration techniques that were not anchored in the old, conservative religious structure and tradition. We ended with former counterculture, now grown-up academics who, while acting with a vision of universal social change, strategically positioned meditation to merge with a globally available model—that of mental and physical health—thus completing the trajectory of secularization and instrumentalization of a former monastic practice. In this last stage, vipassana is a part of the much larger culture of mind and body therapy, advocated by a growing number of institutions and organizations in both private and public sectors who advocate meditation to an extremely diverse audience including prisoners, those who suffer from chronic pain, and elderly people in assisted living.

While each stage is characterized by different actors and audiences, there are overlaps. While meditation practice today in the non-Buddhist world is primarily promoted by the social sphere of body-mind health and subjective well-being, this sphere does not encompass the full range of motivations and experiences of each and every agent or actor. Some practice meditation as a part of their religious-cosmic role in the universe, others use it to strengthen their sense of ethnic or national belonging, and probably there are some who practice it in a countercultural spirit.

Still, when Westerners think about meditation in non-Buddhist locations, the practice is no longer connected to the cosmic role of the meditator in the universe. Outside of Southeast Asia, it has little to do with the integration of society around a collective national/religious identity. In addition, it has lost much of its "counter" spirit, as illustrated by the institutional support of capitalist firms, prisons, and the military. Much of the oppositional force of meditation has been lost as meditation is no longer used as a tool of resistance. If meditation was ever "New Age" (as some sociologists have called the adoption of Eastern spiritual practices in the West), it has gone far beyond, together with yoga and alternative medicine, into the mass self-improvement and self-therapy movement.

The model of physical and mental health is so pervasive that it is not surprising that other spiritual and religious practices attempt to enter this sphere. Coming back full circle to the Dalai Lama and the pope, the body of research on the physical and mental benefits of prayer is growing, and it will be interesting to see whether or not prayer follows in the boundary-crossing footsteps of meditation.[83] What is unique about meditation, and is absent from prayer, is the lack of connections to any local formal religious structure (in "the West") and thus the flexibility with which the diffusing agents translated and adapted it to the language of modern self-care. In fact, even though meditation went through a process of adaptation to the West, it is the "Eastern" connotations, the same ones that fascinated the nineteenth-century groups, that enable meditation to flourish as a space in which one is pushing the envelope, experimenting with something slightly edgy, without the need to cross any red lines.

This stage of meditation practice has been dubbed "the mindfulness revolution."[84] Yet the term *revolution* is something of a misnomer. It was "revolutionary" in the classic sense of a social revolution when, as a resistance to British occupation, Ledi Sayadaw asked his students to meditate until their heads were on fire, or when counterculture young adults embodied meditation as a way to confront the orthodox power structures in their own countries. In this current stage, however, during which meditation has reached the largest audience it has ever reached, it no longer holds social revolutionary significations. One might argue, of course, that it is revolutionary on the level of self-experience and with it the level of social relations. In the eyes of most Westerners, vipassana is about the individual and his or her surroundings, the micro social world. It is this focus, the micro world of self and other, which this book takes as a case study for understanding changing relations between body, self, and others.

3

Collective Solitude

"Why would a sociologist study meditation?" Ron asked when I called him to inquire about an interview. This question did not surprise me at all. Many practitioners of vipassana consider meditation a solitary experience, an activity singularly unsuitable for sociological investigation. Meditation, in their view, is "something that happens between me and myself" or "an experience that cannot be shared with others." As one meditator explained, he was attracted to vipassana practice because "it is something that is mine—I mean, apart from the meditation instructions, whatever follows them is mine." Vipassana, then, is something one experiences alone, in the privacy of one's body/mind.

When vipassana practitioners speak of meditation as an isolated practice, they are relating to meditation in psychological terms. For them, vipassana is technique of internal cultivation that begins with mind and body discipline and ends with certain behavioral changes. Studies on meditation, too, have generally left aside its social dimension, exploring it as an individual endeavor.[1] From this perspective, vipassana meditation practice is distinctly unidirectional, moving from the internal to the external, from introspection to a shift in how one feels and behaves among others.

In this chapter I will argue that such accounts ignore important microsociological facts regarding the training process of meditation. Like other embodied practices, it is difficult to learn meditation from a book or from audio recordings, as is evident from the contemporary high demand for meditation classes.[2] Accordingly, vipassana meditation is usually taught in collective environments, in meditation retreats or courses, in the physical proximity of others. Moreover, while one might assume that meditating among others would interfere with the cultivation of inward looking, it seems that this is not the case. Most practitioners find it easier to meditate with others, and many people report that that their deepest meditation experiences surfaced in collective meditation sessions.

Following the relation between modes of attending to others and modes attending to one's body, I illustrate how vipassana training shifts one's attention and responsivity from the judgment of others to an unspoken synchronization and attunement with the bodies of others.[3] In this move, the projection of self to others (which, as we shall see, is an important part of the training, especially in the early stages) turns tacit. Keeping a tacit or peripheral awareness of others enables practitioners to relax the need for direct response to social interactions, helping them realign focus from the external to the internal. The entwining with the bodily stillness of others produces a safe ground, an anchor, from which meditators turn their gaze inward and attend to the tacit, embodied dimension of their being.

Meditative Environments: Social and Spatial Arrangements

It was evening when I arrived at a vipassana meditation group sitting in Tel Aviv, ten minutes before the meditation was supposed to begin. The door was opened by a young woman, who escorted me into a narrow hall and disappeared into a second room. Peeking into that room, I saw a few computers and three men working. They seemed occupied, so I waited quietly. Shortly thereafter, a few more people arrived. One woman glanced through the door to the other room and greeted one of the workers inside; she seemed to know him. The others took off their shoes and waited quietly in the hall. No one introduced themselves to me or invited me to introduce myself. This felt somewhat awkward, especially since I was planning to make contacts for my fieldwork. Still, I was optimistic; I hoped that after the meditation we would all sit together for a cup of tea. A gong reverberated, and everyone entered a large room that served as the meditation hall.

The next hour passed in nearly total silence. At the end of the hour, after several minutes of chanting, people began to get up. I waited until a few meditators stepped out of the meditation room and followed them into the entrance hall. I watched in surprise as they put on their shoes, some uttering a quiet goodbye as they left the apartment. My participant observation was over—it was time to go home.

Collective group sittings are quite common in vipassana meditation practice. These sittings take place in different locations: meditation centers, apartments owned by local vipassana foundations, practitioners' homes. Home sittings are usually conducted under the auspices of the local vipassana foundation. Practitioners who host such events are instructed to deemphasize socialization. These people have chosen to gather together with the explicit aim for each to concentrate on his or her own breath or bodily sensations. Once the meditation hour is over, the meditators usually go home. When they do stay for coffee and tea (and as I continued my fieldwork, I found that some group sittings do include this ritual), the conversation hardly touches on meditation. Not once did I hear one person ask another, "How was your meditation?" When I myself would venture to ask this question, I would get very brief answers. In contrast to what I expected from this Westernized version of Buddhist meditation, the "twelve-step" culture had not penetrated the scene. Vipassana practitioners do not sit in a circle and share their meditation experiences, nor do they tend to speak with each other about the meditation practice itself.[4]

Newcomers to meditation sittings are frequently taken by surprise when they are introduced to this silent community. A vignette from the field illustrates this reaction. One day I left a meditation apartment with two meditators. A woman whom I had never seen before was walking in front of us. Moving briskly, she seemed to be in a hurry to leave. When she reached her car, she suddenly turned around to face us. Urgently, she asked: "You were there, too, right? How was it for you?"

"The meditation, you mean?" responded Dina, one of the other meditators, in a surprised tone.

"Yes, the meditation—were you able to do it? To do vipassana, I mean."

Still appearing surprised, Dina answered that it depended on her focus; it was sometimes difficult for her to concentrate.

The new woman then continued: "You see, I did my first course just a few weeks ago, and it takes me thirty minutes to get here, and then find parking and everything, and then when I get here I sit and I just can't concentrate— and I can't even follow my breath, not to mention do vipassana, and I wonder if this is worth it; I mean, what is the point of coming here if I can't do vipassana?"

Dina replied that sometimes even one minute was worthwhile, and advised the other woman to speak to one of the teachers.

The woman answered: "The teacher—how is he? I mean, he was sitting there like a statue . . . and you know, I already asked one teacher and got an answer, so what's the point of asking another one?"

This woman wanted to compare her experiences of meditation with that of others. Unable to initiate a conversation of this sort in the meditation apartment, she took it out into the street. But the answer she received was terse, to say the least: it was worth coming to meditation despite the challenges, and if she needed advice, she should ask a teacher. But she didn't want to ask a teacher; she wanted to speak with fellow meditators. This was the last time I saw this woman at group sittings or retreats.

Since practitioners rarely share their meditation experiences, does meditation take place in an utterly private world? Up to this point in our journey, one might well think so. Yet the following will demonstrate that this is not the case. Group meditation involves many nonverbal mechanisms that connect self and other through silent bodily channels, mechanisms that produce a silent community. Nonetheless, as the frustrated novice above tells us, a socialization process is crucial to feeling at home in this silent community. If the process of socialization into this community fails, the adoption of meditation fails as well. Without accepting the silent form of social interactive mode that is embedded in meditation practice, one is indeed left to meditate in one's own world, and to maintain such a world single-handedly is an arduous task indeed.

Progress in vipassana, then, is dependent on sharing a collective space. The main collective space that will be analyzed in this chapter is the meditation center, where silent meditation courses and retreats take place. Like the silent group sittings, meditation retreats offer a silent form of social interactive mode, one that supports the cultivation of meditation practice. In fact, collective meditation courses are central to the training process of many meditation practices. While one can try to learn meditation practice from a book, such attempts tend to produce lukewarm results at best. One can also try to replicate a meditation course in solitude—all that is required is an audio recording of meditation instructions. In fact, during my fieldwork I encountered a vipassana practitioner who attempted to replicate a ten-day retreat while at home. He was able to keep to the schedule for forty-eight hours. After two days, he found himself sleeping instead of meditating and decided to end the effort. Two other practitioners I met spoke about doing such a solo course at home, but three years later they have not yet done so, and my guess is that they never will. The practice of vipassana thus appears to be dependent on the collective environment of the meditation center, where different bodies are positioned in physical proximity.

If you happen to enter a vipassana meditation center in the middle of a retreat, be prepared for some unique sights. The outdoor spaces of the meditation center are empty for most of the day. Participants spend their time meditating in their rooms or in the meditation hall and are specifically instructed not to meditate outside. The sensory stimulation of the outdoors is considered an obstacle to meditation practice: instead of concentrating on the body one senses the bright sunlight or the wind. A gong is sounded on an hourly basis, at which point participants leave their rooms or the meditation hall and walk around for five minutes. This break between sessions allows participants to stretch their sore muscles before they return for another hour of sitting. During this break, sixty or more people walk around the center's grounds in complete silence, not in any way addressing or touching one another. In the harsh winter of Illinois, the space for stretching muscles consists of a small room adjacent to the meditation hall where the students are crowded together, either stretching on the carpeted floor or standing and looking out the large window that offers a view of a small frozen pond.

If you arrive before noon, you will see silent people standing in line waiting for their turn to take food for lunch. After piling food onto their plates (there is no restriction regarding the amount of food they may take, only a recommendation to eat less than usual), they turn to sit silently next to each other in the dining hall. In Israel some participants may choose to sit outside at the few tables designated for dining. The dining hall is filled with people, but one hears only the clink of cutlery and the sounds of chewing. Occasionally someone enters the dining hall to add a dish—such people are members of the volunteer crew that works behind the scenes. They come in quietly, moving slowly. A popular misconception among participants is that this crew is made up of experienced meditators who have come to support them in the course, but the reality is that these volunteers may have taken only one meditation course and are not particularly experienced. Still, they play their role. In the kitchen, the backstage, where participants never enter, they can speak and laugh and move around normally. Yet the moment they enter the course premises, their whole appearance changes: their gaze is lowered, their movements slow down, and most important, they become silent.

When walking around the meditation center, the participants in a meditation course usually move slowly, and I never saw anyone run or jump. At one course, a woman insisted on doing complicated yoga exercises in public, including standing on her head. She was asked to avoid doing these exercises altogether, since they were taking her and others' attention away from meditation. In general, the participants are asked to avoid the following: exercises that are not simple stretching, religious ceremonies (including prayer), reading or writing, listening to music, communicating with fellow meditators, bringing their own food, and using cell phones. They do not communicate with the outside world for ten days, unless there is an emergency, and they are asked not to leave the premises of the course. This does not mean that people do not break the rules. I have watched people speak during meditation courses, eat candies they brought from home, write in a notebook (something, I might add, I also did occasionally). But these were truly exceptions to the rule.

Vipassana meditation centers in Israel, Illinois, Massachusetts (the centers I visited during this study), and many other places have similar physical environments. A meditation center consists of dorms, a dining hall, a kitchen, a meditation hall, and walking grounds. The kitchen and the dining hall are adjacent to one another, but the other facilities are free-standing, with trails or secured corridors connecting the buildings. Few vipassana meditation centers are fenced in, and most are located amid beautiful scenery. In Israel, since the rented meditation center is located close to a small field school, it is surrounded by a blue fence, which blocks it from any view of the external world. In other vipassana centers the view is not blocked, yet there are still clear boundaries. If you start walking on a trail surrounded by high trees, you will soon encounter a sign alerting you that this is the end of the course premises and asking you not to walk any further. The distance between the end of a trail and the course's facilities is not significant, which means there is no place in nature where you can feel isolated. Only in the dorms is it possible to be alone, and even there this is not always the case.

Some differences between the centers are worth mentioning. For example, while in the center in Illinois all the rooms have separate sleeping areas, in Massachusetts and in Israel you will most likely share your sleeping area with at least one other person. Uniformly painted white, these sleeping quarters are plain—no pictures adorn the walls, and no decorative ornaments fill out the spaces. You are given a bed, a place to put your clothing, and a window. The bathrooms are shared by at least two people—in the meditation center in Israel they are shared by five.

If you continue your tour around the meditation center and enter the meditation hall while a group sitting is being conducted, you will encounter the strange sight of more than sixty bodies meditating together. This is the scene that most powerfully contravenes the idea that meditation is a personal or private act, or that people come to a meditation course to be alone. Like the sleeping area, the meditation hall is painted white, with no pictures or statues to be seen. No candles or incense are used, the lighting is dim, and the temperature is comfortable. Individuals sit side by side in rows on the floor. Their eyes are closed, and each seems to be completely focused on his or her interiority. An invisible line separates the women's side of the room from the men's.[5] The space from one person to another is minimal—just enough for a single person to walk between the meditation cushions without touching anyone (figure 1).

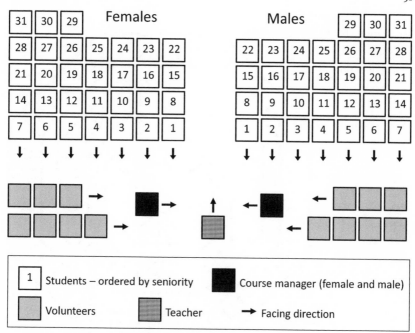

FIGURE 1. Sitting arrangement in the meditation hall.

In some large vipassana meditation centers, like the one in Massachusetts, another training facility is available. This is the pagoda, a large circular building divided into many small meditation cells, each around 1.5 square meters. As shown in figure 2, these private meditation cells are arranged in a few concentric rings within the pagoda. Each cell shares a wall with at least two other cells (in some meditation centers the pagoda has several stories, so each meditator may have other meditators sitting above or below as well). These meditation cells are restricted to advanced students, and each meditator receives his or her cell for the whole course. Here the student sits in relative physical isolation. The cell is empty except for a mattress and a cushion on the floor and a dim light on the ceiling. The meditator enters the cell, closes the door, sits down on the floor, and meditates. When participating in advanced meditation courses, practitioners spend most of their time in these cells, once a day meditating together in the collective setting of the meditation hall.

The vipassana meditation center provides a space where a silent community can be formed, a space based on quietness and minimal stimulation. Yet while the notion of community may evoke connotations of long-lasting ties and mutual commitment, this silent community is different. A typical meditation course runs for ten days. Afterward the participants leave the silent community and return home to their everyday lives. During the course it is

Meditation cell

Facing direction ↓

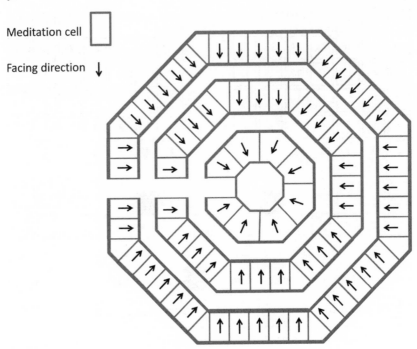

FIGURE 2. A general scheme of a pagoda with individual meditation cells.

not likely that participants will become acquainted with their neighbors; even if they do so, it is quite rare to see participants maintain contact with each other once the meditation course ends. If you arrive with a friend, you are asked to mention this to the organizing staff, since room sharing with friends is discouraged and so is sitting near friends in the meditation hall. A community therefore surrounds you, but this is a community of strangers who have gathered together for one purpose — to learn to meditate. This meditative community of strangers produces the oxymoronic state of *collective solitude*. Meditators have come to learn internal observation, to face themselves, and to practice self-mastery. The cultivation of these apparently subjective abilities, however, requires a supporting group.

A Community of Time and Place

The meditation hall is the most important place in the meditation center. This is where, to borrow a term coined by Alfred Schutz, a silent "community of space and time" develops. For Schutz, a community of space and time is created by individuals in physical proximity to each other who share the same activity or object of attention. The community is based on the mutual sharing of what he refers to as "Here and Now,"[6] leading to the "joint flow of our ex-periences."[7] Through the simultaneous sharing of a place and activity, social relationships and social structures are produced, even in the absence of overt communication.

The constitution of the silent community begins on the evening of the first day of a meditation course, once participants have arrived and registered and the course is about to begin. The participants stand outside the meditation hall, and each one is given a number. This number corresponds to the mattress and cushion upon she or he will sit for the rest of the course. Only by special request—for example, if one asks to be seated next to a wall—are students permitted to change position. Since students are requested to refrain from touching or sitting on the cushions of others, meditation spots are considered personal. After receiving their numbers, the students enter the meditation hall. A volunteer shows them silently to their cushions. If a student happens to speak, a volunteer will put a finger on her own mouth and smile. Each student sits down on his or her 70 cm² blue mattress and smaller blue cushion. At the beginning of the course, all meditation spots look exactly alike. In time, each spot will acquire personal characteristics—extra cushions for comfort and support or a piece of cloth to cover the body during meditation.

As the numbers are distributed, the rows become occupied with students. They sit facing the front of the room, where the seat of the teacher is located. On the right and left sides of the meditation hall, the volunteers sit facing the teacher as well. Let's look for a moment from the point of view of a new female student sitting in the meditation hall. The only face she can clearly see is the teacher's. Then there are the volunteers, whose sides she can easily see. The main view, though, is of the backs of other meditating women in the front rows–one next to the other, in straight lines. The backs that our student observes are not randomly positioned; teachers assign those positions on the basis of the forms that students filled in during registration. Students are seated in the hall according to their seniority in meditation practice, seniority determined by the number of courses they have taken and the intensity of their daily practice. In figure 1, female number 1 sitting in the front row will be the most "senior" female student, meaning she has most likely participated in several meditation courses, perhaps even a long course of twenty days, and practices daily at home. Female 2 will be the second in terms of seniority, and so on. Most students, then, observe the backs of more advanced students.

This order of sitting adds complexity to the silent community that is beginning to form. The participants in this community are not equal in status. They each have a place and a role in a hierarchical system of expertise. Although the new students are not told in advance about this spatial arrangement, they quickly grasp it.[8] Despite the fact that students do not wear any marks of seniority and in general are asked to keep their eyes closed during meditation, those in the back rows soon discover that the students whose backs they can see sit more quietly and for longer periods than themselves. In this way novice students understand that those sitting in the first rows are more experienced.

The basic social structure that is built into the silent community lays the ground for one important microsociological mechanism of meditation practice: vertical imitation. Once a novice student realizes that the students in the front row are more experienced, the natural tendency of a training process leads the novice to imitate those senior students. For example, the students receive no instruction on which position to assume. The instructions tell them only to sit with their backs and necks straight. However, since the teacher sits in a cross-legged position and the meditators in the first rows usually do the same, the majority of the students will begin their meditation in this position as well (some teachers sit in a lotus or half-lotus position, but students rarely imitate this, as it is physically difficult). Through personal improvisation, some meditators change their position over time, but most students will end the course sitting with their legs crossed. Hand position is determined through a similar process. Students sometimes begin by resting their hands on their knees, as is common in yoga practice, but as the course advances, the majority will shift to a position in which the arms come straight down from the shoulders and the wrists rest on the upper thighs, imitating the meditation teacher and the advanced students. In response to a query I made about the position of the arms, I was told that it is not particularly important. Only once was I informed that having the arms close to the body can help in the more advanced stages of meditation, when the meditator scans the whole body in one breath.

A vignette from a one-day vipassana retreat I observed illustrates the search for role models which occupies the mind of novice participants. The participants in this relatively short retreat had all participated in a ten-day vipassana course in the past, but most were not experienced in meditation. The person in charge was an advanced practitioner, Peter, who had once participated in a twenty-day course. After the retreat was over and people began talking, one of the women asked Peter about his unfamiliar meditation posture as she noticed that "he was slightly rocking back and forth." He answered in a tone of surprise, "Oh, I just fell asleep," and laughed. The woman started laughing as well, saying that it looked so intriguing she'd thought this might be some sort of unique meditation reserved for advanced students and tried it, unsuccessfully, herself.

Though most imitation takes place vertically, with new students imitating more advanced students, horizontal imitation is also an important mechanism. As mentioned above, in the first meditation session all students sit on plain blue cushions. The next day other cushions, which are stored in a closet outside the meditation hall, suddenly appear. These supplementary cushions vary in shape, size, and color. In my observations, when one new student improvised and put an extra small round cushion under her knee for support, the next day a few others tried the same arrangement. The same day that one student asked for and was given a back support, three others asked for a similar support as well. In one course a student decided to move and sit against the wall while the evening lecture was played on video. This improvisation was well accepted by the group, and the next evening during the lecture, ten students were resting against the wall.

Students are thus quite aware of the other participants who share the meditation hall, and they constantly search for cues that could assist them in their meditation training. This awareness is first centered on the practical aspects of meditation practice, such as sitting positions or the use of cushions. As the course advances, another dimension of meditation practice becomes central to the social relationship produced in the meditation hall—the importance of bodily stillness. From the beginning of the meditation course, the participants are asked to minimize movement while they are meditating. When they do move, they are asked to do so slowly and consciously. From the fourth day onward, during collective meditation sessions, participants are asked to keep completely still for an hour-long period three times per day. The advanced students, who sit in the front rows, can sit still, while the novice students struggle. Here processes of mutual imitation and bodily synchronization become central, as the stillness of one body affects the stillness of another.

Self through the Eyes of Others

Vipassana meditation involves shifting the body to the center of attention, turning it into an overt object of observation. The main instruction of vipassana is to "observe" bodily sensations—from breathing to pain to itchiness to a tickling in the hand, without reacting or responding to these sensations. Observation here is a metaphor, as students are not asked to actually look at or imagine their body parts. They are asked to "feel" them. In other words, they are asked to transfer the regular, everyday focus of attention from the world to the inner lining of experience. To feel themselves feeling the world.

Bodily silence is central to training in this shift. When people are in movement, attention quickly shifts back to the world. Of course we are never completely motionless. Our bodies are in constant movement and touch with the world—the breath comes in and out, the leg is pressed against the mattress, the cloth touches our skin, there is noise, light, itchiness. During meditation different sensations "tempt" the practitioner to move and lose the focus on the internal milieu, to move from feeling myself feeling the world back to sensing, perceiving, acting, and reacting. Teachers discourage such distractions by asking the meditator not to move, or to move with as much awareness of the movement as possible. Such movement helps the practitioner to focus on feeling the body, even when moving around or acting. This explains the slow and precise movements of volunteers and teachers in the meditation center. It also explains why the physical proximity of bodies plays such a significant role.

The physical proximity of others produces an interaction chain in which the first step in the initiation into feeling one's own body is the observation of other bodies. Through observing other bodies, novice practitioners learn the significance of bodily silence. Such silence is not trivial, as it requires a great deal of effort that sometimes seems contradictory to the aim of meditation. Take the following exchange I observed between a teacher and a student who was attending her fourth meditation course. When asked if she could sit without moving for one hour, the student answered that she could sit still for only fifty minutes. Instead of offering the usual advice given to novice students, which permits movement as long as it is slow and monitored, the teacher insisted that she not move.

The student answered, "But I keep generating all this hate toward the pain, and I am not internally peaceful at all, so I just keep reacting internally—isn't it better just to move a bit and quiet the pain?"

The teacher smiled and told her to keep still: "You are an advanced student; you can do it."

For the student, the insistence on nonmovement seemed irrational; stillness did not bring about peacefulness at all, and if she kept reacting to the pain anyway (at least mentally), why did it matter whether the reaction was internal or external? The teacher's answer shows that it does matter. Training toward detached observation of sensations begins with external physical reactions, ones that can be tracked by observers.

A silent and peaceful body is not a natural, passive outcome of meditation. In fact, it requires active doing. And this active doing is supported by the existence of an audience to whom one projects the "right" self. Even though students are asked to concentrate on their own sensations and ignore others, meditators always spend a part of the meditation practice time in the mind of others.

Those who sit in the front row, for example, spend time in the minds of those sitting behind them, aware of the fact that they are serving as role models. Rachel was seated in the second row in one course. Although she had taken a few meditation courses in the past, she still could not sit for one hour without moving. She was concerned about her positioning, wondering, "What will they think of me? I keep moving all the time . . ." Tom, for his part, was not aware that students were tracking him when he was sitting in the first row in two meditation courses. He then took a more advanced meditation course in which he was one of the less experienced meditators and therefore was moved to the third row. He found that sitting in the first row had helped him reach a high degree of equanimity. In the third row he tended to move more and had difficulty cultivating peacefulness. Thinking back, Tom felt that he had not been conscious of the fact that others were observing him from behind when he was in the first row, but somehow their presence behind him had been extremely influential.

Neighbors sitting next to one another also spend some time in each other's minds. Daniel, who sat next to an advanced meditator, was sure that the still body and calm face of his neighbor signified that he was having an easy meditation course. On the last day, when talking was allowed, he found out that his neighbor had in fact been going through a difficult course, experiencing significant pain and discomfort. Another participant, Ben, was tormented by a pressing need to swallow saliva continuously during meditation. This disturbed him greatly, and he was certain that others suffered from the sounds that his body generated. When the course was over, he approached his neighbor and apologized for "making so much noise," but the neighbor responded that he had not been aware of any noise and was certainly not troubled by it. These observations confirm Goffman's claim that "when nothing eventful is accruing, persons in each other's presence are still nonetheless tracking one another and acting so as to make themselves trackable."[9] Even though meditators are asked to "ignore" others, they track the movements of others and assume (though not always correctly) that others track their own movements.

Spending time in the mind of others, then, does not always disclose correct information about others' experiences or thoughts. In a meditation center one can feel extreme pain or depression while one's neighbor experiences erotic sensations or euphoria. This special form of togetherness, which keeps some experiences hidden from others, enables a form of intersubjectivity that is unique. People in a meditation center are not united by a shared culture or history. They are also not united by a shared object of attention, such as seeing the same movie or hearing the same music.[10] Everyone in the meditation center concentrates on their subjective feelings—and these may vary radically from one student to another. What unites people in a meditation center is the

fact that they are all involved in a shared activity that is performed in proximity to one another—that they share a general form, regardless of the specific content each person observes.

Being able to see and hear others during group meditation also generates
a competitive urge. Though meditation formally advocates acceptance of the
present moment with no reference to the future, since meditation is a practice that relies on progress, it certainly ignites a desire to succeed. I frequently
found myself in the last ten minutes of a meditation session, with extreme
pain in my legs or back, telling myself: "You can do it—just a few more minutes before moving." Such internal conversations may not be an official part of
the embodied attention mode that is taught in meditation, but they are quite
common among novice practitioners. Crucially, these conversations are not
disconnected from the silent conversation that takes place between self and
other in the meditation hall. Your neighbor's ability to sit still for a whole hour
is likely to increase your motivation to do so. Conversely, if five minutes before the end of the session your neighbor suddenly moves, the temptation to
move grows and your own chances of moving rise.

While students are specifically told not to compare themselves to others,
comparison is unavoidable. To some extent, it is even encouraged by the
teaching structure. In general, course participants do not hear conversations
between their fellow participants and the teacher. If a student wishes to speak
with the teacher, she must sign up for a private meeting that takes place during the lunch break. These meetings are limited to five-minute blocks. Shorter
questions to the teacher can be brought up at the end of the day, at 9:00 p.m.
At this time the students who would like to ask a question stay in the hall, and
each student approaches the teacher separately and asks him or her a question
in a soft voice. Unless you were sitting in the first row, it is unlikely that you
would hear either the question or the answer.

These arrangements for keeping students' questions private suit the solitary and individualistic approach of vipassana meditation. But they stand
in opposition to another teaching session that takes place on certain days
during the course. In this session, referred to as "checking," the teacher asks
short and simple questions designed to check each student's progress. In the
middle of the day, when the students are in the meditation hall, the teacher
invites groups of five to sit in front of her. The five students sit down close to
the teacher, each on a cushion. The teacher then asks each student the same
question. For example, on the first day the teacher asks, "Can you feel your
breath?" On the third day, "Can you observe your breath for one minute?"
On the fourth day, "Can you feel sensations?" On the sixth day, "Can you sit
for one hour without moving?" The question is repeated to each student, and

after all five students have answered, the teacher invites them to meditate with her for a few minutes. When the few minutes are over, the teacher instructs them to continue their meditation in the meditation hall or in their rooms. She then calls up another group of five students.

Although these questions are merely answered in a yes-or-no format, they supply important information regarding other students' progress. A student thinking to herself that concentrating on the breath for one minute is an impossible task may learn that the other four students in her group can do that easily. Such a discovery may lead to frustration, but it can also kindle a competitive urge in participants, who then tell themselves that if others can do something they can do it as well. This also explains why even though students can ask to sit on a chair or ask for back support, the majority choose not to do so. Seeing others, and the teacher, sitting on the floor for long hours, they recognize that this is the "right" way to meditate, and assume or hope that they will become accustomed to the position.

Rhythmic Coordination and Mutual Attunement

As we have seen above, the projection of a self to others through the use of the silent body is a crucial part of meditation training. Here others function as an audience, and in these moments of self-evaluation they are at the center of attention, as meditators dwell in the minds of others and adjust their bodies accordingly. This channel of training is particularly important in the first stages of meditation training. However, with time awareness of others recedes to the background and turns tacit. When this happens, we witness another channel through which others are used in meditation training: rhythmic coordination and the production of mutual bodily attunement.

Imagine a meditation hall, full of meditating bodies. No one is speaking and no one is moving. You observe perhaps sixty faces; some people seem to be concentrating, and some seem calm. Here and there you see or hear the briefest of gestures. Many long observations have taught me that patterns emerge out of this silence connecting the movements of different meditators, despite the apparent lack of communication. Following the movements closely, I have noticed that movements cluster and form bundles of noise: the movement of one woman leads to a movement reaction by a few others. One person's cough triggers others to join in. The movement of one person leads to the movement of another.

This became apparent when I participated in a group sitting at a meditation apartment. Sixteen people were sitting silently in meditation, when a phone in another room began to ring. One woman quickly got up and stepped out of the hall to disconnect it. A moment after this interruption, two people changed their posture and two people coughed. It was as though the break in silence opened a narrow time slot for communal noise. A minute later we were all in complete silence again. Following this incident, I began to monitor movements in the meditation hall at the meditation center. In one instance, a loud cough was heard from the men's side. As the man continued coughing, a woman in the third row moved her leg and changed her posture. Her movement was noisy, and it activated two other movements—another woman moved her hand, and another straightened her back. In another episode, fifteen minutes before the end of a one-hour sitting, a woman moved her leg. Almost concurrently another woman, sitting a few spots away, straightened up, and her neighbor then took a deep, audible breath. In fact, after I became aware of this mutual influence of movement, I found myself while in meditation taking a heavy breath a second after the woman next to me let out a heavy breath.

This attunement to others is usually quite minimal, but it can grow into a live orchestra. On the ninth day of one meditation course, during the individual meditation hours (when there was no teacher in the hall), a woman sitting in the first row began to giggle. Trying unsuccessfully to control herself, she giggled, was silent for half a minute, and then giggled again. During her third round of giggling, a woman sitting behind her began giggling as well. They shared a short laugh together. To an outside observer it looked as if they were acquainted with one another (as I later learned by inquiring, they were not). At the next giggle, a third woman joined in—her giggle was more restrained but audible nonetheless. All three were giggling while sitting with eyes closed and bodies still. The incident lasted a few minutes, and then they all returned to silence. Throughout the entire episode, the other students in the hall sat quietly.

This orchestra of sound and movement tells us that even when attention is diverted inward, a part of us is still tracking the external world of social interaction and adjusting our bodies accordingly. It reflects the fact that as humans we react to others, and this reaction is embodied. Even though meditation students know that they should not move, when someone else moves their body demands movement as well. This influence can take place even without direct intention or awareness. Students have reported that on occasion they find their hand moving though they don't remember making any conscious decision to move anything. The joint giggling episode is an excellent example of the mutual influence of physical proximity. Though these women were not concentrating on the same amusing object, they were certainly influenced by emotional contagion.[11] At the same time the other people in the room, by continuing their own silence, conveyed to these women that they were expected to end their interruption and return to meditation. By keeping silent and nonengaged, the other students performed the emotional attitude that is cultivated in the meditation center. The women that giggled responded to this performance and quickly silenced themselves and returned to the joint calm.

Such rhythmic coordination and emotional entrainment are quite common in a meditation center. There were days when four or five students in the hall suddenly began shedding tears; later they reported that they had no conscious awareness of one another. There were days when the whole group was quiet and still during meditation and days when interferences produced a wave that carried many participants into restlessness and movement. Entire meditation courses can be affected by such synchronization. Meditation teachers rate courses—a good course is one in which serious meditation took place, while a difficult course is marked by frequent emotional outbursts, movements, and disquiet among practitioners. The attempt to produce a "good course" explains why one third of the places in each ten-day meditation course are allotted to advanced students. Having more advanced students in the hall helps to control the number of movements and generates a general tendency toward silence and seriousness.

The effects of both social monitoring and mutual attunement account for why meditators report that they find it easier to meditate quietly in a group. The group, with its nonresponsive attitude of silence and stillness, keeps that part of me that is attentive to the external world quiet and relaxed as my body synchronizes with others and my attention is diverted inward. When comparing their meditation in the meditation hall to that done in their rooms, many meditators discover that in the meditation hall they can sit without moving for longer periods, and their meditations are deeper and stronger. If in their rooms they tend to move once or twice in an hour on average, in the meditation hall they find that they can maintain nonmovement for a whole hour. In a real sense, the stillness of the individual body is a collective endeavor.

Silent Communities in Private Meditation Cells

As meditators progress, they are expected to reduce their dependence on the physical proximity of others. The training toward becoming an independent meditator takes place in the private meditation cells described above. The small cells allow vipassana practitioners to cultivate independent practice. Typically, only experienced students who take courses of more than ten days' duration are offered meditation cells.

When Alex participated in a fourteen-day special course for experienced students, he was shocked to find that he had difficulty sitting alone in the meditation cell without moving. As he told me in our third interview, he found that in the cell he became tired and restless:

> There was a big difference. I felt lazy and drowsy. So for the majority of the time, I decided to sit in the hall and not alone in the cell. It was very surprising—I would go to the cell, sit down, and suddenly I open my eyes, I do not feel like meditating. I tried fighting it, and it was really hard—I was not able to concentrate, I did not feel like meditating. So in the first days, I tried to give the cell a chance and meditate there, but as the course continued, I found myself more and more in the hall, where it was much easier to meditate.

Alex had been practicing in solitude for a whole year at home before he participated in this course (which is one of the requirements for participating in long courses, which can last up to sixty days). Nonetheless, he still found it extremely difficult to meditate for many hours alone. He discovered that he needed the silent bodily co-presence of others for deeper and more relaxed meditation.

Though meditation cells do not allow for bodily co-presence, they are not completely cut off from the silent community. In the meditation hall the physical proximity of others has a direct influence—you can hear and see other bodies—and an intersubjective space is produced where different bodies are engaged in the same activity. In the private meditation cell you cannot hear or see others. And yet the others are still in proximity, not much farther away than in the meditation hall. Each cell shares a wall with at least two other cells. In addition, the practitioners who sit in meditation cells are asked to sit facing the center of the structure. Those in the cells, then, are all oriented toward the same place. If we were to take away the walls, an intimate arrangement would appear, one that is even more intimate than that of the meditation hall. Instead of sitting in rows, meditators essentially sit in two or three concentric circles facing one another.

The influence of this sitting arrangement is revealed in a story that Rachel told me after her first twenty-day meditation course:

> For the first time, I had my own meditation cell. I was sitting in the cell, and something felt wrong. I cannot explain it. I just couldn't meditate, and I felt restless. So I asked to speak with the teacher, and she asked me where I was facing when I sat—and I found out I was facing the wrong direction! I was sitting with my back pointed to the center of the pagoda! And I went back and this time sat with my face toward the right direction and then it just all clicked in, as if I was out of tune and now I was back in tune.

To demonstrate this experience of "clicking in," Rachel moved her body so that she was not facing me, stretched her hands out in front of her, and moved her body around until she faced me again, then made a gesture with her hands as if she was now anchored in place. We can imagine how Rachel felt when she realized that while everyone else was sitting facing each other in a circle, she was sitting with her back to the whole community. Despite the fact that Rachel did not see the other people around her, the knowledge that upon changing her position she was facing the center and that others around her were sitting as she was, produced a "tuning in" that was essential for her practice.

This tuning in is further supported by a temporal alignment of meditation sessions in private cells. The schedule for meditation sessions is fixed, with timing signaled by a gong that reverberates through the meditation center. That is, the times at which people enter and leave the meditation cells are synchronized. When a participant completes a meditation session and goes to lunch, she sees all her neighbors leaving their cells and taking their lunch break. When she returns, she sees the others returning and entering their cells. In addition, once a day all the participants gather in the meditation hall for a joint meditation sitting, where they are back under the influence of bodies of others.

Private meditation cells therefore reduce meditators' dependence on physical proximity, but they definitely do not constitute solitary practice. Physical proximity and temporal synchronization remain, even if they are not accompanied by bodily co-presence. The people who sit in private meditation cells continue to be part of a silent community of time and space, even with walls separating them from one another.

From "Doing Meditation" to "Being Done by Meditation"

The above observations, which illustrate the dependence of meditation practice on the physical proximity of others, are not unique to meditation. Similar observations can be made in a fitness class, where imitation, competition, and emotional entrainment all play a role for participants in proximity to each other. When we are learning a practice that involves embodied knowledge, proximity to others is crucial for the training process, since learning such practices requires a mentor and a supporting community. When surrounded by other people, an individual can reach a much higher level than he or she would alone. This does not always require a deliberate awareness or conscious self-control. In fact, by immersing oneself in a social environment one can cultivate certain abilities without any need for constant self-discipline, which can be exhausting. The social environment provides one with energies for action that are difficult to locate when one is alone.[12]

These energies and mutual influence are highly dependent on the body, as we use our bodies to project internal states both to others and to ourselves. Through our bodies we bridge the divide between the external and the internal. On the one hand, the body carries a subjective intimacy — we can feel our bodies, and this feeling is unique. We cannot feel other people's bodies in the way that we feel our own. And yet at the same time, the body is also always in the world. We constantly use our bodies to sense the world, trying to locate our position in relation to the world (and others within it). Simultaneously our bodies are seen, heard, and interpreted by others. Like a radar, we send out signals through our movement, action, and expressions, and react when these signals bounce back from the external world. This explains why a meditation practice that accentuates awareness of internal processes puts so much emphasis on quieting the movement of the body — the least "internal" part of our being.

By quieting bodily movement, a meditator quiets the "active-sensing" part of his body, the part that mandates a response from the body, the part that perceives change and reacts to it (even through the minor change of the rhythm of breathing). The fact that the body is simultaneously internal and external makes it an ideal medium for the process of self-exploration. While no one can track the quieting of another's thoughts, a whole group of people seated one next to the other can track the quieting of each other's bodily movements.

This tracking takes place through two distinct channels. The first is through dwelling in the minds of others and evaluating one's performance through their eyes. The second is joint bodily indwelling, submitting oneself to bodily synchronization and attunement with others. While these two channels are interrelated, progress in meditation is dependent on a shift to the second channel, moving others from the foreground of attention to the background, shifting from focused awareness of others to tacit awareness. In fact, as we saw, too much awareness of others, being too "self-conscious," can inhibit meditation as one spends time thinking about the judgments of others instead of concentrating on the inner lining of experience. This is why meditation teachers ask students not to compare themselves to others. This is also why meditators do not discuss their meditation experiences with each other. And this is why the final goal of meditation training, the isolated meditation cells, remove the external gaze completely while keeping a dimension of joint bodily indwelling that is produced through the physical proximity of the cells and the temporal alignment of meditation sessions.

Jack Katz has introduced the notion of "doing emotion" versus "being done by emotion."[13] One can say that the first stage of meditation relies heavily on the active, conscious, self-aware in the symbolic sense stage in which participants "do meditation." This includes mimicking others, searching for cues, learning how to act, performing for the teacher and others in the room, aligning performance with certain external rules, competing with others and with oneself. Gradually, as the practice gets anchored in the surrounding environment, this self-aware mode can be relaxed. At this point the external world disappears, and one finds oneself in deep meditation, a stage in which the stillness of the body takes care of itself (through mutual attunement) and one is immersed in the nuances of bodily sensations. It is in this stage that strong meditation experiences appear, including experiences of flow, experiences of peacefulness and equanimity, and experiences of liberation. In this stage, meditators no longer "do" or "perform" meditation but are "being done" by meditation, as the practice takes over the self and brings about new and transformative experiences.

Communities of Solitary Practice

Meditators decrease their dependence on the physical proximity of others as they become more advanced in the practice. They start meditating alone at home, and meditation turns into a relatively solitary practice. However, this form of solitude is based on their previous social encounters in the meditation center. Solitary meditation practice is not disconnected from the silent community described above. In fact, home practice frequently re-creates the original environment of the meditation center through the use of certain spatial and temporal arrangements.

Outside the meditation center, many meditators participate in collective group sittings once a week. These sittings, like the one described at the opening of this chapter, re-create the silent community that is constituted in the meditation center. Though this community exists only for one hour, it suffices for reconstitution of all the mechanisms discussed above—imitation, social monitoring, rhythmic coordination, and mutual attunement—and the effect of these mechanisms lasts beyond the meditation hour: it spills into everyday solitary practice. If we also consider a meditation retreat of ten days and a few days of volunteering at the meditation center once a year, then meditators' everyday life is not that distanced from the previous or the next participation in a silent community, and meditators remain aware of the existence of this silent community even when they meditate alone at home.

The use of certain devices reinforces this awareness. One important device that helps produce a meditative atmosphere is sensory cues. Sensory cues are based on the body's reflexive capacity to react to perception of specific elements in its surroundings that index a certain environment. For example, the sight of the kitchen when one returns home from a day out at work often produces a craving for food, even when one is not particularly hungry. In American culture, a bedroom lighted with candles may trigger sexual desire. High heels or a silk dress serves as a bodily cue that produces the right mood for participation in a formal event. In all these cases, sensory cues serve as reminders of previous encounters with the same environment and generate a certain bodily state and state of mind.

The teachings of vipassana meditation seek to minimize the ritualistic aspect of meditation. There are no uniforms, no candles or pictures of the teachers. You can choose the cushion you would like to sit on, and you can choose your posture. You can meditate at home, at the office, or on the train. In fact, this is one of the features that attract many meditators to this type of meditation: a sense of a secular, nonritualistic practice. In vipassana there is a clear effort to reduce meditators' dependence on external devices and a general emphasis on cultivating a continuous attitude of meditation in every moment of everyday life.

Still, while vipassana meditation does not provide formal ritualistic devices, practitioners tend to produce their own sensory cues. Meditators practicing alone usually practice in dim lighting and in silence, as in the meditation center. They sit for an hour, which is the timeframe for a sitting in the meditation center. They sit in the same posture, and though this is not required, the posture is usually the same for all meditators. Many have cushions identical to the ones they have used in the meditation center. Some even have a favorite piece of cloth that they cover their bodies with while meditating, the same cloth they use in meditation retreats.

Novice practitioners take further steps to reconstruct the atmosphere of the meditation center. Some use the same audio recording that is used in collective group sittings, which includes a few meditation instructions and a short segment of chanting. The voice of the teacher, S. N. Goenka, brings the community of meditation practice into their home. In one instance, Sarit, who participated in two ten-day meditation courses, had difficulty sitting alone. She was able to practice meditation for one hour in group sittings, but when alone, she would stop meditating after fifteen minutes. When she heard that I had a CD of meditation instructions, she asked if she could use it. I gave it to her, and after a few days she called and thanked me—she found that when sitting with the CD she could sit for as long as in a group sitting.

Some practitioners report that when they are having a difficult time meditating they use a sensory trick—they imagine that they are sitting in the medi-

tation hall surrounded by people. This imaginative moment is very brief—
a mere second in which the collective community is summoned and they see
themselves surrounded by meditating people. This second suffices to summon a change of mood in both body and mind, as the body relaxes into subtle
and warm sensations. Though others may not use such overt tricks, the use
of any sensory cues works in a parallel way, metaphorically summoning an
invisible community from the past. The dim lights, the silence, the chanting,
sitting on a familiar cushion, and covering oneself with a familiar cloth all
aim to produce an environment of meditation by reminding the meditator
of previous collective meditation sittings and meditation courses. These are
external anchors that induce a specific inner state. They call for a particular
attitude from within, of bodily stillness, of sensitivity to sensations, and of
introspection. The external repetition cultivates an internal repetition: as one
hears the chanting or sits in a posture, one invokes the internal attitude of
meditation. There is no specific significance to the posture one chooses, but
there is significance in mimicking the posture of others. The significance of a
particular cushion lies in the fact that it was chosen for its similarity to those
used in the course.

Though this phenomenon only emerged close to the ending of this research, the recent use of meditation applications, such as Headspace, produces the same effect. While using an application may produce a feeling of
being in a solitary space (no need to be in the physical presence of others), this
is not the case. Each session includes meditation instructions repeated in the
same familiar voice, and in most sessions you are consistently accompanied
by that voice and thus are not "left alone." The meditations are based on fixed
time slots, you get email reminders regarding your progress, and you can even
see how many people around the world are meditating using the same application at the same time. Like other virtual networks, the application removes
physical proximity while keeping you embedded in a social world.

As a meditator's practice develops, these physical and temporal cues are
internalized. Take the one-hour timeframe for meditation. As mentioned,
novice practitioners frequently use a CD that creates a one-hour frame by
giving meditation instructions at the beginning and the end of one hour. As
meditation becomes more natural in practitioners' lives, they usually switch
to using a simple alarm clock, setting it for sixty minutes. Eventually even the
alarm clock is no longer required. The body becomes habituated to a one-
hour frame, and practitioners can sense how much time has passed.

In one of the meditation sittings I attended, I witnessed an incident that
demonstrates this internalization of the timeframe. The sitting took place in
the house of a longtime meditator, and all the participants (except for my-

self) had taken at least one twenty-day course. As is customary in joint meditation sittings, we sat on the floor in rows, and a CD with some chanting
was played. Five minutes into the meditation the chanting stopped, and we
entered silence. The plan was for the chanting to resume after fifty minutes,
signaling the end of an hour—but the CD got stuck. Since we were all sitting with our eyes closed, we did not know about the problem and continued
meditating. Nevertheless, after around sixty-five minutes of completely silent
meditation, sounds of movement were heard as participants stretched. Two
minutes later the host got up, checked the CD, and announced, "Guys, the
CD got stuck." No one answered, and we all continued to meditate for a few
more minutes. After these few minutes people started moving, and someone
turned on the light. When people went back to speaking, the conversation
revolved around the stuck CD. "I felt it was too long," said one practitioner.
"Yes," added the host, "we sat for almost seventy minutes." Another woman
added that she considered opening her eyes to check but then thought, "What
the hell, a longer meditation session is even better."

As practitioners become habituated to meditation, they may cease to rely
on external cues and frames. They meditate alone easily, they do not use a
recording, they can change the hours of their meditation, and they can more
readily change their place of meditation. For many meditators, meditation
practice is not confined to sitting on the cushion. Some meditate while they
eat by turning attention to the sensations on their tongue and in their mouth.
Others meditate while driving, by turning attention to sensations on their
hands. Some serious meditators claimed that they had gotten to the point that
a part of their mind was constantly aware of sensations on the body. For them,
the practice has become so habituated that meditating, as a senior meditator
told me, "is like brushing the teeth in the morning."

Still, even these advanced practitioners require maintenance in a collective sphere. Meditators who have not taken a meditation course for a year
commonly say that they feel they are losing their sensitivity to bodily sensations and need a meditation retreat of a few days to regain the practice. They
need to go back to the environment where the social, temporal, and physical
dimensions are most supportive of meditation.

*

In our everyday lives, the "normal" direction of attention moves from body
to the world, from body and its sensations to the projection of self to others,
or, to borrow Polanyi's terms, from the proximate to the distal.[14] In everyday interactions I am aware of my body, adjusting it in relation to others and
in relation to the way I think they perceive me—but this awareness is tacit.

Someone waves his hand in greeting and I wave back, but I don't direct full attention to my hand or to the movement. My attention is set on the social situation, on the meaning of the gesture, on the way the other sees me responding.

Vipassana and other practices of heightened embodied awareness reverse this direction. In these practices, attention is placed on what is in "regular" daily interaction the proximate—bodily sensations—while the distal, the others, turns into the anchor, the ground from which the practitioner attends to the inner lining of experience. This inversion of attention entails moving others from the role of the audience to the role of co-bodily indwellers. While doing so, a part of my body is monitoring others, but such monitoring is done through synchronizing movement and nonmovement, a monitoring that does not require focused attention. Such bodily interdwelling allows for a relaxation of awareness of the outside world, a function that is now held and exercised by the silent body, permitting diversion of attention to the subtlety of sensations. Instead of projecting a self to the world and to others, I align my body with others' bodies and turn my attention inward.

There is a great deal of sociological inquiry on the connections between a social group and the self. But unlike Cooley's "looking glass self" or Goffman's "face work," in the silent communities described in this chapter, the group does not take center stage as an ever-present self-judge.[15] When others are at the center of attention, the attention cannot be reversed. As long as others are in the limelight, you are "doing" meditation but not "being done by" meditation. As the others move into the background, as tacit social attunement is achieved, one can trust the social surrounding to provide the grounding in others necessary for being completely focused on the internal.

Paradoxically, meditation participants use others to forget about others. The group enables them to put aside their social concerns and enter deep meditation. It is the "collective solitude" generated by the group that allows them to feel that they are "facing themselves" on their own.

Meditation in Daily Life

You see, now, while I am talking to you, I can feel the ends of my toes. Isn't that an amazing thing? (Gabriel)

Gabriel's statement, and others like it, pushed me to rethink relations between the body, self, and the world. As I participated in and observed meditation retreats, following my informants' and my own experiences, I began to understand that Gabriel's remark goes a long way toward accounting for the allure that vipassana carries for its practitioners. I found that the people I studied take the experience they encountered within the situated practice of vipassana into their lives outside of meditation. They make the practice relevant to their everyday lives, infusing it with meaningful and pragmatic use.[1]

By tracking the significance practitioners give to vipassana in their lives—showing how they perceive vipassana to pertain to a wide range of life situations, from managing workplace stress to negotiating conflicts—I demonstrate in this chapter how feeling "the ends of my toes" can become a significant and even liberating experience. By illustrating how my informants harness their meditation experiences to shape their selves, the strategic uses they employ, and what they see as being "discovered" through meditation, I shed light on potentials, possibilities, and variance in making and experiencing the embodiment of the self. At the same time I explain the motivation behind the decision to invest time and effort in practices that increase awareness of the embodied dimension of everyday life.

Vipassana practice as it is exercised and experienced in meditation retreats is introduced first. Then we'll step with my informants out of the meditation centers and into their normal routines, following the varied and creative ways they use vipassana in different situations and contexts—first in daily meditation sittings and second while moving and acting in the world. We will track how they perceive and interpret meditation practice as influencing their lives and selves.

Shifting Attention to the Inner Lining of Experience

I met Tanya in the Israeli vipassana center during a meditation course in which I volunteered as a course assistant. She was a recent immigrant from Russia, around fifty-five years old. This was her third meditation course, and she seemed quite accustomed to meditation. Most women her age ask to sit on a chair while meditating, but she sat on the floor in the first row. She was meditating without moving and seemed to be completely concentrated on her embodied sensations. On the fourth day, when the evening meditation session was about to start, I noticed that she was sitting in her spot in the meditation hall and quietly crying. The teacher looked at her but did not approach her. After a few minutes Tanya stood up and left the hall. The teacher asked me to follow her to see if she needed help. She was standing outside the hall sobbing. It did not seem as though she could go back and meditate, so I told her (at the advice of the teacher) that she could go back to her room and rest. Several minutes later I went to check on her and found that she was weeping more loudly than before. I returned to the teacher, who suggested I sit next to Tanya to keep her company.

I went back to her room and sat on the bed in front of her. During this whole episode she had not uttered a word, following the rules of silence in the meditation center. But when I asked her if she would like to see the teacher, she started talking: "The teacher cannot help me. You see, I am alone now."

I asked her if her husband had passed away, and she said, "No, I am divorced. But my daughter left the house a year ago. I thought it would be fine— that I would be fine alone. But I found out I can't be alone. Last year was so difficult. I was depressed a lot." She stopped for a few minutes and then continued: "The meditation helps me. I am a different person. I love people now. I feel I have so much strength in my hands—I want to help people. But my family is in Russia, and my two daughters are now away, I have no one to help." She then calmed down, though she was still sobbing a bit.

She had not looked at me once during this whole monologue—she was looking at the wall in front of her. Now she smiled, looked at me, and said, "You can go, I'll be fine, go back to the hall." I went back, and after ten minutes Tanya rejoined the group and continued to meditate for the remaining half hour.

The next day Tanya's roommate informed me that she had continued crying all night and morning. When I told the teacher, he asked me to approach Tanya again and see if she would like to speak with him. She agreed, and we went to see him together. The teacher was sitting on his small podium, and Tanya sat on the floor in front of him. Since the teacher did not speak Hebrew,

I sat next to Tanya and translated from English to Hebrew and back. Sitting there, I was sure that Tanya was going to repeat the story she told me. But to my surprise, that did not happen. The teacher asked her how she was doing, and she said, "Not so good—I cannot stop crying."

He smiled at her kindly and told her, "It is OK to cry. If you cry, cry, but cry like a vipassana meditator—feel the sensations. Tears come down: watch them. A tear is coming down, and another tear is coming down . . . When a storm comes, do not let it overpower you."

When I later reviewed my notes on Tanya's conversation with the teacher, I realized that he strictly avoided prompting her to tell her story. He did not ask her to narrate her state, to enter a discursive self-reflexive mode. Instead of searching for the cause of her emotion or asking her to translate how she felt into words, he encouraged her to concentrate completely on the physical aspect of her emotion. The story she attached to her emotion, the one she had told me the day before, was irrelevant to the self-awareness mode practiced in meditation. She was asked to cultivate a new kind of self-awareness: an embodied one.

In everyday "natural" crying, the wetness on our cheeks is but a small, unimportant element in the full experience of crying. While we are certainly capable of being aware of internal bodily sensations—breathing, muscle tension, or wetness of tears—only rarely do they command the focus of our attention. These sensations are a background from which we act as our attention is directed to the meaning, significance, and consequences of our expressions and movements. Vipassana practice subverts this directionality. One is asked to observe the tacit dimension, the invisible, the inner lining of experience.[2]

In vipassana, the first common object of attention is the breath.[3] The precise place of observation of breath varies. In the Goenka vipassana school that I studied, students are asked to concentrate on the movement of air in the nostrils and above the upper lips. In other popular vipassana schools, the breath is observed in the rise and fall of the abdomen. There are no special breathing exercises. The only instruction is that if one finds it difficult to concentrate on the breath, one should start with a few deeper breaths and then return to regular breathing.

After the student can concentrate on breathing, the meditation technique involves moving one's attention slowly, patch by patch, from head to toe, feeling whatever is happening in the body in each specific patch.[4] A patch is an area approximately one or two inches square. If the meditator does not feel a sensation on the body in one patch, she is asked to wait one minute, concentrating on this area, and then move on. After the sensitivity to the surface has increased and there are no "blind spots" left, the student is asked to speed up the process and, instead of moving patch by patch, to glide attention through the body, sometimes in one breath, a technique that is called sweeping, and then to return to a slower body scan, again moving patch by patch.

As the meditation retreat progresses, the students are advised to be mindful of their sensations when they are not formally meditating. For example: When walking, focus your attention on your legs, feel the pressure when the foot touches the ground. When eating, focus your attention on the touch of the food on the lips, the movement of the teeth and tongue, the change of taste in the mouth. While not all the participants in a meditation retreat extend the meditative attention mode to these contexts, they are still exposed to the idea that vipassana is not limited to sitting on a cushion.

When novice practitioners try to track their sensations back to a source, they are asked to suspend conceptual or discursive thinking. A dialogue I recorded between a teacher and a student illustrates this request:

STUDENT: When I feel sadness, I ask myself, where this sadness is coming from?
TEACHER: Don't ask it, don't think about it.
STUDENT: Not to think about it?
TEACHER: Observe sensations; sensations are the mind.

This dialogue reveals the ideological foundation of meditation and Buddhist philosophy in general. There is no Cartesian hierarchy of mind over body; in fact, the body is considered the main channel for influencing the mind. In complete contrast to the "talking cure" in psychoanalysis, which involves a search for the causes of an emotion and attempts to raise embodied sensations into the verbal realm, the attempt here is to remain in the nondiscursive realm of feelings.

To make sensations the main object of attention is not a natural move. The observation of sensations aims to "bracket" the regular significance that they carry. Instead of acting from or through our emotions and feelings, we are asked to observe them. Pain, a sensation familiar to all meditators, serves as a good example. Although vipassana teachers do not place much importance on the exact posture of meditation (unlike in Zen, for example, where posture is central), students are still instructed to sit straight and not to lean back, and most meditators sit on the floor. Cross-legged sitting on the floor usually leads to pain. Even when one is sitting on a chair, pain in the back is frequent. In general, meditation teachers view discomfort in meditation as an important part of the training, and indeed this is a common challenge for meditators.

The excerpt below is one example of encountering pain, taken from an autoethnographic vignette which took place while I participated in a seven-day meditation course:[5]

> In the last meditation session, I experienced a very strong pain in my knee. It was very difficult not to move. I knew I should observe the pain, but every time my attention was brought to the knee [as part of the body scan], the pain became so strong and unbearable that my leg almost moved involuntarily. The area of the pain seemed to grow. It climbed up my feet. There were moments in which I felt my whole body was in pain, even though I knew it was just the knee. It was very unpleasant, and it took a lot of self-discipline not to move and slowly divert my attention to the pain. When I "looked" at it for one minute or so, my impression was that it suddenly became smaller. Or maybe it would be more exact to write that it returned to its original proportion that was limited to the knee. I started giving attention to the nuances of the pain. I found that the main sensation is pressure on the knee. When the pain turned into pressure it was much easier to focus on it. It became very clear where the pain was concentrated. It was a small patch of pressure on the muscle. I concentrated on that patch and then moved on to scan my body. The pain was still there but it was significantly reduced. Interestingly, it came back when the session ended and I moved. The moment I moved the pain hit me again, and only after a few minutes of stretching did it disappear again.

When we experience pain, we experience it as carrying a message regarding the state of the self. Pain does not need our thought or cognitive interpretation—it is already an interpretation of the situation, an interpretation presented through a somatic medium. As a message regarding self-world relations, pain calls for action. In the above vignette, pain led to a strong desire to move. In ordinary life, the reaction to pain would have taken its course and I would have moved, perhaps even before I noticed doing so. But in a meditation course, one is asked not to move. This means that I was asked not to act from my pain but instead to turn the nuances of pain into a central object of attention.

Sitting there, I felt a powerful urge to return my attention to the world of action, to change my position and posture. But I resisted, instead, training my attention on the particulars that constitute "pain." I felt the muscles, the pressure, the nuances. This was not an easy task. I found out that by doing so, however—by concentrating on the inner lining of what we call pain—I was able to momentarily bracket the interpretation of my current state. I found out that my pain was no longer painful. I say "momentarily" since the moment I switched my attention back to the world and moved, the pain returned. This was striking, as it revealed meditation as a practice that brackets full engagement, a bracketing that requires maintenance. In other words, the signification carried by sensations is pushed to the background, but this bracketing is dependent on the modality of self-awareness that is exercised.

In his discussion of self-awareness, G. H. Mead writes, "If you can actually keep yourself from reacting against suffering you get rid of certain content in the suffering itself."[6] This description neatly captures the sense I described above, with one important difference. For Mead, the process of not reacting to suffering is made possible by a self-transcendence in which one engages in conversations about oneself while adopting an impersonal stance. The distance, according to Mead, is produced discursively through taking a new, impersonal point of view of another person toward myself and thus reducing my identification with this suffering. It requires a kind of "zooming out" from the particulars of the suffering, seeing it from a more "objective" perspective. In contrast, the embodied awareness exercised in meditation is not based on "zooming out" but instead on "zooming in," on attending to the particulars which rest at the root of the pain. This focus blurs or brackets the previously attached meaning of the full picture. Both techniques—zooming in and zooming out—achieve a distance from the signification that suffering carries to the self. Both lead to experiences of transcending the pain, but the kind of transcendence, and its experience, is different.

In the meditative mode of attention described here, something is gained but something is also lost. Try touching the table—you feel the smoothness of the table. Now try to feel your hand while it is feeling the table. This is not easy. Such an attention shift requires diverting the attention away from the table and to the hand, as it is impossible to concentrate both on the table and on the hand simultaneously.[7] In the "regular" attentive mode of everyday life, I pay attention to the smoothness of the table, while the awareness of the muscles in my hand remains tacit, in the background or at the margins of attention. When I am trying to concentrate on how my hand feels, the table and its smoothness are pushed to the background.[8]

When I zoomed in on the particulars of pain, the cause, significance, and consequences of pain turned tacit. When Tanya was asked to zoom in on the wetness of her tears, the significance of her life circumstances was pushed into the background. When I feel pain in everyday life, it is a holistic experience, enriched with meaning. When I zoom in to it in meditation, pain is no longer painful. When I first spoke to Tanya, her crying was a holistic emotional experience connected to her life story and biography. After she spoke with the teacher, her tears were no longer connected to her identity and her unique biography. Observing the tears (or any other bodily sensation) for an extended period isolates the sensation from the relevance it carries for acting and engaging with the world, encapsulates it in an inward-looking, embodied mode.

The way sadness and pain lose their meaning during meditation resonates with Polanyi's explanation for why during action in the world, the proximate or the inner lining needs to remain tacit: "Repeat a word several times, attending carefully to the motion of your tongue and lips, and to the sound you make, and soon the word will sound hollow and eventually lose its meaning. By concentrating attention on his fingers, a pianist can temporary paralyze his movement. We can make ourselves lose sight of a pattern or physiognomy by examining its several parts under sufficient magnitude."[9] My meditation experience confirms Polanyi's argument that one cannot zoom in while holding on to the full picture. There is a trade-off. When the projection of the self to the world is at the center of attention, feeling the body and its sensations is pushed to the background. When the bodily based inner lining takes center stage, important elements that pertain to the social world are pushed to the background.

I encountered one extreme incident that bears recounting in this context. On the final day of a ten-day vipassana course, in the middle of chatting and preparations for departure, a student reported to the teacher that he could not stop feeling sensations. He could not sleep, could hardly speak with others, and he compulsively performed body scans. The teacher suggested that he stay longer in the meditation center without meditating so the return to everyday life would be more gradual, and indeed after a day the student felt much better. Thus diverting attention to the body and its particulars without being able to reintegrate these particulars back into a meaningful background for action can be disruptive to competent action in the social world.[10]

In Buddhist tradition, such distancing from everyday sense-making and biographical self serves the practitioner in his or her attempt to bracket "conventional truth" and experience "ultimate truth." The focus on the inner lining of experience, on the nuances of sensations, is meant to help practitioners let go of the conventional meaning given to these sensations. Ultimately vipassana seeks to lead practitioners to the realization that the self, that "thing" that in conventional reality we experience as an object that we can identify with, is nothing but a mass of ever-changing sensations and thoughts. Such realization of not-self, *anatta* in Pali, is key to the achievement of *nibbana* (Pali for nirvana).[11]

Here arises a puzzle. Few meditators I met were seeking enlightenment. From their perspective, meditation, as a practice that brackets everyday life, is first and foremost about everyday life. Moreover, as I demonstrated in chap-

ter 2, contemporary meditation schools, including the school I studied, promote meditation practice by emphasizing the relevance of vipassana to action
in everyday life. This is how friends convince their nonmeditating friends and
relatives to join a meditation course. This is why psychologists suggest that
their patients give meditation a try.

Such relevance of meditation to everyday life is actively produced by practitioners as they forge linkages and resonance between vipassana practice and
their search for solutions to daily concerns. Not everyone who encounters
meditation creates such links. For some the retreat will remain a one-time,
not-to-be-repeated, experience that is disconnected from daily life, like a
backpacking trip to an exotic location. Still, for others, those who continue
and meditate, vipassana does end up resonating with their daily life concerns
and experiences. How, then, did my informants use vipassana as a practical
tool? How did they extend the situated practice of meditation to serve them
when acting in mundane reality?

Stepping into Everyday Life

Peter is in his thirties, a professor of computer science at a top university
in the United States. He took his first vipassana meditation course when he
was studying in France, a few years before our first interview. During this
time in France he felt intimidated by the French students and their somewhat
anti-American attitude, as he perceived it. Here he describes his return from
his first meditation course, when he first realized the potential hidden in the
meditative attitude for daily life:

> I was in France, and I just did two years in a very demanding and high-pressure
> school, and there were some foreign exchange students there, but I was the only
> American student that was actually enrolled in the school, and France is some-
> how anti-American, especially in the fortresses of culture. . . . My French was
> far from perfect—it was pretty lousy. It was getting a little better, but it was still
> bad. . . . I didn't want to open my mouth because I felt I didn't have the right to
> be there, which meant that I couldn't improve in French and that I built very
> little connections with people because I was afraid to talk to them. So during
> the [meditation] course—and this is always the case—you are brought very
> violently against your anxieties and your fears, and so that really strong under-
> current of fear was something I was clearly aware of during the ten-day course.
> And just to skip ahead to what happened when I got back, *I saw the physical
> aspect of that fear immediately; that was the thing that changed the most.* I got
> back on Sunday, and Monday went back to school, and I'm just walking down
> the street, and it is a fairly long street, and you know that that is where you are

heading and that everyone that pass you are coming from that school. And I saw right away the clenching in the stomach, and my shoulders going up and my heartbeat, my heart started racing, my breath getting shallow. And I mean, that was nothing new: just *noticing* that was something new, and everything I heard in the course, that every reaction has a physical component, and that if you learn to be detached from the physical component your state of mind can also be detached. And it was immediately clear, and also incredibly liberating, *that if I stop and watch my heart racing I could stop that process, slow it down.* (emphasis added)

What Peter had discovered is the background embodiment of the self, the background mechanisms that are at the base of our actions and expressions. Behind the expression of fear and anxiety there is a heart that is racing, a clenching in the stomach, or a breath that is becoming shallow. What Peter discovered is that fear has an inner lining, an invisible dimension, that others cannot see. The fact that Peter knew that these sensations were not new points to the fact that we are all tacitly aware of the inner lining. But to place these sensations at the center of attention, to "notice" them, was something new, and according to Peter, that "was the thing that changed the most."

I found that people who continue to meditate rely on moments like the one described by Peter—moments in which they realize the potential hidden in meditation as a solution or tool for their daily concerns. When explaining why they meditate, they stress the resonance between experiences they encounter outside the meditation center and those they encountered within it. For Peter, this was what he labeled "the undercurrent of fear." For others it could be the observation of sadness, anxiety, or pain, and with it the aftermath experiences of calmness, equanimity, and peace.

Some encounter this resonance already in the meditation retreat. Rachel, for example, realized on the fourth day of her first retreat that her depression had disappeared, and stepping out of the meditation retreat she searched for ways to maintain this experience in her daily life. Others, like Peter, encountered such moments of pragmatic use only after they left the retreat. For still others, such moments appeared only after weeks or months—one of them is Tom, who after a year of not meditating turned to meditation as a way to deal with work-related stress.

When practitioners of vipassana attempt to extend the experiences they have in the meditation retreat into their everyday life, they do so in two main contexts. The first is the context of daily meditation, which holds a special space for reenacting meditation experiences and maintaining heightened awareness of the embodied self. The second is awareness of the body in everyday life, in situations where people interact with the external world, from driving or washing the dishes to social encounters. That being said, while I distinguish between these two contexts, as I shall show, meditation and everyday life are lived in loops: over time the boundaries between the two can become rather blurred.

Daily Meditation Sessions

As a situated practice, daily meditation is separated from the flow of daily life. You enter a separate room, dim the lights, sit down in solitude, silence the phone, and close your eyes. In this sense, daily meditation includes a small-scale replication of distancing from daily life that takes place in the meditation retreat. Yet since the practice of meditation and daily life are lived in loops, daily life seeps into the meditation session. Such seeping turns the daily meditation sitting into a space where meditators purposefully redefine and redirect their relations with everyday social life and events.

In the year I attempted to meditate daily, I wrote notes after each meditation sitting. These reflections were quite consistent in tone and theme. Here is one such representative description:

> I sat down in the evening after a long day. I was tense. I could feel the tension in my body. My mind was in a constant rush—jumping from one thought to another. It took me almost forty minutes to clear the mind and settle into a quieter zone. I almost gave up after half an hour, but in the end, something in me gave up and at last I was in silence. After that I felt much more relaxed. As if I washed away all the worries of the day.

In each such meditation practice my mind and body were occupied by something else—depending on what happened during the day. If I meditated in the morning, I could feel the emotional burden of the day before or of the dream I had dreamt at night. If I meditated in the evening I could feel the tension, the enthusiasm, or the restlessness of the day. The object of meditation was sensations, but these sensations were not random—they were generated by my daily engagement with the world.

My interviewees used two interrelated descriptions to explain how daily meditation pertains to their daily life. The first is a "pause" or a "break" from the hectic nature of daily situations and events, a break that enabled them to return to daily life with "charged batteries" or "refreshed." The second is a space where life events, and especially emotional situations, are "dismantled," "cleansed," or "processed."

To elaborate on the first theme, many of my informants referred to vipassana as a turn inward that stands in contrast with the "external" world. Yet this turn inward was not understood as escapism but instead as a buffer or balance that helped them to return and engage "better" in daily life.

Tony, an organizational adviser, described meditation sitting as a need. "I need this hour a day for myself," he said. "I am constantly outside, in work and with people, and I need the space to move inward or I lose myself." He gave an example of the previous day, when he'd had no time for meditation in the morning. That day his car was hit by another car, and he was so angry that he shouted at the other driver. The rest of his day was full of tension, and he had a hard time waiting to return home and meditate. "So in such cases, when I lose myself, I know that I will have the time in the evening and that I will be able to *charge back the battery*. When I have time for meditation, my whole coping with the world is much easier" (emphasis added).

Likewise George, a PhD student, stated: "I have five big projects now at work. . . . And I find that I do not have time to myself. . . . I really hope to get back to a state of one hour [meditation] a day since if I don't my life will start deteriorating. I don't see my life without [internal] observation." The identity that George registered between "time for myself" and "time for meditation" is revealing, as it illustrates the use of meditation as a self-reflexive practice (or in his words, observation) that maintains a separation between "myself" and the world. Continuing this conversation, I asked George, "If your life deteriorates, how would it look?" He answered: "Enslaved to some goal, without time for the important things . . . enslaved . . . I would become addicted to competition, to aspiration . . . to all that nonsense." From George's perspective, the daily practice of meditation enables him to keep a distance from being completely engrossed in the academic world, to preserve a part of himself that is not "enslaved" to the social game of competition and aspiration.

Both descriptions reveal an attempt to use vipassana daily sittings as a buffer that enables one to eventually act better in daily life. Tony does not want to stop driving. George does not want to quit his job. But both have concerns regarding the way they act and live their life. "Coping with the world," as Tony said above, is difficult, and vipassana makes it easier. Academic work, says George, can become an addiction, and vipassana helps him to maintain balance. Both see vipassana as helping them keep a part of themselves alive outside of the social game—preventing a "loss of self" or "enslavement."

Such search for a balance to daily engrossment in social life was also revealed when vipassana practitioners spoke of meditation as permitting a moment for the suspension of social roles and identities. Yoav, an Israeli BA student, put it aptly when he remarked that meditation is a time in which "I don't have the need to be in a form. Just to sit and breathe and find a whole world in it." His use of the notion "form" alludes to the visible, outer dimension of experience—that daily self that needs to be maintained in interaction, the projection of self into the world, the way others see me and respond to me. Of course, in meditation Yoav is actually in a form—that of a meditator, sitting with his legs crossed and his back straight without moving. Still, the form of a meditator represents a place outside of structured social roles, replicating, to borrow anthropologist Victor Turner's notion, the "liminoid" space of the meditation center.[12] For Yoav and other vipassana practitioners, the relaxation from "being in form" is both liberating and refreshing, producing a break that enables them to return to "being in form" more easily.

From a sociological point of view, self-reflexivity involves attending to ourselves through taking the role of the other, judging and evaluating ourselves through social perspectives. It is this self, the self as an object that is viewed from an external point of view, that meditators hope to stay away from in daily meditation, and thus to gain a break, or a pause, from its centrality in their life.

Such making sense of vipassana daily sittings is captured well in the following quote from the vipassana teacher and psychiatrist Paul Fleischman: "I sit to be myself, independent of my own or others' judgements. Sitting enables me to slip beyond that second, commenting, editor's mind, and to burrow in deep towards immediate reality. When I sit, no one—beloved or enemy—can give me what I lack, or take away what I am."[13]

Let's draw our attention to the words "no one . . . can take away what I am." These words express a hope, or desire, to liberate oneself from the social gaze, a gaze represented by "my own or others' judgments." These words echo the above-cited fear of loss of self or anxiety regarding enslavement to social expectations. In all these examples the social world is portraited as a threat to the self, a source of ontological insecurity.[14] In contrast, for meditators the body offered a secure space that is out of social reach, an anchor for the continuation and stability of "what I am."

The second interrelated theme that recurred in the interviews I conducted was the use of daily meditation sittings as an emotional management tool.[15] Practitioners of vipassana used different notions to explain the use of daily meditation sittings to redirect or influence emotions. Some used the word *processing*, which evokes a pop-psychology connotation. Others used the term *cleansing* or *washing away* or *getting rid of* all the tension and stress of the day. In some cases, interviewees mentioned using daily meditation sitting to deal with a specific event that triggered a strong emotional reaction. In these cases, as in the one described above by Tony, they identified an unwanted emotional state and waited till the evening meditation in order to confront it. In other cases, interviewees talked about a more general "cleansing" process not attached to a specific event or situation. However, even in such general "cleansing" processes, it was clear that what one clears oneself from is connected to daily life.

The daily situations that practitioners described from which they wanted to "cleanse" themselves varied, but they all related to familiar scenarios in contemporary middle-class Western social life. Work-related challenges came up again and again. Some explicitly told me that without meditation they would have difficulty sleeping, as work-related worries tend to seep into their sleep. Other recurrent themes concerned money or expenses. For university students, anxiety regarding exams was another regular theme. Conflicts around intimate relationships appeared repeatedly, including dealing with a broken heart and loneliness.

Sitting in a cafe in Tel Aviv, Shira and I drank coffee while she complained about her work. Shira teaches children with special needs, and her job places strong emotional demands on her. There are too many children in the class for her to be able to give proper attention to each one. "It is so difficult," she told me. "They need me all the time. They have so many problems." At the end of a working day, she said, she feels overwhelmed. She tries to meditate every evening. When she is too tired, she lies in bed and meditates for five minutes until she falls asleep. "Vipassana helps me to make a separation," she said, "that there is me and then there is [her student] Ron or Beni."

Avi, Israeli and married, participated in his first ten-day retreat a few weeks before he was supposed to start a new job. During the retreat, he found himself worrying about this new job. As he told me, already in the retreat he found that "if I observe sensations and don't think about what awaits at home, about all the things I want or need to do, the future that awaits me with my new job, if I don't think about it, time goes faster and it is easier. . . . I found a way to experience peace and quiet." When Avi returned home he continued to meditate daily; he told me that it helps him to deal with work-related stress.

Ron, an Israeli MA student, spoke of vipassana as a tool to manage what he named "obsessive thoughts"—a term that represented the stress and anxiety he experienced in daily life. When I asked him what he means by such thoughts, he answered with examples:

Will I be accepted to the MA program? Is my suitcase too heavy and they will charge money at the airport? Any little thing that bothered me would turn into these obsessive thoughts. And then I took a few meditation courses and it disappeared. Of course, it didn't just disappear—it disappeared since I recognize it when it starts, and then I sit for a while for vipassana and I decrease it. . . . It is not that it cannot appear anymore, but now I have a way to deal with it.

Ron's story exemplifies the situations of uncertainty that people in contemporary affluent society often encounter, uncertainty that can induce stress or anxiety. It illustrates the fractures that people may experience when moving between social situations, when lacking security regarding how to act, or under the pressure of social evaluations. Vipassana here turns into a strategic tool that helps Ron to regain an experience of control over his life and self.

Family conflicts were mentioned quite often in the interviews as daily events that practitioners try to process or confront in meditation sitting. While a full development of the theme of intimate relations is reserved for the next chapter, I want to offer one example here.

Thomas, married with two children, used vipassana quite often to manage his anger especially in relation to family conflicts. The following is a vignette regarding an argument he had with his wife:

So an argument started, and we both got annoyed . . . and then I went to the room and sat and watched my sensations. And it was extremely difficult, since it was much more tempting to go over the argument and to tell myself I was right. . . . But slowly I was able to watch the sensations, and subtle sensations appeared, and in the end I was able to leave the room and tell her that I love her.

Thomas and his wife had a fierce argument which he found disturbing. As he recount, he utilized vipassana to effect a break in the interaction and to begin the relationship anew without dragging in the prior tension. When he was sitting for meditation, the argument he had with his wife leaked into the meditation session, tempting him to concentrate on his judgments of himself and his actions in the situation ("tell myself I was right"). In the attempt to manage his anger, he diverted attention away from these judgments and turned inward to track the inner lining of experience. This turn inward produced a pause in the engagement with the conflict, and the "zooming in" eventually led to a deliberate and purposeful cultivation of love.

Note that the managing of emotions in the above case did not take place through interaction or a dialogue. This type of emotional management is further elaborated by Don:

The way I handled life was that when I was stressed or sad I would call someone—one friend or a few, and talk with them all. . . . I used to run away to others. And now, this is the first time I run to myself. . . . I go to my room and close the door and sit with myself, and meditate, and this way I am less dependent on others, less needy, and this way my connection to others becomes better since it doesn't come from that needy place.

Don's example shows a shift in managing his emotions, from talking about them with friends to "running to myself." From Don's perspective, vipassana liberated him from the need for others as emotional management tools or therapeutic agents. He used vipassana both to distance himself from social dependency and to return to his social connections from what he considered as a "better" place.

The above examples illustrate how vipassana produces a break in the full engagement with the world. Daily meditation serves as an extension of the meditation retreat, a space where identities and social roles are temporarily bracketed, where one trains in relaxing the attention given to the self as viewed by others. When daily events seep into meditation sittings, practitioners try to focus on the inner lining of these experiences, a focus that pushes the social consequences and significance to the background of attention. When the practitioner flips back and returns to social interaction, the prior significance given to the events seems to lose its intensity. From the perspective of my informants, they return to the same social world, but this social world is now interpreted somewhat differently. Meditation in this sense produces a break that meditators use to recalibrate.

Everyday Situations and Contexts

Most of the people I spoke with did not limit the tracking of the inner lining of experience to the relatively isolated moments of sitting on the meditation cushion. They tried to be aware of their body at other moments as well. In this sense, the intermingling of meditation and daily life goes both ways. Just as daily life seeps into the practice of daily meditation sittings, vipassana seeps into daily life, utilized by practitioners in different situations and contexts.

Attending to the inner lining of experience when acting and engaging with the world is not a simple task. It requires shifting some of the attention from whatever you are doing to the body. In some contexts, such as driving, the attention that the world requires is quite limited and the shift of attention is easier. In other cases it can become more complicated.

How can I observe my sensations while in the middle of a conversation? I asked meditation teachers this question, and I received different answers from

different teachers. One instructor told me that it happens naturally: "It is habitual. A part of the mind is always tracking what is going on. It is less deep
when compared to meditation since I am doing something else at the same
time, but it is still there." Another teacher told me that when she talks she is
aware of her voice, as she is "hearing herself talking." Last, one senior meditation teacher from India said that while speaking, she observes the sensations
on her tongue, on her lips, around her mouth. Wondering aloud whether this
interferes with the talking, the teacher laughed and remarked, "It certainly
slows it down."

Since tracking the inner lining of experience "slows you down," most
of my interlocutors used vipassana in their daily life for brief moments or
when engaging in relatively habitual actions. Some used only observation of
breath, some concentrated on sensations that are relatively easy to track even
when in movement, and some scanned their body very briefly. As illustrated
below, these deliberate and brief moments of attention shifting were used for
a variety of ends.

My informants discussed feeling that their mind is occupied and that they
are not "in the present." Sara, an American meditator, exemplifies a search for
returning to the present: "If I am in a state that my mind is wandering to whatever, I try to notice my hand . . . to feel the tips of my fingers, the connection
to the chair . . . notice my breathing. . . . And this way I return myself—where
did you go? where are you?" When I asked her in what situations she exercises
this noticing of the hand, she answered that originally this happened in daily
meditation sittings, but today she tries to extend it to daily life. One example
she gave was driving. I will return to this example later in this section.

Sara's reflection reveals an interesting relation between self, body and
mind. We are all familiar with such states in which we "find ourselves" daydreaming, busy in internal dialogues, occupied in planning ahead or rethinking the past. During such moments our body can be doing something completely different, such as driving or swimming or washing the dishes. At these
moments the body takes care of the present in such an efficient way that I
might not remember what I have done, and a moment later wonder, "Did I
brush my teeth or not?" At such moments the awareness of the present becomes completely tacit, as our mind is busy with the issues of everyday social
life that await us. I write "tacit" because whatever is happening does enter our
consciousness; otherwise we would break a dish or crash our car. We are aware
of the present even in such habitual actions, but this awareness is at the background or periphery of attention. Only when something suddenly changes—
a dish slips, the car in front of me slows down—do we divert our attention

back to the present and to our body as we try to catch the falling glass or jam on the brakes.

Vipassana practitioners offered many descriptions of using vipassana when their mind wanders in lecture halls or during work—in all these cases they used awareness of sensations to "bring themselves back" to the present. An example from my own experience is illustrative. While reading a book to my son at night, which does not require complete concentration, I will sometimes notice that "I am not here." Instead I am thinking of my next article or a work-related concern. When that happens, I turn my attention to the movements in my mouth that create the spoken word. Attending to the movements allows me to stay focused in the present situation and listen to my own voice reading the story out loud.

In the above accounts, including my own, there is a hidden morality that holds the value of "being" in the present moment.[16] It would be quite efficient if I could read books to my son while at the same time contemplating the next chapter of my book. But when I am contemplating my book, the book reading is pushed to the background of attention, and with it my son. Since I value my relationship with my son—since I want to be present when interacting with him—I use vipassana to push back the seepage of my work into our moments together.

In this example, vipassana is used as a tool to maintain the infamous work-family balance that is so difficult to achieve in contemporary society. As a similar but opposite example regarding work-family balance, consider Shai, an Israeli psychologist, who described situations in which while listening to a patient, his mind wanders to his own family-related problems. In such cases he "gathers" himself back by observing his breath for a moment. As he said, "This enables me to divert my attention back to the patient and listen, to truly be with her." In this case Shai uses vipassana to push back his family-related issues while prioritizing full engagement with his work.

Another common use of tracking sensations in everyday situations related to labeling emotional states. Dov, an Israeli social worker, stated: "Once you feel it, you can't lie to yourself. I feel the anger. I can no longer deceive myself as if I am not really angry." The contrast of "truth" versus "deception" reveals an understanding, shared by many vipassana practitioners, that feeling the body provides the most "authentic" possible representation of one's present relation to the world. The body, in this sense, was interpreted by my informants as having a higher status in terms of "true knowledge" of the self, especially when compared to the world of thought.

Such centrality of feeling is not unique to meditators. Relying on "feel-

ing" and not on "thinking" has become a common guiding principle in contemporary culture. Contemporary psychological and neuroscientific perspectives emphasize feeling the body in emotional and cognitive processes even
when making rational decisions.[17] The potential hidden in turning embodied
awareness into a deliberate, explicit, and central source of knowledge regarding the self prompted the psychologist Daniel Goleman to coin the now well-
known term *emotional intelligence* (EI).[18] Importantly, however, in contrast to
EI, which also stresses being aware of others' emotions, my informants considered such awareness to be only indirect. Dov, for example, explicitly said,
"I think it would be pretentious to say that I am more sensitive to the emotions of others. I am more sensitive to my own reactions. These reactions may
indicate something about the emotion of the other person I am interacting
with, but it can also be my own misinterpretation, so I try not to go there."

Such "authentic" knowledge of the self is used by many meditators as a
tool in an ongoing project of self-improvement. Oren, for example, is highly
conscious of his behavior when interacting with others. Describing himself as
not very good at communication, he has used vipassana as a way to improve
his presentation of self:

> An example of a space where I try to be very aware of bodily sensations is inter-
> personal interaction. It is being aware of the body, but somehow that means
> being aware of the place that drives me to do things. It helps me to see that I
> might seem as if I am nice to this person, but I am really just patronizing him.
> Or that I am not saying this because I want to, but because I am stressed, and I
> need to talk just to keep the silence out. So I try to be with the body.

Oren has turned the awareness of the inner lining of experience into a technique for projecting self-authenticity. This quote reveals a search for a way to
align feeling with acting, sensations with behavior. Being nice to another person is viewed negatively if it does not align internally with wanting to be kind.
Talking to another just to keep the silence at bay is not the "right" drive for
talking. In other words, for Oren to "be with the body" means a more accurate
understanding of internal, often unconscious drives, and such understanding
helps him to monitor his behavior.

In addition to using the body as a source for gaining knowledge about
one's emotional state, meditators use vipassana to manage their emotions
while acting in the world. "I do anapana [observation of breath] a lot when
I am in a situation that makes me angry or frustrated or impatient or any of
those things," Lian told me when describing how she uses vipassana in everyday life. When I asked for examples, she said: "It could be anything, from
being late to the bus to someone hurting me. Observing the breath grounds

me; it helps me regain proportion, that all these things don't actually matter. It really calms me down."

The act of driving a car was raised repeatedly in the context of managing emotions while acting in the world. In his book on experimenting with Zen attitude as a sociological exercise, the sociologist Bernard McGrane writes, "The social institution of driving engenders a certain kind of mood . . . of aggressiveness, competitiveness and a very definite goal orientation."[19] When one enters a car, one is tempted to enter the social "role" of the driver and "play the game" of driving. McGrane encourages students to practice Zen while driving so that they become aware of this unspoken game. Moreover, as Jack Katz claims in his sociological account of anger in driving, social interaction while driving is a "dumb interaction." The term *dumb* is used here to stress that communication is experienced as asymmetrical—I see you (another car) and take into account your behavior (by slowing down, adjusting the car), but you do not seem to take into account my behavior or even bother to "see" me.[20] Such perception of myself through the eyes of other drivers leads to anger and frustration and frequently ends with one driver attempting to force the other driver to acknowledge him or her (by cutting back, signaling, cursing, gesturing and so on . . .).

In attempting to avoid the driving game, and with it, feelings of anger and frustration, many practitioners of vipassana said that when they drive they try to divert attention to the sensations on their hands, thus returning to "present-state" corporality. This return to present-state corporality helps them to push the self as viewed from the eyes of other drivers to the background of attention and avoid road rage. For example, Ben, who according to his mother (whom I interviewed) used to curse and get upset quite often when driving, told me that today when he drives he tries to pay attention to the sensations on his hands that rest on the steering wheel. This helps him to remain calm and ignore certain gestures or actions of other drivers, actions that in the past he found extremely irritating. Such meditative driving represents an attempt to resist entering the aggressive mood that the social institution of driving induces.[21]

Scanning, Checking, and Catching Selves

In time, especially for those who practice meditation daily, managing the self through tracking bodily sensations turns into a natural part of their daily life. Practitioners, especially the more experienced ones, said they attempt to do "bodily scans" regularly to "check themselves." This checking involves moving their attention throughout the body, from top to bottom. It can be done at any moment in everyday life—sometimes deliberately and sometimes as a habit. The checking helps a meditator to "catch himself," another phrase favored by meditators. To catch oneself means to catch a change in bodily sensations as early as possible and to monitor this change, and the reactions it triggers, by observing the inner lining of experience. To check oneself and to catch oneself are both practices of self-monitoring that are anchored in bodily awareness.

Thomas is in his mid-thirties, a young, successful lawyer working in a large firm in Israel. A few years ago he began feeling that his life had lost some of its sense of satisfaction. He felt exhausted from his work, and the whole pursuit of money seemed irrational to him. He began reading different books on Eastern philosophies and Western psychology and also started practicing yoga. The desire to change his life quickly turned into a desire to change his self, based on a logic shared by both Eastern philosophies and Western psychology. Being an ambitious man with strong self-discipline, he invented a self-reflexive practice: writing down the things he would like to change in himself. This would include commands to himself like "Stop eating so many sweets" or "When you work, concentrate on your work." In order to increase the self-reflexive aspect of this exercise, he used to go back to this "ideal self" list and mark the accomplishments he had made and the changes that were still needed. This was his central self-reflexive tool before he started meditating.

When I met Thomas after his first meditation course, he had completely stopped the management of this list. He told me that he didn't need it anymore. And yet after a year he gradually came back to the habit and started writing again. This time the commands also included many references to meditation: "When meditating, don't move for the whole hour," or "Remember that when in everyday life you react, then the whole point of meditation is lost." He even told me that while in a meditation retreat he missed having this tool (since he was not allowed to write) and tried to remember insights he had during the course, hoping to add them later to his list.

Six months later I asked Thomas again about his ideal behavior list. "I still have it," he answered, "but you know, I haven't looked at it for a while. I don't know—I think that in the last period my meditations were good and now I don't really need that list." I asked him why, and he said it seemed to him that when the meditation was good, the things in the list just fell into place; he ate fewer sweets, and when meditating he didn't move for an hour. "It just works." I then asked him what he meant by "good meditation," and he answered that it meant "that I am with the bodily sensations all the time."

Thomas's main channel of self-monitoring changed, from writing down the way he acted to an embodied management of his urges and desires. In the above description, he exemplifies two techniques that are oriented to the same goal: managing and controlling behavior and expression. The goal is therefore the outer lining of the self, the crafting and shaping of myself as an ethical and moral person. The first technique—that of the list—dealt directly with the outer lining, commenting and judging the way one behaves from an "external" point of view. The second technique, meditation, shifted to tracking the inner lining of the behavior, the background embodiment of eating sweats or "reacting."

Here we see the circular movement between the inner lining and the outer lining, how both are, in fact, two sides of the same phenomenon. When meditating, practitioners focused on the inner lining of experience, pushing to the background the pre/postmeditation life. But, for many of my informants, the ultimate goal was postmeditative, that is, to return to their conventional social life, to the projection of self, and act closer to ideals they held, both in the sense of ethical behavior toward self and others and in the sense of ideal emotional states of calmness or comfort. When returning to daily life, meditators reflect on the outer lining of the self and find it "better," attributing the change to meditation practice. Notions such as "good meditation" or "it just works" reaffirm this circular movement, and with it the pragmatic use of meditation toward this-worldly ends.

The continual monitoring of the self through awareness of the inner lining requires constant maintenance. With the decline of meditation, this mode of self-monitoring declines. Most vipassana meditators reported that when they do not meditate they feel their emotional reactions begin to get out of sync, and their control over their behavior and responses decreases. Many told me that they needed a meditation retreat of a few days' duration to rebalance themselves and regain access to their bodily sensations. They needed to go back to a collective environment where normative social life and identity are bracketed, and where the presence of others facilitates the cultivation of focused, nonreactive attention to the sensations.

*

Coming back full circle to feeling "the ends of my toes," for vipassana practitioners the encounter with the inner lining is an encounter with the background embodiment of the self. This encounter is put to use in varied ways that all converge around the same mechanism: by zooming into the particulars of their experiences, by focusing on sensations, practitioners purposefully push to the background the "full picture" of social life, the self as viewed by others. When doing so, they gain a break from the demands of the social world, keeping a private sphere alive outside of social reach. This is what turns feeling the ends of the toes while in conversation into an exciting experience. They find that "behind many masks and many characters"[22] there is a breathing and feeling body that transcends all social situations and provides continuity and stability.

Contemporary Western culture of the self encourages individuals to work on the self, examining and enhancing it.[23] This culture is not isolated from other cultures of self, borrowing and exchanging different techniques.[24] Since the body is key to the production, representation, and projection of self in daily life, it should not come as a surprise that people search for ways to increase awareness of the embodiment of the self. Vipassana serves as an entry point to the body that individuals use in varied and creative ways to negotiate and maintain their complex lives.

Vipassana adds a dimension to the culture of self-search and self-improvement, a dimension that the people I met said was missing from their premeditative life. Studies on the culture of self in the Western world tend to emphasize discursive self-reflexive techniques and the "textualization of subjectivity."[25] These include, for example, talking to a psychologist, writing in a diary, or having intimate and revealing conversations with friends and partners. In contrast, vipassana, and with it other reflexive practices that are anchored in the body, offer a self-reflexive mode that is not based on language but instead is anchored in awareness of the embodied background of daily life.[26]

The cultivation of such embodied self-awareness is not unique to meditation. For others it could be jogging, fasting, dieting, or dancing. Shifting attention to sensations in the body is an experience that transcends all social situations, offering a refuge from the looking-glass self, and with it from the projection of self to others. Such refuge, however, does not necessarily oppose daily life. On the contrary, for the subjects of this study it is this refuge, and the self-knowledge and self-anchoring it offers, that helps them to return to daily life in a "better" and "refreshed" state. In a somewhat paradoxical turn, the technique that originally helped monks to disconnect from "conventional" worldly reality is now helping individuals to return to and maintain mundane social life.

Negotiating Intimate Social Relations

Following an evening meditation session of a ten-day meditation retreat, a woman approached the teacher with a question. Midconversation, she raised her voice and said: "I cannot do it anymore; this is too much." She then turned an irritated and frustrated gaze toward the hall and at someone sitting and meditating with his eyes shut. Later I discovered that he was her partner. He did not look back, and his expression did not change. She left the meditation hall at a quick pace and returned to her room. That night she told the course manager that she wished to leave the course. When her partner was informed, he decided to join her, and they left together.

A few months later I met the partner, Roi, and asked him about the incident. Roi was an experienced meditator who had once participated in a twenty-day course, but at the time we spoke did not practice regularly. He had met Galit a year before, and recently they had moved in together. At his suggestion, she decided to participate in her first vipassana course. Although they arrived together, as is customary in vipassana retreats the couple did not share a room and did not interact during the course.

Galit found the silence and noninteraction to be alienating and had strong negative feelings about the course content. Amplifying her annoyance was the knowledge that vipassana was important for Roi but she could not share her feelings with him. Roi told me that when he heard her speaking in the meditation hall, he knew that her words were intended for his ears. He added that his first reaction was to get up and hug her. She must have felt disappointed, he figured, and he felt a strong need to do something. He told me that it was painful, but he was able to keep himself from reacting and instead he observed the sensations in his body and attempted to keep calm and send her *metta* (loving-kindness).

Roi's story reveals the collision of two spheres that were meant to be kept separate—the everyday sphere of significant others and the sphere of the meditation center. As such, it lays bare the tension between two social orders and interactive modes. The first is social interaction based on acknowledged and reciprocal engagement, putting the other at the focus of attention. This is the kind of interaction that Galit was seeking—she wanted Roi to acknowledge her difficulty, to respond to her behavior, to talk to her, to hug her. The second is social interaction that pushes others to the periphery of attention, being aware of them without directly attending to them, relying on their presence to divert attention inward.

The first interactive mode is a part of everyday sociality, in which self and other are defined in relation to one another and people are expected to meet the expectations and demands of others with whom they have differentiated relationships (e.g., partners, parents, friends). The second interactive mode is a part of a meditative, monasticlike community of collective solitude in which strangers help one another to "forget" the existence of the others.

Galit demanded that Roi return to his social interactive self of her romantic partner, and Roi resisted this demand, choosing to pursue the microsocial order that is institutionalized in the meditation center. Though I did not speak to Galit, I can imagine that she interpreted such a reaction as withdrawn, cold, and disengaged. It is here that the world of meditation and the everyday life of social engagement diverge.

Entering the ordinary intimate relations of practitioners, relations that are far from the original monastic ideal in which vipassana was developed, I follow different everyday interactions: those that meditators and their significant others (whom I also interviewed) describe as resonating with vipassana and those that expose tension and incompatibility. I argue that although vipassana moved from the monastic sphere into everyday life, it carries with it what the sociologist Max Weber terms "otherworldly" traces, manifested in the solitary or joint attempt to decrease attention to the self as viewed by others. I illustrate how the inversion of attention described in previous chapters carries with it a specific type of social relation that differs from intimate sociality, and this social relation is sometimes in tension with the world of families and friends.

In the analysis to follow, vipassana is not an independent variable that leads to a specific effect on people's lives or selves. Such a causal explanation is beyond the scope of this study. I do not know if the lives of the people I met would have been different without vipassana meditation, even though they themselves, and their family members, may believe so. Thus whenever a causal explanation appears in the text, it is offered from the point of view of the subjects of this study, who themselves tend to use such explanations to make sense of their lives. At the same time I do not regard vipassana as a mere rhetorical device that people use to explain or justify changes that were already taking place regardless of their practice. This would turn meditation from a lived practice into a dead "discourse" and miss the active microsocial dialectic movement between self to other that I aim to uncover. Instead I focus on how people who take vipassana into life outside the meditation center negotiate tensions and search for resonances between their experience in vipassana and their intimate relationships. By focusing on the process, on the "how," I shed light on different ways in which meditators use vipassana for initiating and negotiating changes in their social life.

Otherworldliness, Inward Looking, and Social Life

The sociologist Max Weber considered Theravada Buddhism, from which vipassana meditation emerged, the quintessence of his ideal type of other-worldly mysticism, or "contemplative flight from the world."[1] According to Weber, religions of salvation tend to abnegate the world, either through flee-ing from it (otherworldly) or through active attempts to change it (inner-worldly).[2] Such abnegation includes a stance toward what Weber calls "natu-ral kin," or what I refer to as "everyday sociality."

Everyday "natural" sociality stems from an emotional differentiation of the social world. It involves attachments to particular people, who are granted significance and value. It consists of friends and family, of togetherness and distinction, of pride and shame—which includes not only self but also other people who become a part of this self (such as parents and offspring). In con-trast, religious abnegation of the world is based on what Weber dubbed "acos-mic benevolence," or universal brotherliness, which "had always clashed with the orders and values of this world."[3] This kind of benevolence is also referred to as "world-denying love," since "as opposed to worldly love, which is always love for particular persons, is love for all, without distinction—love for who-ever comes, friends, strangers, enemies."[4]

From this perspective, the search for salvation, and with it the abnega-tion of the "natural" order of the world, goes hand in hand with an attempt to establish a new social order and a new kind of social and emotional relation to others. This new social order can be established away from society, in the otherworldly monastery, or in society, in the inner-worldly attempt to change mundane life which includes others who are not necessary believers.

The extreme version of otherworldly world abnegation is represented in the order of contemplative monks who relinquish their possessions, sexual interactions, and family life and seek salvation through contemplative practices that distance them from daily engagement.[5] These monks spend long periods in solitude and have a supporting community that acts as an anchor for their practice and path. This supporting community differs markedly from the social order of family and kinship. It is the "otherworldly" direction that unites a group of salvation seekers, connecting them with a shared attitude and purpose.

Different monastic orders have different levels of interaction with the "laity"—that is, those in the social order of family life. For example, certain Christian monastic orders proselytize and offer salvation also to the laity and thus tend to be involved with the nonmonastic population. Others, such as the forest monks in Thailand and Sri Lanka, focus on meditation; traditionally their interaction with the laity was restricted to the receipt of donations or alms.[6] In all cases, when monks do act and interact in "this world" and with those belonging to a "this-worldly" social order, they follow strict behavioral codes. Such codes are acknowledged by the whole community, including the laity. Thus Catholics know the rules for interacting with the priest and acknowledge the different social order in which he lives. Lay Buddhists know how to treat a monk and respect the rules he is following. These rules help the otherworldly oriented person to act in this world and shift between moments of inward looking (meditation, prayer) and moments of daily interaction.

Such ordering of daily "this-worldly" interactions also characterizes insulated religious groups that adopt an otherworldly orientation even when not choosing abstinence or monastic life. For example, the Jewish Hassidic Gur community, while not a monastic order, is known for its rigor regarding the regulation and supervision of its members' social life, including sexual relations, in an attempt to produce what scholars have called "a society of sacredness."[7] Such regulations help members of religious groups structure their relations with nonbelievers or with those who are not a part of the "sacred community." An important part of these regulations are special uniforms or religious signs that distinguish the insulated religious group from others and create clear boundaries between the "sacred" group that has renounced the world and the external, profane world. These religious signs enable outsiders—be it other religious groups or secular individuals—to recognize and affirm the religious identity and otherworldly orientation of the person they are interacting with.

With the reformation in Theravada Buddhism described in chapter 2, vipassana, as a contemplative religious practice, moved from the monastic sphere into the life of family holders and kinship. In this step it went from being a "world-fleeing" practice to a practice that is also oriented to this world. For the first time, we find people who are vipassana teachers and at the same time have families and occupations. They are using an inward-looking spiritual exercise not solely for reaching enlightenment but also for improving and influencing their ordinary life.

As part of this process, the logic and infrastructure of the social world of monks was replicated in nonmonastic spheres. This order is established in the relatively "otherworldly" social space of the meditation center. It is in the meditation center that people can take on the monk's attitude toward the social world. And it is in the meditation center that people can share collective solitude and be a part of a group that enables them to forget about the social world and turn their attention inward.

At the same time, since vipassana is not restricted to the meditation center, the world abnegation, and with it the attempt to establish a new social order, seeps out into "this-worldly" life. Given this process, it is not surprising that the Theravada Buddhist reformation is sometimes referred to as Protestant Buddhism.[8] In this reformation, monastic and ascetic dimensions were introduced into everyday social life. The social life of kinship and the social life of the monastery were thereby blended. Sociologists think that these monastic elements left traces in modern secular culture, a culture that carries the values of "absolute individualism and absolute universalism,"[9] which characterize monastic orders.

In Buddhist locations, the monastic elements and meditative attitude have been adopted by many individuals and are shared in the community of believers. This process is captured by the notion the "monastization of the laity" that characterizes the mass meditation movement in Burma and Thailand.[10] In contrast, outside Buddhist locales the attempt to "monasticize" daily life is limited to individual meditation practitioners and is rarely shared by a group. Most meditators' significant others and friends do not meditate and do not share a "sacred community" in which emotional and spiritual attitudes are mutually maintained.

Unlike monks, priests, or ultra-orthodox Jews, whose interactions with people outside of the "sacred" group is highly regulated, vipassana meditators receive minimal guidance regarding the preferred ethical relation to others (i.e., loving-kindness and compassion), even though these "others" are frequently those with whom they share their lives. Vipassana meditators constantly encounter others who are not a part of this way of being, others who do not necessary recognize, acknowledge, or respect the different social order and interactive mode that meditation carries.

What happened when meditators attempt to introduce the meditative social order into their intimate social life? Has meditation turned into a self-constituting practice that is completely oriented toward this-worldly social relations, or does it still carry monastic traces? In order to answer this question, I enter the microsocial life of vipassana practitioners, first in the meditation center and then outside it, analyzing closely the kind of engagement with social life that vipassana entails.

Tacit Awareness of Others: The Meditative Social Order

While vipassana holds otherworldly dimensions, it is not an asocial practice. Quite the opposite: vipassana practice is embedded in a social world. However, this is a social world with singular qualities. The meditation center is not only a training space for inward looking—it is a training space in a specific kind of social order and social interaction. This kind of social order stands between full engagement and disengagement and is in resonance with the overall project of vipassana meditation and the Buddhist path.

To replicate the social conditions in the meditation center, participants frequently share a room, a shower, walking trails, and dining hall. They sit near each other in the meditation hall. They see one another, smell one another, and, most of all, hear one another. Yet at the same time they are asked to avoid direct communication of any kind. They are in the presence of others, but they are not interacting in the full sense of the word.

A brief point about acknowledged and unacknowledged interaction might help to make sense of this strange social situation. In an elevator or on a train, I interact with others to adjust where I stand to equalize distance, to gaze without offending, but this interaction is not openly acknowledged by any of the parties. Exercising what Erving Goffman dubbed "civil inattention," I do my best to ignore others in a polite way, but to "ignore" them, I must actively adjust myself to them.[11] I am aware of the others, but this awareness is pushed to the background, as all parties involved synchronize and adjust to one another while doing something else—reading a book, looking at the cell phone, or daydreaming. Likewise the silent proximity that meditators share means that they need to find the right balance, the right form of unacknowledged interaction, that allows them to become a part of this social world.

The following description exemplifies the search for such a balance and the kind of microsocial order that is offered to practitioners. I heard this story from Aaron about a powerful experience he had during his first meditation course:

> I had one experience I remember clearly. My roommate had this alarm clock that ticked, and I hate ticking clocks—they get on my nerves. But I told myself, OK, this person needs a clock and they allow us to have clocks. But then

I noticed that he also had a watch, and he did not even use the alarm on the ticking alarm clock, he did not use it at all—it was facing the wall! And for a whole day I walk around like crazy that it cannot be that I suffer from this clock and the man does not even use it! Then I had an idea—since he does not use the clock anyway, I can go to the room when he is not there and just take out the battery. And I did it, but then I started to feel very guilty and ran back to put it in again. So I asked the instructor if he can tell my roommate, but he said he does not want to bother him. So I asked maybe I can say one sentence, just tell him to stop the clock, and I won't say anything else, and the instructor said it is better not to and that I should try to accept it. And on the third day of the course, I was trying to sleep during the break and that clock was ticking and I was trying to ignore it, and then I told myself don't ignore it, just listen to it and feel whatever sensation comes. . . . Every tick I feel anger building up . . . for half an hour or so . . . and I observe this anger . . . but after an hour I felt a feeling I never felt in my life, a feeling of deep peace . . . a feeling of kindness to everyone in the retreat.

Let's unpack this vignette. Anyone who is sensitive to noise knows how irritating a ticking clock can be. In the meditative atmosphere a ticking clock can be mind-piercing. However, Aaron's tale reveals that there is more to a ticking clock than mere noise. For Aaron, the noise of the clock is not a natural entity like the noise of raindrops. Raindrops do not trigger anger. The clock is the person who uses it.

Since the noise of the clock represents a person, it tempted Aaron into a social role, tempted him to perceive interactively. To perceive interactively means that the clock represented a relation with the roommate, and Aaron reacted to this relation. The anger and frustration that Aaron describes are most likely connected to the feeling that the roommate does not "see" him. In the clock, he could hear indications about himself and the way he is perceived by his roommate as "nonbeing." It is thus not surprising that he wanted to communicate with his roommate and tell him, "I am here—please show consideration."

In Aaron's story we see that the silence in the meditation center leads to asymmetrical interactions in which one is aware of the other but this awareness is not reciprocated. It is this asymmetry that tends to trigger anger. If Aaron could have talked to his roommate, he could have corrected this asymmetry and this whole episode would have come to an early end. Through talk he could have turned himself from a "nonbeing" into a being that is seen and heard, a being that deserves consideration. But he was asked not to talk or signal. He was also denied the possibility of someone else fixing the asymmetry for him. Instead he was asked to try to accept it. This is not surprising; the whole point of vipassana is detached observation of whatever sensations you have, even if these are painfully unpleasant. Such observation of sensations, I argue, produces a new kind of social relation and entails a social attitude toward others that is a part of vipassana training.

When shifting the focus from his roommate to the sound of the clock and the sensations on the body this sound produces, Aaron practiced bracketing his tendency to perceive interactively and sought to turn the clock into an asocial thing. He trained himself to turn the ticking from sounds that represented a social relation with his roommate, to random asocial disturbances. When the ticking no longer carried social indications about self vis-à-vis others, it no longer triggered anger.

Aaron inverted the direction of attention: previously the focus of attention was on the roommate and how the self was perceived by the roommate (or not perceived, which was the source of anger), while the feelings of the body were the tacit base from which he attended to the roommate (anger). He attempted to transpose this mode of attention by moving the focus to the body while moving his roommate to the periphery of attention. In this process the awareness to the self as perceived by others (in this case the roommate) turned tacit.

Such peripheral or tacit awareness of the self as perceived through the eyes of others is a way to be in the social world and interact with it while keeping a certain embodied distance. Instead of directly engaging with the social sources of his anger, Aaron shifted attention to his bodily reaction to the situation. As he remarked: "Just listen to it and feel whatever sensation comes . . . every tick I feel anger building up . . . for half an hour or so . . . and I observe this anger." Interestingly, the outcome of this exercise was "a feeling of kindness to everyone in the retreat." Such kindness is a social relation that is oriented toward others, but it does not require engagement with a particular person. Such kindness is an important part of what Weber termed "universal brotherhood," a social world that is not based on significant others. I will return to this point in the subsequent sections.

I have claimed above that the meditation center is a social space where people help each other to disattend to each other. Recall, from chapter 3, the three giggling women. That was emotional contagion in action as each woman "caught" laughter from the other. For the purposes of our analysis, however, the significant part was the other bodies in the meditation hall who were not giggling. In fact, far from giggling, they made absolutely no contact. By keeping silent and nonengaged, the other students performed the emotional attitude that is cultivated in the meditation center. They signaled to the women that their little interaction ritual, their responsiveness to one another, was not the kind of social order that was expected. They offered an alternative social world that negates the disruptive nature of social responsiveness (disruptive to meditation). And indeed, the gigglers quickly silenced themselves and returned to the joint calmness.

Later that day, during the one-hour joint meditation sitting, one of these women began giggling again. She attempted to keep her mouth closed, but the bursts of laughter were clearly heard. After a few minutes, her laughter became a loud sobbing. Her whole body trembled, and tears ran down her cheeks. She was trying to control her crying but again without success. She opened her eyes and looked at the course assistant, who came to her and whispered in her ear that she could leave the room if she wanted. She left the room, sobbing.

The day after, on the tenth day of the course (when students are allowed to speak), I asked that woman, Rina, about the incident. My exact question was "You laughed the other day in the meditation hall, right?" She answered by saying that she had been having a difficult day, and everything seemed to her completely irrational—the course, the people, and the meditation. And then she heard a dog barking outside and thought it was funny. She did not know why she found the barking funny, but she did remember that she tried to control her laughter, which quickly turned into crying. She told me that after leaving the hall, she walked around the yard until she calmed down, and in fact, after the incident she experienced a strong peacefulness that stayed with her to the end of the course. We drove home together the day after, and she seemed completely taken by the meditation. She was sure that she would return to participate in a future course.

Outbursts of laughing and crying characterize situations in which one responds to a loss, or fallout, of the ongoing embrace of self in the social world.[12] In such emotional outbursts one is forced to turn attention to the parts of the body that in everyday interaction are routinely kept tacit, thus shifting away from attending to the social world and seeking a way to regain a new embrace and tranquility. As shown above, the meditation center is a space in which people train in stripping away the self as lived in everyday life. To be viewed by others as "nonpersons" (in the sense of not being directly attended and acknowledged), and to react to others and to oneself as such, may lead to a sense of nakedness, of a lack of social clothing. This sense is captured in Rina's perception of the social world around her as irrational, suggesting that she lacked a social script that offered her order and anchoring. Such experience may trigger strong emotional outbursts such as laughing, crying, and laughing again until one regains a new stability, a new anchoring of self.

Rina laughed and cried without social engagement with those around her. Such "solitary" crying (while surrounded by other people) might seem to an outside observer as lonely, and one might wonder about a coldness or heart-lessness projected by others. These others did not attend to Rina's crying. Even the course assistant did not begin a conversation or offer empathy. Instead she suggested that if Rina wished to, she could leave the room. But Rina did not talk about feeling lonely. She did not expect others to attend to her crying, and thus their lack of attention was not experienced as cruel or cold. The others offered her support in the collective effort of each individual to observe his or her sensations (and emotions) without the requirement to attend to others or respond to them.

From Meditative Social Order to Daily Social Order

The meditative social order we have observed implies a built-in tension be-tween vipassana and full social engagement with others. This is why practices of heightened embodied awareness, be they yoga, jogging, or self-cutting, are usually somewhat compartmentalized to specific temporal and spatial frames, and thus the inversion of attention does not necessarily take place in the regular social world. This is why meditation centers were invented. How-ever, as noted in the previous chapter, practitioners frequently take the prac-tice into their daily life and daily interactions, and here a tension may emerge.

In the meditation center, the nonresponsiveness of the other meditators helps me to relate to my sensations as distinct from action in the world. In daily life, friends and family members will not do what other meditators do. They will attend to me and respond to me; they will perceive me, and I will see this perception of "me" through their eyes. They will try to draw me back into concentrating on the outer lining of experience, to fulfill their interactive an-ticipations. In other words, in interaction, when others attend to me as a family member or friend (and not as a meditator), pain will go back to being painful, tears will go back to expressing sadness, and the answer to "who am I?" will go back to being embedded in specific contextualized relationships.

The experience of being drawn back to the self as lived in daily life is fre-quently encountered on the last day of a meditation course: this is the day that participants are permitted to speak. On that day, practitioners talk and inter-act but also sit in three silent collective meditation sittings of one hour. They move from one mode of interaction (speaking and laughing together) to the other (meditating together) and back again.

Roy's experience, described below, illustrates the tension between these two modes of interaction. During fieldwork I met Roy many times. I thought he was a very social guy and found that in many situations he tends to tell jokes and dominate the interaction. Roy has high social competence, with which he influences the emotional mood of an interaction. Here is a quote from an interview I conducted with him after his fifth meditation retreat:

> When the silence was over, a few of us sat together outside on the grass and I told some kind of joke and everybody laughed, and then after a while we entered the meditation hall to meditate together for an hour, and I just couldn't meditate! I kept going back to the interaction outside and how I told that joke and the reactions of others. . . . It made me feel very elevated and excited, but I completely lost my equanimity and could hardly meditate.

Roy describes a "normal" acknowledged everyday interaction that includes shared excitement and elevation, or what Randall Collins refers to as emotional energy.[13] As social creatures, we would think that such excitement would be viewed as positive, and indeed Roy seemed to have enjoyed his social status and the positive self-reflection he received from others. But as his comment reveals, for him such excitement stands in sharp contrast with meditation and equanimity.[14]

To tell a joke successfully, I must notice the reaction of my audience. I need to attend to the "me" that they perceive, which emerges through their gestures, and adjust my conduct accordingly—by modifying my tone, expressions, and hand movements. The body parts to which I attend tacitly in this interaction are the parts that are relevant to my performance—I do not observe the end of my toes or my breathing. If I were to focus on my breathing while I told a joke, the whole performance would likely break down, and I would fail to produce the shared excitement.

Roy's remark shows us how difficult it is to shift from one side of the interactive continuum to the other, to shift from carefully attending to others (and to myself through their responses) to pushing others to the background and "forgetting" their existence. Roy could decide to stop telling jokes and remove himself from the center of social attention. This would most likely make it easier for him to reduce the need to put others in the focal of attention. That could be easily accomplished in the meditation center, where his partners for interaction are aware of his need and desire to focus on the inner lining of experience and can help him by lowering their expectations regarding social involvement. When one is interacting with significant others, however, especially significant others who are not themselves meditators, the dilemma is much more acute.

Before meditators leave the meditation center, they receive some guidance regarding their relations to others in daily life, guidance that aims to ease the shift back to conventional social order. On the last day of a ten-day vipassana course, students learn a new type of meditation—*metta* meditation, also known as meditation on compassion or meditation on loving-kindness. This meditation is practiced throughout the Buddhist world and aims to cultivate love and compassion toward others.

The kind of "love" that is referred to in *loving-kindness* differs from the commonly held notion of love. In both everyday love and loving-kindness (or in Robert Bellah's words, in this-worldly love and in world-rejecting love), the notion of love includes a motivation for "selfless" behavior that is oriented toward the other, a need and desire to give to the other. However, in the normative order of the "regular" social world, feelings of love are oriented toward specific others, separating these others from the rest of the world. Love makes specific others unique for us and thus is an important part of sociality. Parenting exemplifies such love. It entails extreme altruistic behavior oriented toward another, but this altruism is based on a strong attachment, extending the self to include the offspring being a part of my flesh and bones. In my son I see and experience an extension of me. In contrast, loving-kindness is oriented toward all others and thus circumvents singularity or social differentiation. It is based on the cultivation of universal identification (but not attachment) with the suffering of all living creatures.

The instructions for metta meditation are very brief. On the tenth day, after the first session of vipassana meditation, the teacher instructs the students to relax their previously motionless bodies and lean back or sit comfortably. After a full session of bodily scanning, students usually feel subtle sensations on different parts of the body. The students are asked to concentrate on these subtle sensations, which are usually prominent in the area of the head and the hands. As they focus on these sensations, a chanting is played with the following words: "May I be free from all anger, hatred, ill will, and animosity. May I generate love and goodwill, peace and harmony. May all beings share my peace, share my harmony, share my merits, share my dhamma. May all beings be happy, be peaceful, be liberated . . ." This is the only time in vipassana training that the meditator is asked to purposefully focus on words and purposefully increase specific sensations.

Teachers do not check to see whether meditators feel the "right" feeling, and I found *metta* to be a term open to many different interpretations. Some students refer to it as a "soft feeling." Others spoke of a sense of kindness and positivity toward others. Some spoke of a feeling of identification with the suffering of others. Teachers tend to refer to it as an actual "thing" or "vibration" that can be sent from one person to the other and can in fact influence others. Thus, for example, when the teachers meditate in the meditation hall in front of the students, they "send metta" to the students to help them in their difficult training.

Feeling more positive toward others is easier in a social world in which you do not need to attend to the way others perceive you and your sense of self is less dependent on others. In other words, metta relies on the bracketing of the conventional social relations that we are used to in our intimate social life. This explains why after Aaron transformed his relation with the clock and the roommate to an asocial relation, he felt a feeling of kindness to everyone in the retreat.

Nevertheless, while offering guidance in terms of ideal relations to others, metta still carries monastic dimensions and does not necessary solve the tensions that may arise when one is attempting to integrate vipassana into daily interactions. Many practitioners I spoke with noticed the gap between the general positive attitude toward nonspecific others encouraged in the metta part of vipassana training and actual intimate social relations. In their words, vipassana training does not include clear instructions or recommendations on how to reintegrate into a social interactive world.[15] One of the more advanced students I interviewed put it aptly:

> There is not an explicit connection between the cushion and social relations, and it is not necessarily made explicit in the teachings. . . . I think it is so highly experiential, and it seems that how to deal with your own mind and your own body, that is the focus and the teaching. How to deal with other people is not the focus of our teachings, so it is something that I came to a little bit more through experience and on my own.

This lack of "explicit connections" means that when meditators take vipassana into their daily life, they experiment and negotiate intimate social relations, negotiation that can take different routes depending on the specific social relations they are embedded in. In what follows, I review various themes that arose in connection to relations with significant others. I open with meditators' perspectives revealing their experimentation in integrating vipassana into their intimate life. I then move to the perspectives of significant others, and the ways in which practitioners of vipassana react to these perspectives, revealing moments of tension and doubt.

Meditators' Perspectives: How Vipassana
Pertains to Intimate Relations

Even though there is no explicit connection between vipassana teachings and intimate life, I found that the practice of meditation is frequently oriented to the social world as a tool for controlling, monitoring, and influencing close social relations.

Vipassana is an interesting instrument in this regard, as the teachings do not involve communication skills for the improvement of relationships. People do not use vipassana in relation to significant others through empathic perspective taking, sharing of emotions, or any other such communication technique of mutual alignment and social attunement. Instead vipassana practitioners use the inversion of attention to create disruptions in the taken-for-granted interactive structure or script, a disruption that they see as enabling them to divert the specific interaction to what they see as a better or desired place, or sometimes even to influence the relation as a whole.

When my son was two years old, I tried to put him down for a nap at noon. Lying in bed with him, I did what I usually do—pretend to be asleep so he would fall asleep as well. Being more energetic than usual one day, he kept moving his legs in unrest, kicking me. I soon felt waves of heat and unrest going through my body. These waves were not from pain: his kicks were not very strong. What drove me to anger and unrest was the perception of myself through the eyes of my child as an entity that could and should be kicked, and with it the frustration that arises from an inability to achieve cooperation. The frustration that emerges in such parenting situations hides the wish to be seen and acknowledged, as the conversation in my head moved from "Please go to sleep" to "I order you to go to sleep" to "Don't you see how tired I am?" or "You are kicking me—don't you see I am here?"

I found it very difficult to lie still while I felt an adrenaline rush, but I knew that any active reaction would destroy my attempts to have him nap. So I tried to meditate, to invert my attention and concentrate on my sensations. I tried to scan the body, or observe my breath, but every kick came in a surprising new place and my focus would jump back to the outside world (the source of the kick), again attending directly to my son and to his attitude toward me. With every kick I could feel my muscles contracting, and I had to force myself not to move. But instead of moving my son's legs away, I deliberately relaxed my muscles and returned attention to the body. It was interesting, and frustrating, to realize how much easier I found it not to react to aggravating pain in the leg when sitting alone on a cushion, than to not react to the relatively painless kicks of a two-year-old. It was a fight I eventually won. He fell asleep.

In the normative, taken-for-granted interactive script, I was supposed to align myself with my son's signals and move my body away from the kicks, ask him to stop kicking, or respond in some other way that affirmed my part in the interaction. Already at the age of two, my son knew this script and expected my cooperation. By turning inward, I pulled myself out of the dramaturgical role in this interaction ritual: I disrupted the taken-for-granted mutual alignment. My son soon discovered that he had no interactive partner for kicking and playing. By introducing disruption, I attempted to move the interaction into a different interactive script—that of sleeping.

This vignette shows how vipassana can be used to influence relations with significant others—in this case mainly in one contextualized situation. My interviewees, however, often attached significance to vipassana that transcends single social situations—they perceived vipassana both as a tool in influencing specific social interactions (like in the above vignette) and as having the potential to affect their intimate social relations as a whole. Five themes emerged from their stories which represent different social contexts and situations in which vipassana was perceived as relevant to intimate relations: conflicts and arguments, emotional connection and openness, sexual passion, autonomy and independence, and separation from loved ones.

CONFLICTS AND ARGUMENTS

Time and again, my interviewees told stories of using vipassana to manage anger and conflict situations that involved significant others. We often share moments of emotional togetherness with friends and family. Social life includes participation in an emotional intersubjective space in which we are influenced by the bodies of others and they are influenced by ours. Sometimes this space is enjoyable, such as sharing a moment of joint laughter. But sometimes we may find this joint emotional space problematic and unwanted, and we may search for ways to control and manage it. We do so through managing and controlling our own emotional expressions, while the true target is changing the social event we are a part of, including the emotions of others.

Ruth, for example, told me of previous conflict with her husband. Today, she said, she uses observation of breath so "I do not react to him as I used to. We used to have many fights—because I would react and then he would. Now I just accept him as he is. So he doesn't have someone that plays his game—which means that he is also more tolerant and easy." The words "does not have someone that plays his game" ring distinct bells: that is precisely the thought I had in the aforementioned interaction with my son. As Ruth states, she uses nonreaction not only to manage her own anger but also to manage and control her husband's anger and divert their relationship to what she sees as a better place.

Likewise, Joanne recounted arguments with her father:

Anything he would throw in the air, any type of teasing, I would catch and throw back. My mother would tell me, "Don't react, let it pass," and I could not handle it, no, I wouldn't let it . . . . Today I see that it is like a swing—if he "throws" something and I don't respond back, it is over, it is extinguished. And today he does not throw because he has no reason—he sees that it is extinguished.

Family conflicts are famous for people feeling frustrated in their inability to influence each other. When you are doing things that affect me (in unwanted ways), I feel that I cannot affect you back, which leads to anger and frustration and an attempt to rebalance the situation by provoking anger and frustration ("throwing back," in Joanne's words). By declaring (without words) that I am not influenced by you or that I am "not playing your game," I attempt to strike a new balance: I won't be influenced by you, so the fact that (as I see it) you are not influenced by me is no longer a moral problem of unfairness or inequity—that is, no longer a source of anger.

Let's note that the recommendation "do not react" is not unique to vipassana teaching. Joanne's mother, who is not a meditator, applied this idea long before Joanne met vipassana. In fact, family counselors have long suggested this as a means of calming tensions during a family fight. In this sense vipassana is used as a tool to execute a culturally approved interaction-management technique of not letting another influence you emotionally.

For some meditators, especially the less experienced among them, observing the breath or sensations while interacting with others was too difficult. They found it impossible to both be in the interaction and track the inner lining of their experience. They thus initiated a break or disruption in the interaction by avoiding physical co-presence. Take Thomas, whom I introduced in the previous chapter. The following is the full account of the argument he had with his wife:

> Yesterday evening I sat and meditated, and Shira was sitting in the other room watching television. We have an agreement that if I meditate and she watches television, she keeps the volume down. And in the beginning the volume was indeed down since she was watching a movie with subtitles. But then she moved to a different show and had to turn the volume up. So in the last twenty minutes of my meditation, I had a hard time ignoring the noise. So when I finished the one-hour meditation, I told her that the television was really a problem and that it bothers me. And she answered, "I am sorry, but maybe you should put in earplugs when I am home watching television." And that made me angry. I told her something like "No, I think it would be more considerate if for half an hour you keep the volume down . . ." So an argument started, and we both got annoyed . . . and then I went to the room and sat and watched my sensations. And it was extremely difficult, since it was much more tempting to go over the argument and to tell myself I was right. . . . But slowly I was able

to watch the sensations, and subtle sensations appeared, and in the end I was able to leave the room and tell her that I love her.

This is a familiar scenario: the sound of the TV annoyed Thomas not just because it was disruptive but because it sent him signals regarding how Shira perceived him, that she did not respect his needs. Even in meditation, Thomas was not able to disattend to Shira and concentrate on the inner lining of experience. He was drawn to fulfill the outer lining of "who you are," which from his perspective was reflected to him in Shira's lack of consideration. He responded to Shira as a life partner and family member (not as a meditator), and she responded back. She demanded consideration (earplugs), and he demanded consideration (lowered volume). Both projected to each other their experience of not being "seen" by the other.

Thomas then initiated a break in the interaction. First the break was produced through physical withdrawal from the situation. But this break was not enough, as Thomas was still thinking about the conflict, still engaging with it. So he meditated with the explicit aim to create an embodied distance that would calm down his anger.

When Thomas returned to his wife to tell her he loved her, to hug her, or to talk with her about the situation calmly, he shifted back to the everyday social interaction of co-presence—but this was a completely new interaction, one that did not take into account the previous moment of tension. His turn to meditation thus produced a rupture in the interaction, which he used to influence the relationship. This rupture, however, was initiated by one side and forced upon the other. Thomas did not "talk it over" with Shira. There was no joint overcoming of anger or a resolution of the argument. From his perspective, he began the relationship anew. We do not know if Shira did the same. I will return to this theme in the next section.

EMOTIONAL CONNECTION AND OPENNESS

Even though meditation is an inward-looking practice, many meditators attributed to vipassana a change in the way they connect to others emotionally. One meditator told me, "I love people more in general. Even in the supermarket. In the past I used to choose the handful that I could stand being with." Another practitioner stated, "My instinct today is to like people and not to hate them. It used to be the opposite." Meditators thus tend to interpret the influence of vipassana as "bringing me closer to people," as another practitioner put it.

The general statements of "love people more" were oriented to the world of strangers, thus relating to the "brotherly love" discussed above. This is a kind of love that attempts to deconstruct the differentiated nature of intimate social relations by extending feelings of warmth to everyone, friend or enemy. However, alongside this cultivation of brotherly love, I found that vipassana practitioners saw these feelings of warmth and openness as relating to their intimate social relations in two ways: first, helping them feel closer to existing significant others, and second, helping to create new intimate connections.

Regarding the first theme, feeling closer to current significant others, let's consider Daniel, age twenty-six, an American practitioner and graduate student. When Daniel completed his first course, he felt a sense of closeness to his family. He told me, "I connected with my family, with my friends, and it was a sense of real heart-opening; with my father, since they [my parents] were divorced, especially I felt a real sense of overcoming years of fear and avoidance and hiding and tension." As Daniel described it, his relations with his family had been marked by tension and fear. Vipassana helped him to connect anew, jettisoning the negativity. Likewise Meir, an Israeli PhD student, told me that thanks to his vipassana practice, he can for the first time in his life embrace his father.

In its ideal form, the "others" toward whom metta is directed are all living creatures, all of whom suffer. And yet in the nonmonastic lay version of meditation practice, both teachers and practitioners are flexible in their understandings of love and compassion. Most of the practitioners I spoke with tried to feel metta to specific others, their attached loved ones. This created an interesting twist. While loving-kindness in its ideal type negates everyday sociality, meditators found ways to take such feelings of loving-kindness and incorporate them in their daily life in their interactions with significant others, thus connecting between in-worldly love and world-denying love, between attached love and detached love.

The second theme broached in interviews in regard to emotional connection was an enhanced ability to forge intimate connections. This theme was mainly mentioned by practitioners who considered themselves shy and self-conscious in social interactions. Michael, a fifty-four-year-old American with serious meditation experience, so defined himself:

> A lot of the way we act is dependent on our perceptions of how we want other people to see us. I spent a lot of my time in social situations trying to fit it. Being somebody different from who I really was. I am by nature shy and not outgoing. So finally after meditating it became much more natural for me not

> to try to fit in but just to be comfortable with who I was or who I am. I don't have to pretend to be something, or pretend to like something I don't like, or socialize in general. I am much more comfortable being in my own skin.

Michael knew in his gut what microsociologists have long claimed: social interaction requires effort. It entails attending to the way others perceive me, which for some people, those we tend to call shy, leads to a feeling of playing a role "different from who I really was."[16] For some people, Michael included, the task of socializing is difficult, and the judgment of self through the eyes of others is acute.

According to Michael, vipassana enabled him to push to the background of attention self-judgments and with them the feeling of awkwardness. As a result, he not only felt more comfortable with himself but also felt more comfortable with others. As he told me, although he still lives alone, he has friends with whom he likes to spend time, friends he did not have before. He attributed to vipassana the new intimate connections he produced.

Elli's story paralleled Michael's, but in the context of a romantic relationship:

> I am not saying that in the past I did not have any friends and now I have a lot. I am not a social person and will never be. I just feel that now it is easier. I used to have very strong negative feelings from people, from being with people, and now I feel much less; when I have these feelings they are less intense, I can observe them, and that enables me to be in a [romantic] relationship.

The way that Elli told it, vipassana enabled her to have a romantic relationship after many years of painful solitude. Both Michael and Elli derived from vipassana practice a way to be with others without constantly attending to the "me" others project back, to their self as reflected through the eyes of others.

I suggest that the meditative mode of being with others is less likely to generate negative feelings such as social anxiety, shame, and embarrassment, as these feelings are an outcome of self-judgments. In other words, in an interaction mode that liberates you from the need to attend to others or to respond to their judgments and evaluations, people may find it easier to forge new intimacies or refresh old ones.

SEXUAL RELATIONS AND PASSION

My interviewees held varied views on sexual passion and romantic relationships, some siding with the Western/modern encouragement of sexual passion, while others adopted the Buddhist approach, which perceives sexual passion as contradictory to enlightenment. The attitudes expressed about these themes varied by age and meditation seniority.

Contemporary popular culture portrays sexuality and sexual passion as vital, healthy, and normal, integral and required dimensions of romantic love. Sexuality is cultivated and celebrated. The medical industry supports the attempt to prolong the sexual drive even after a certain age at which it naturally declines. Marriage counselors write books on how to maintain healthy sexual relations even after twenty years of marriage.

Theravada Buddhist ethics, by contrast, does not celebrate sexual passion. Sexual and romantic love are situated on the "in-worldly" side of emotional attachment. Therefore Buddhist monks are forbidden to be involved in any sexual activity (including self-sex), and householders are asked to avoid "sexual misconduct," which means to limit sexual activity to the marital partner. Moreover, Buddhist teachings see the decline in sexual drive in old age as a positive step, since in Theravada teachings enlightenment and sexual activity oppose each other.

Interestingly, even those I interviewed who had little knowledge of Buddhist ethics recognized that the practice of nonresponsiveness may contradict sexual passion. This led to different debates regarding sexual passion. For example, when he was taking his third meditation course, Avi, age twenty-eight, became concerned:

> I went to the teacher and told him I am worried, since I am afraid that if I continue to practice in the end I will lose my sexual passion. I mean, after all, this is a practice that aims to increase equanimity and decrease passion. So I went to the teacher, and I remember he looked at me and smiled and said I don't have to worry about it, as it takes a very long time for sexual passion to disappear.

When I asked Avi what he feels regarding sexual passion, he answered that in fact he thinks that the pleasure he derives from sex has improved. In many ways, he said, sex had become a more sensual experience. Indeed some of my interviewees, especially women, found that the heightened awareness of the body heightened their sexual experience. A forty-seven-year-old married meditator told me, "I found my body in vipassana, and my sexuality with it."

This makes sense. Vipassana's interactive mode involves diversion of attention to the body while suspending self-judgments. It brackets the social roles that people usually feel a need to play for one another even when having sex. It thus silences internal conversations such as "What does my partner think of me?" or "How do I look from this posture?" and involves a shift from objectification of "me" as a sexual and attractive partner (as viewed by my partner) to being focused on feeling myself through the touch of my partner. In fact, we can think of sex as a practice that invites an inversion of attention, as it has the potential to draw one's focus to the inner lining of experience.

Still, as practitioners advanced in their meditation practice, dilemmas regarding sexual passion became more acute. I followed Oren, a PhD student in chemistry, for a period of two years. He was single, lived in Tel Aviv, and like many young Tel Aviv residents, made a hobby of seeking random sexual encounters. He kept up this activity for some time into his meditation practice. In fact, he felt that vipassana helped him to control and manage his anxiety, thus relaxing more on dates. In other words, he felt more successful in finding sexual partners, and he attributed this success to meditation. But as Oren continued to practice, he felt that something was changing. After completing his fourth vipassana retreat and starting to meditate more frequently, he expressed a conflict regarding this change:

> I felt that I was killing something inside of me with this practice [of medita-
> tion]. For example, the problem with sexual passion — if you teach yourself
> not to be disappointed, to live well even if you don't get what you want, you
> are killing something inside of you — this passion, that doesn't let you live in
> peace, is part of you, it is a part of what it means to live, to experience life, and
> practice is killing it.

When I asked Oren about this passion, he said that while sexual passion was his first thought, he meant passion for everything — for his work, for his ideas, for science. In his words, "When you get into this mode of need, of 'I need to solve it,' something inside you pushes you forward to find the solution, the discovery, and I don't know if this can be done without experiencing this need." Oren here extended the notion of need from the sphere of sexuality to the sphere of achievement and discovery, and wondered about the emotional state that enabled this kind of engagement, an emotional state that was being "killed," as he described it, in meditation.

Oren thus expressed a strong dissonance in regard to vipassana. I anticipated that he would stop practicing or remain at an amateur level — attending the occasional vipassana retreat but not practicing regularly. Yet by our next interview Oren had upgraded his practice and even started to volunteer at the meditation center. When I asked him about sexual passion, he said that he stopped searching for random sex. He added that it was a source of suffering and that he was much happier and calmer without what he now categorized as "obsessive need."

For Noa, a fifty-year-old married Israeli, the dilemma was different. Noa felt a decline in her sexual passion, which she first attributed to her age and then to her daily vipassana practice. Her husband, however, did not meditate and did not experience the same decline. This created a tension around her practice that was strengthened by her husband's dislike of her ten-day absences for meditation retreats and his feeling of being excluded from a big part of her life. Noa added that while many couples go through similar difficulties around this age, she did not feel the urge to revive her sexual passion, even though she knew that she might pay a price for this in her marriage. Her efforts to convince her husband to attend a meditation retreat with her had failed, and the tension between them was not resolved.

When I spoke to meditation teachers, I found that they had adopted the Buddhist attitude toward sexual passion. This attitude was also associated with age. For example, one American teacher told me that at around the age of forty-five she lost her sexual passion and did not feel a need to revive it. Since her husband was also a meditation teacher, he accepted it. Younger teachers I spoke with were still sexually active but spoke of sex as a need, like food, and said that they expect this need to decline with age. Thus it seems that when vipassana becomes a way of life, the practitioner's attitude toward sexual passion resonates with the Buddhist ideal of abstinence. Such an attitude worked well when both partners shared this perspective but created tension in cases when only one partner meditated.

AUTONOMY AND INDEPENDENCE

Another way meditators said vipassana pertained to intimate social relations was when they found themselves in relations where they needed to protect or negotiate autonomy and independence. This theme appeared depending on the kinds of relations practitioners had in different periods in life.

Dena's partner took his first vipassana course two years before she began meditating and was immediately hooked on the practice. As Dena recalled, "It was very difficult. After eleven years of being together, I can testify that he went through a huge change . . . and there were all these worries. . . . It was very difficult." When I asked Dena to specify the difficulty, she responded, "You want the old person back. Also, you are not a part of something that is important to him—he disappears for ten days and who knows what goes on there." Then she articulated what had worried her most: "I felt that maybe he does not want to be in a relationship with me, or in a relationship at all. He was so self-contained." Here Dena hit the nail on the head. It is precisely this self-containment that can feel dangerous to partners and family members as it threatens the reciprocity of mutual dependence.

After two years, Dena decided to participate in a vipassana course, and she and her partner now meditate together. While Dena is not as serious a meditator as her partner, the practice helped her to confront her feels about being alone:

> Vipassana gives me the power to be alone. . . . I am not very good at being alone. I am a people person. . . . And I think it is a very important part of a healthy relationship that each person has his own life and that there is the life together. . . . And it prevents frustrations because each person understands that the other is a whole person and can do what he wants, and he should do what he wants, what is good for him, and everything from acceptance and the desire that the other person be happy, but not to sacrifice yourself, because this is not good for anyone.

Dena expresses here an ideology of independence and self-containment that is common to the individualistic culture she is a part of. Her words are in full resonance with psychological discourses that view codependency as a problem, as a source of unhealthy relationship.[17] Interestingly, until Dena meditated it was difficult for her to accept that model, to accept the self-containment of her partner. Thus from her perspective, vipassana enabled her to join her partner and together maintain a nondependent relationship model, a model that can work only if both sides agree to it.

Josh, a thirty-six-year-old American who had practiced vipassana for more than a decade, including participation in long courses, was seeking a life partner. When I asked him what kind of relationship he imagined, he was very clear: "I don't want the kind of relationship in which my happiness is contingent on something someone else does, and I don't want anyone's happiness to be contingent on what I do." Like Dena's view, this ideology regarding relationships is not unique to vipassana practitioners—nor is it shared by all my interviewees. But for Josh this perspective was directly connected to his experience in meditation and his belief that his own happiness is not dependent on the external world. Such an expectation of independence in intimate relationships opposes the idea of differentiated sociality, in which significant others are deeply dependent on the actions of each other. In many ways it opposes the "natural order" of family life.

We might expect someone who rejects the dependency inherent to romantic relationships and family life to decide to remain alone. This is indeed the growing tendency of many young people in American and European societies.[18] However, Josh did not reject the idea of long-term relationship. On the contrary, he was looking for one. Not surprisingly, while he did not limit his search to vipassana practitioners, he said that such a relationship would be easier with someone who meditated or practiced some kind of inward-looking technique that would enable him to cultivate his own happiness without dependence on significant others.

In addition, I found that meditators use vipassana to gain some distance between themselves and the demands of family members and friends. For example, Roy told me that vipassana taught him to say no to invitations to family dinners in his parents' home. "Not all the time," he smiled, "but once in a while." If in the past he had felt he must play along with the invitation even though he did not want to, today he feels he can manage the guilt that is directed toward him by his disappointed parents.

Phrases such as "learning not to sacrifice my needs to please others" or "I learned that what is good for me is good for others" or "I learned to say no" reflected the kind of social order some meditators envisioned, a social order that did not necessarily match that which their significant others envisioned. Such expressions may seem strange in light of the compassion and loving-kindness that Buddhism advocates, but it did not strike as contradictory to those meditators who strove for independence. While they acknowledged that Buddhism supports compassion toward others, they stressed that compassion does not mean they are in charge of their significant others' happiness and well-being.

SEPARATION FROM INTIMATE OTHERS

The final theme that emerged was the use of vipassana to manage separation from intimate others and loved ones. This included separation due to death of a loved one or to the breakup of romantic relationships. I met people who decided to join a meditation retreat or started meditating daily after such partings from those they loved. Vipassana in such cases was used as a tool for detaching from those to whom they had been attached in the past.

Rebecca, for example, described a few difficult months after a romantic breakup. During that period she meditated daily, confronting feelings of depression and misery and attempting to manage them through meditative observation. She spotlighted a specific meditation session from a time when she volunteered in the vipassana apartment in Tel Aviv. One night she found herself alone in the apartment. She entered the meditation hall and set up for meditation alone: "I sat down and I was so sad about the breakup I started crying, feeling so sorry for myself. I truly sobbed—my whole body was shaking; I observed this shaking, and slowly I felt the calmness entering." Rebecca characterized that moment as crucial in redirecting her relation to the breakup: "I remember that at the end of that session I laughed from relief. At last I could think about him without feeling that ache in the belly. I felt free."

During one of my volunteer periods at the Illinois vipassana meditation center, I met an older Indian woman who was working in the kitchen. As I helped her chop vegetables, I found out that she had participated in one vipassana retreat in the past. Now she had come to stay at the meditation center for a month. Her husband had just passed away, and she was searching for a way to deal with his death. Staying at home was difficult for her—too many neighbors and family members. "Here in the meditation center," she told me, "I find peace." With tears, she added that she misses her husband very much. We then fell into silence and continued to chop the vegetables.

The meditation center, with its unique social community, presented this woman with a social space that differed from the one she had at home. She chose to volunteer, a role that enabled her to stay in the center while not being completely occupied by meditation. As she told me, she thought it would be too difficult for her to join a retreat. She needed something to occupy her mind, and cooking in the kitchen gave her the right balance between being with others and being alone, between engagement and disengagement.

Significant Others' Perspectives

Meditators do not experiment with vipassana in a vacuum. My interviewees' attempts to apply meditation to different situations were noticed by their significant others, who frequently defined what they saw as a "change" or "transformation" in the behavior and personality of their loved one. Such change or transformation may or may not be a direct outcome of meditation practice, but both practitioners and their family members tended to attribute this change to vipassana and on this basis judged the practice positively or negatively.

In this sense, while vipassana is a practice of following the inner lining of experience, a dimension that is hidden from the eyes of others, it was also understood as affecting the observed projection of self—the way I am perceived by others. This is communicated by significant others to practitioners, who respond to this feedback, sometimes taking it as validation of their decision to practice and sometimes finding themselves at a crossroads.

When I interviewed Elli's parents, they told me that their daughter had become more tolerant since she began meditating. It seems that prior to beginning her practice, Elli lost her temper regularly when interacting with her parents.

FATHER: She inherited my character—I was born without a delay wick. I lose my temper extremely fast, like someone without brakes. Over the years I

learned to keep myself. When I feel I am getting angry, I turn around and
walk away. And Elli, she acquired her brakes [i.e., like car brakes] through
vipassana. Before she used to get angry so fast—

MOTHER: [interrupting] I used to say one word, or repeat myself twice, or just
say something without thinking, and she would get so annoyed . . .

Elli's parents appreciated the reduction in angry interactions. Her father, who
does not meditate and does not share Elli's enthusiasm for the practice, also
practiced an anger-management technique, in his case turning around and
walking away. From his perspective, Elli learned an anger-management technique that gave her a delay wick, a temporal distance between the gesture of
the other and her response, thus slowing down the social process that leads to
the escalation of joint anger.

When I interviewed Ben's mother, her first remark about Ben concerned
anger: "Ben was totally transformed. He is suddenly calm, relaxed, and quiet.
The change was very good for him. He used to be quite anxious before—he
was angry a lot." Ben's mother treated this change as a direct cause-and-effect
process—once Ben started meditating, his anger reactions disappeared. But
Ben describes it as a process, an actual effort that must be maintained. In fact,
family disagreements still made him angry, but since he is now more aware of
sensations, he catches his anger at an early stage and manages its expression.

By and large, significant others were favorably impressed with the use
of vipassana in anger-related situations, but some noted an unwanted influence. When I spoke with Thomas's sister, she told me that Thomas used to
be enthusiastically involved in political arguments and debates around the
family table. As is common in Israeli families, such debates were an important part of their family's interaction ritual every Friday night. These debates
frequently escalated into arguments, but these arguments were considered
by most family members as a lively part of their gathering. Now, whenever a
political debate arises, Thomas seems to retreat and fall into silence. His father
had also noticed it and wondered about it. They both noticed that Thomas
no longer contributes to interactive "doing" of familial togetherness when
it comes to lively arguments. They no longer had an interactive partner for
political debates.

When I asked Thomas about this observation, he agreed that he no longer
takes part in political arguments. From his perspective, these political arguments were disturbing the peace around the family table: "My brother-in-law
and I have very different political perspectives, and often the argument would
spin out of control." Thomas still finds his brother-in-law's perspectives dis-

turbing, and he is frequently tempted to speak up but prefers to observe this urge to speak instead of expressing his opinion. According to Thomas, the outcome is more pleasant and harmonious family dinners.

The significance of arguments, however, is culturally dependent. In contemporary "folk" perception, arguments are frequently understood as disruptive to social relations. This was also the opinion of most vipassana practitioners I encountered, who viewed arguments as a violent form of communication. Yet this is not necessarily so. Some families, especially in Israeli culture, thrive on such disagreements, and it is withdrawal from arguments that is interpreted as antisocial and disruptive to familial togetherness.[19]

In some cases I found open disagreements between meditators and significant others regarding ideal social relations. When Dov began meditating, he took a break from his family for a while. For one year he moved far away from them, hardly visiting or calling. He felt that since they tend to fight a great deal, it was better to keep a distance. In fact, because he found it so difficult to control his anger around them, he considered becoming a monk. After a year of practicing, and with the understanding that he does not really want a life of solitude, he started visiting more often.

While his family members were glad to see him back, they experienced a shift in their relationship; his sister told me, "Something has changed." She went on: "He was fun! He used to come into my house and eat all my food and annoy me and then we would have laughs together." Today, his sister said, they don't have such laughs together anymore. When I asked Dov about his family's impression, he answered:

> I told [my parents], "Remember how I was before vipassana? I used to smoke grass, drink alcohol, I couldn't work, I couldn't hold a relationship, and look at me now, at my life and state of mind." And they hold back and answer: "But you used to laugh more and have a good time."

Later he continued:

> I used to be one of those social guys. I would make an effort! I would contact people and organize social events and put in a lot of energy so people would have a good time and like me. I feel much more comfortable today.

In his first year of practicing vipassana, Dov told me, he found that he was not able to produce an embodied distance when interacting with his family. He was drawn back to his old anger reactions, being the Dov that they were used to. He thus disengaged in the physical sense of staying away from interacting with them, choosing a life of solitude. The experience allowed him to realize that he is not cut to be a monk. "I need and want people around me," he told me. But the kind of being together in which he feels comfortable, the kind of being together that he creates with his family, is different from the one his parents and sister seek.

While Dov states that his feelings toward his family members are in general more positive, they report a growing distance in the relationships and say they miss the "old Dov." What they miss, I argue, is not necessary a personality trait but a mode of interaction. They miss the social alignment and togetherness they had with Dov—either in disagreements or in laughter. They notice that the turn inward produces a misalignment between their expectations of the interaction and Dov's responses, a misalignment that ruptures the family bond.

Such disagreements regarding ideal social relations triggered different responses from practitioners, depending on the nature of the relationships. For example, Josh, introduced above, told me: "I think there are relationships that have become less significant in my life since I take more responsibility for myself and I am not ready to take responsibility for things that are not my responsibility." He told me about a friend who went through a difficult period and accused Josh for not being there for her. Josh recounted how he resisted the accusation and with it resisted the social expectation of guilt and apology:

> For instance, this friend of mine . . . it is not my responsibility if she is going through a hard time, to know when she needs me to call or whatever. . . . If she would have called me I would have provided some support, no doubt about it, but I know my—and this is something vipassana taught me—I know my intentions were good and seem OK to me, and I did not have the intention of disregarding that person, but I also know I have responsibilities to attend to, I'm busy . . . and would have been more than happy to accept the invitation to support her, and my intentions were good so I didn't take that on. I didn't say, "Oh, I'm really sorry," and beat myself up about it, and I think maybe that does—that may shift my pattern of relationships. . . . I feel much clearer that my happiness is really my responsibility and that the best thing I can do for myself and others is to keep this view and grow in my happiness and share it with others when I can. And for some that formula doesn't work.

Here Josh expresses a value that is in strong resonance with American cultural norms—"my happiness is really my responsibility." While this value of personal responsibility is not specifically Buddhist or vipassana-related, Josh uses vipassana to justify and make sense of this value, recognizing that some of his friends, including this specific friend, interpret his behavior as cold. In this sense the social order in the meditation center, in which all participants are working "together" in collective solitude while not attending to others, resonates with the American values of individualism and personal responsibility, values that were carried from the monastic world into Protestantism and from there into secular modern life.[20] As Josh said, for some of his friends this formula works but for others it does not, and these others, like Josh's friend described above, may decide to end the relationship.

Yet not everyone can end relationships. In a visit to the home of an assistant vipassana teacher, I found the teacher's teenage daughter in a flurry of anger and resentment toward her mother. Her mother replied quite calmly, although this reply did not seem to have much effect on the daughter for better or for worse. When I later spoke with the mother about the incident, she herself expressed frustration with the fact that no matter how you attempt to keep social relations harmonious, you can change only yourself and not others. Her attempts to encourage her daughter to meditate had not succeeded, and she felt that her daughter constantly tried to prove that her mother "is not as calm as she [mother] thinks."

Attempts to persuade family members that they are "not as calm" as they think were not limited to rebellious teenagers. One way that significant others resist vipassana is to invalidate practitioners' perceptions of the influence of vipassana on their behavior. Such statements on the part of family members hide an assumption that vipassana should influence behavior for the better, so that when they do not see this influence, they question the motivation to meditate. For example, when I interviewed Noa's husband, who, as noted in the previous section, resisted her involvement with vipassana, he said that he sees some influence after retreats, especially in the few days after Noa returns, but this influence does not last. "She has always had a temper, and she still does," he concluded.

Likewise a meditation teacher told me, "My family likes to remind me, 'Look, you are just the same, you have not changed . . . even after all these years of meditating.'" When I asked how such remarks influence her, she answered, "It takes time to change, it depends where you started, we are not Buddha, we react, we are humans, what really matters is what you feel inside, not what others tell you."

When significant others explicitly inform their family member or friend that they do not agree that vipassana has a positive influence, they try to force the meditator back to her differentiated social role and to the personality scheme they are familiar with. They reject the role that meditators play for each other when disattending to one another. They want and demand from their meditating loved one to attend to their perception of "who she is" in their eyes. This demand may lead to doubts and uncertainties for the practitioner. As Rachel said:

> He [her friend] said to me, "Rachel, you are not fun anymore." And it is true—
> I don't have that fire anymore. And I wonder about that sometimes—it is just
> like people that are on antidepressants, or people that are bipolar and don't
> have the highs and downs anymore—not that I was bipolar, but when you
> don't have these extreme feelings. And I always was known as a person that
> had very strong feelings—feel very strong about this or that.... And I am not
> the same person anymore. And I don't know if it is a loss or not.

Rachel attributed the change that her friend perceived to vipassana practice. She added that interactions with other meditators tend to be relatively calm and are very different from the interactions she used to like having with her nonmeditating friends. Rachel was not able to maintain a "fun" self with her nonmeditating friends and a "calm" self with the meditating circle. Her account shows that meditators understand vipassana practice as something that seeps into different social relations even when this is not intended, influencing their projection of self in different social circles. Such stories reveal that the same practice that is used by practitioners to keep away from the gaze of others, and with it from the anxiety and doubt of social interactions, may paradoxically lead to anxiety and doubt regarding the kind of person one has become, the new "me" that others see.

*

This chapter opened with vipassana stepping out of the monastery into family life and ended with the monastic traces that can be followed in daily interactions of practitioners with their significant others. It uncovered the flexible and creative ways people can harness a cultural practice for their own purposes, but also disclosed the limits of this flexibility as the practice itself carries its own logic.

The meditation center is a sphere for training in tracking the inner lining of experience, training in looking inward. At the same time, it offers a unique social space for training in a specific mode of social interaction. In the meditation center participants learn to be with others while decreasing the awareness of the self that is projected to them from the eyes of others, keeping such awareness tacit. They learn to disengage from the self that is outlined for them by their significant others. This disengagement is what turns meditation into a practice with otherworldly traces even when practiced in the contemporary nonmonastic world. It provides a pause from everyday symbolic evaluations and social engagements, allowing people to step aside. Such stepping aside does not necessary entail complete withdrawal, but it does imply a different mode of being together, one that allocates much space for the internal, frequently at the expense of the external.

This meditative interaction mode tends to seep into everyday life and into different social circles, sometimes in resonance and sometime in tension with intimate relationships. Significant others notice changes in the behavior of meditators, changes they may attribute to vipassana, and these changes are not always welcomed. While the management of anger is considered a positive and useful use of vipassana, significant others also notice a level of social withdrawal, of reduced motivation to play the social game.

Significant others' perception of change is then picked up by meditators, who react to these judgments and evaluations either by defending their "new self" or by negotiating uncertainties and doubts. Since there is no explicit connection between the cushion and social relations (as aptly put by one of my informants), meditators find themselves shifting on the continuum between a focus on the inner lining of experience to a focus on the "me" as perceived by others, trying to redirect social interactions in ways that will allow them to maintain a meditative attitude.

Since my research ended, I have noticed increased efforts to create connections between meditation practice and social relations. Books about mindful parenting and mindful relationships have proliferated.[21] Some meditation teachers have started inserting psychological theories such as Rosenberg's nonviolent communication into their teachings.[22] They turned to Western psychological sources that deal directly with questions of communication and intimate social relations to fill a gap that exists in the teachings of Buddhist-based meditations. Though putting social relations at the front, such hybrid combinations are still based on decreasing the attention given to the self as perceived by others, and on bracketing and challenging expectations and norms of interaction in ordinary social relations.[23]

Sociologists of contemporary postindustrial urban society claim that we are moving away from closed engaged communities into a different social world in which one is "bowling alone"[24]—a social world of loose connections.[25] The growing phenomenon of living alone, or couples that do not share the same household, point to the increased search for social spaces and relationships that allow for decreased engagement.[26] The meditative "collective solitude" in this sense may offer a synopsis of a social order that fits the urban modern life of being together and apart. It is thus not surprising to find that vipassana is used as a tool to maintain independence and autonomy and help

people "be alone," either within relationships, like Dena above, in between relationships, or when separating from loved ones. Meditation here becomes a
tool to negotiate the paradoxes that processes of individualization have introduced in terms of the place of the self vis-à-vis significant others. In this view,
it is one among different ways that have emerged to sustain a society of individuals.

Becoming a Meditator:
Life-Course Orientations

Tom's response to his first vipassana course was tempered in the extreme; it was, as he put it, "an interesting experience," but that was as far as he planned to go, "as it was so difficult and demanding." When Tom later found himself sleeping poorly because of work-related stress, however, he began meditating for fifteen minutes a day. "Slowly, I felt this was helping," he said. After a year he decided to try a second meditation course. This time his response was different: he found it "very strong." He continued to meditate every day and began volunteering at the meditation center. In time his wife began to meditate as well. When we last spoke, Tom was planning to participate in a twenty-day meditation course.

Rebecca, for her part, was completely taken by her first meditation course. "In vipassana I found myself," she told me; "it completely changed who I am." Yet despite her efforts, she was not able to sustain the practice in her everyday life. During the three years that followed her first meditation course, she returned annually for a ten-day vipassana retreat. Nonetheless she did not meditate daily. Before each of these retreats, she would report intense daily demands and high expectations of the retreat: "after the retreat everything will look better—I won't care so much about everything." This pattern continued for three years. At that point Rebecca stopped participating in meditation retreats, explaining that she felt that meditation was "flattening things inside." For Rebecca, vipassana was an important part of her life that was now anchored in the past. In terms of practice, she sometimes diverted her attention to breathing or to sensations so as to calm herself down and feel more grounded, but this was as far as she went.

Tom and Rebecca represent two common trajectories taken by the meditators that I followed. While these trajectories seem strikingly distinct, they reveal a central dynamic in vipassana practice: for my informants, meditation was not a mere background to their biographies, and its meaning was not confined to the situated practice. Meditators understood meditation and explained it in light of their long-term biography and life course and vice versa: their life stories received meaning and trajectories in light of meditation practice. Meditation triggered self-reflection that referred to the past, present, and future, oriented one's life course, and organized the meaning given to the autobiographical self. To meditate, then, is not only an in-situ practice that focuses on the present; it includes a trajectory of "becoming."

Processes of becoming are anchored in the social world and are entangled with social institutions, recognitions, and relations. Becoming a parent is based on a radical transformation of social relations. Converting to a new religion includes new identity markers recognized and shared by others. Such processes of becoming usually have shared and recognizable stations—one may even say a "career"—in which one progresses toward a certain shared and recognizable goal.

Meditation, however, offers an unordinary case. When vipassana was a monastic religious practice, the trajectory of meditators was set by the institutional frame of Buddhist thought and practice, including a conception of progress toward enlightenment that is anchored in the recognition of the surrounding Buddhist community. With the movement of meditation to "the West" and as part of the secularization of meditation, this social institutional frame can no longer be taken for granted; in fact, for many meditators it plays no role at all. Many practitioners thus had to develop their own answers to the question why they meditate, answers that help them make sense of their practice, offer biographically based meaning and motivation, connect past and future, and attach personal hopes and goals to the practice.

These answers developed over time, changing in accordance with context and social relations. Becoming a meditator is not a linear process with clearly defined stations, markers, and identifications. The appeal of meditation hinges on one's circumstances. As a practitioner who stopped meditating told me: "Right now, I am too happy to meditate. But when things get tough, I know I can always go back." Meditators integrate within their biographies the experiences they have during meditation, but such integration follows their own personal trajectory. One experience can be interpreted in multiple ways: frightening, therapeutic, or mystical-religious, perhaps, depending upon the person and where he or she stands in life. Certain "truths" about the self that are "discovered" in meditation can be attractive at certain moments and disappointing or useless at others.

When integrating meditation practice into their biographies, my informants used the practice in different ways to orient themselves in relation to their past and future. In what follows, I introduce three life-course orientations I identified as central.[1] The first of these is an orientation that focuses on the future, seeing meditation as a tool in departing from an unwanted past toward a more desirable future, anchored in a therapeutic imaginary of self-transformation and healing. The second orientation focuses on the past, as meditators experience the reversibility of selves and find that their desirable self is fragile and difficult to sustain. The third and final orientation is one in which meditation becomes a way of life or a superordinate "career," a life-course orientation reserved for those who are so taken by the practice that they become serious meditators. While each of these life-course orientations is analytically distinct, meditators sometimes expressed two orientations simultaneously or switched from one to another in the course of their practice.

In Search of Change: Departure from
the Past toward a Better Future

The title of Jack Kornfield's book *After the Ecstasy* jumped out at me as I entered Rachel's living room.[2] What did she think about the work? I wondered aloud. She replied that she had not yet read it but that his previous book, *A Path with a Heart*, was too "new age" for her taste. This genre, she added, "presents everything as if it is easy and charming and forgets to say that we have to work hard." Rachel's shelf also held other meditation classics, such as Thich Nhat Hanh's *The Miracle of Mindfulness*.[3] In evidence as well were more than twenty black notebooks, which I later found out were her personal diaries.

Rachel and I began our interview with a joint meditation. This was far from the first time I had meditated with my informants: perhaps a fifth of my interviews began this way. We sat on the floor in her living room, her normal meditation space. Her gray cat rubbed his head against my leg throughout the sitting and even licked me once. The windows were wide open, and the loud noises rising from a busy Chicago street contrasted starkly with the silence in the room. After an hour had elapsed, Rachel got up, said, "Wow, this was noisy," and smiled. She offered me tea, and we began the interview right where we had just meditated.

When I interviewed her in May 2006, Rachel was a forty-year-old divorcee living in Chicago and working as a graphic designer. She was raised Catholic, the oldest of four children. When Rachel was in high school, her parents turned to charismatic healing. She and her siblings found the conversion process difficult, and even today they feel a certain reluctance about religiosity. When I asked her about her interest in meditation, she answered:

> I remember when I was young I was driving with my mom and there was a story on the radio about TM [Transcendental Meditation], and I said, "Mom, I want to do TM," and she said "What?" and totally freaked out and pulled to the side of the road and said "No, you cannot — we are Catholics." She totally freaked out, which I found quite intriguing and thought, "Oh, I should really do it."

Although Rachel speaks of meditation as something she was interested in from a young age, it was only in 2004 that she took her first meditation course. The previous year Rachel had undergone two personal crises: she divorced her husband and her mother died. "I was going through a really rough time. I cried the whole summer. I was really, really sad. Extremely sad." Rachel heard about vipassana from an acquaintance while at dinner with friends. This type of meditation was virgin territory for her, and none of her friends meditated, but "When I heard about it, I immediately thought, 'This is what I need.'" Nonetheless, it took six months before she began a course. Initially Rachel had serious concerns about the demands of the course while she was feeling so low, but these fears disappeared on the fourth day:

> After four days I felt, "Oh, OK, this is it." As the days went on I felt better and better. I realized that the feeling I had, that sadness, dissipated . . . and I understood that I was going to be fine. That everything is going to be fine. I was one of those people who came out of the course with a big smile [smiling a very big smile]. I couldn't believe how wonderful I felt. How I felt like I didn't have to worry anymore about things, that it is all going to work out.

Rachel had come to vipassana quite unprepared. But she was equipped with strong motivation and hope. Three intersecting factors led her to meditation: a personal crisis and its attendant depression and search for recovery; a long interest in self-exploration (as the pile of personal diaries suggested) and, more specifically, in meditation as a counterconservative (or in this case counter-Christian) practice; and hearing about vipassana through her social networks. But for Rachel, all these are just details that summon the climax of her meditation biography — the moment of liberation from sadness and unhappiness. This moment of liberation anchors her orientation toward meditation as a practice of recovery, a practice toward a better life.

The anthropologist Edmund Leach distinguishes between two experiences of change: the first is change in which there is clear continuation with what came before, while the second is rupture, a change in which the past is irreversibly separated from the present.[4] The moments we mark as significant in our biography tend to take the latter form. We all change from day to day: our moods fluctuate, our bodies encounter new sensations, we have ups and downs. Although we all experience daily change, when narrating our biography we tend to concentrate on specific moments that represent rupture, moments that had a crucial impact on who we are today.

Some of the more familiar moments that appear in our biographies are accompanied by a sense of self-transformation—falling in love, becoming a mother, suffering from a serious illness, or finding God. These moments are frequently regarded as small enlightenments—something about the world or about ourselves was revealed to us and changed us in a profound and irreversible way. Such moments can be encountered unexpectedly, without any previous search or planning. However, in the contemporary culture of the self, we find people who are deliberately searching for such moments, and some use meditation as one possible channel for self-transformation.

For the participants in this study, the first encounter with vipassana, and usually their first vipassana course, serves as such a moment of seminal self-change. For the vast majority of the people I interviewed, the first ten-day vipassana meditation course was the one they remembered best and considered critical to their choice to continue meditating. Almost all of them reported having strong emotional experiences during or after the course, experiences that were accompanied with a new relation to their body and emotions. Some described major change and some described more minor ones, but they all marked a point of crucial change in their experience and perception of the self.

The place of this rupture in the biographies of practitioners of meditation becomes clear when we review their life trajectories prior to their participation in the first vipassana course. I found that in terms of both social and personal trajectories, life before the first meditation course was already characterized by rupture or transition. First, the timing in the life course is important—the majority of participants in this study took their first course when they were between twenty-two and thirty-five years old. This period is considered a transitional one in the lives of many Americans and Israelis (especially those belonging to the educated, mid to high socioeconomic strata), as this is the period in which decisions regarding work, education, and family are made and questions regarding self-identities and chosen lifestyles are dealt with. Moreover, for the middle/high strata in first world locations, this period before having children and settling down is considered one in which self-searching is legitimate and even recommended. This is in stark contrast to

Southeast Asia, for instance, where it is only after one's children achieve a degree of independence that one is expected to engage in self-searching.

Second, discussion of the personal life trajectories of practitioners revealed that many of them perceived the period before meditating as emotionally or existentially challenging. Common themes included major illness, romantic breakups, death of a loved one, and job loss. It appears that meditation centers are filled with people who are experiencing stress and unhappiness and are seeking answers or change. This pertains to participation in meditation retreats in general and not only to a first encounter with vipassana. I myself met a woman who came to stay at the Illinois meditation center for a month after her husband died. In becoming temporary refuges from daily difficulties, the centers take on the function served by temples in East Asia.

Long-standing unhappiness with one's emotional state was another recurrent theme. In such cases, people were desperately *seeking* rupture so as to stop their suffering. Their motivation was therapeutic in nature: they hoped that meditation would alleviate their depression, chronic pain, or debilitating anxiety. The third description I encountered portrayed a period of self-exploration for frames of meaning that included alternative forms of spirituality. Here people said that they were "searching" for something—be it meaning, direction, or an otherworldly experience that would ground or center their life. These were the participants who were more interested in the Buddhist background of meditation, and some were already quite familiar with Buddhism.[5]

Not everyone found what they were looking in vipassana. Those who did not moved on to other spheres and practices. Those who did anchored their practice in the belief that meditation offered them a solution, one may even say salvation. This salvation, however, is not metaphysical or religious in nature but instead a this-worldly, everyday-life-anchored salvation.[6] And like many salvation stories, these featured a before-and-after narrative: "this is how I used to be before meditation, and this is how I am today." Such accounts of transformation recall tales of religious conversion or enlightenment episodes, in which one feels that something new about the world and the self was revealed and that this new "truth" altered something fundamental in one's life.[7]

When we spoke, David, an Israeli vipassana practitioner, was in his mid-twenties. He was born to a secular Jewish family and defined himself as agnostic. I interviewed him after he had taken two ten-day meditation courses and was meditating daily at home. Three years before, David had been in the middle of his military service. This service was a part of his childhood dream of a lifelong military career. The dream was shattered when his unit was involved in a battle and he was seriously injured:

> I did an officers' course and was the commander of a small unit of fifteen "high-quality" soldiers. Most of our service was in Lebanon. The goal was to kill as many terrorists as possible. We were in a stakeout, it was the third day, and we were just sitting there, not very excited or anything, and then on the third day we got information that terrorists were detected. I raised my binoculars and suddenly saw an Arab-looking person with a gun approaching me, and another and another. The moment I had been waiting forever since the age of eight was materializing; they were just in front of me on the weapon's sight, getting closer. I could kill them in a minute and get the army medal of honor. But something felt very strange. I could not kill them. Suddenly the bush beside us was shaken and an Arab came out. We shot him and killed him. A very, very difficult battle began—we found out we were surrounded; they were twenty, and we were five. During the battle I tried to raise myself to see what to do and a bullet hit me, through the back and the shoulder.... The fight lasted twenty-five minutes, which is very long for a fight. Then we got the order through the wire to stop shooting and to start shouting "Zahal" [IDF—Israeli Defense Force], and then everyone around us from all the bushes started shouting "Zahal" and we realized these were not terrorists—these were South Lebanon Defense Force [SLDF is part of the IDF].

David was released from the army and diagnosed with posttraumatic stress disorder. His dream of a military career was gone. In his attempt to cope, he did what many young Israelis do after their compulsory military service—he traveled to Southeast Asia, first to Thailand and then to India. In Israel the obligatory army service produces a break between graduation from high school and higher education, a break that prolongs the stage that David Brooks has dubbed the "Odyssey" years, the stage between adolescence and the starting of a work career.[8] In the past twenty years, a journey to a developing country has become a rite of passage from the stressful period of army service to the demanding life of adulthood.[9] Thus this trip—like similar trips taken by Israeli backpackers—was tagged in David's eyes as a transitional aid, a break from everyday social concerns and structures before he moved on to mainstream adult life. For many, including David, the journey entails a quest for answers—where do I ground myself? what is central in my life?

David first heard about vipassana while in India, but as he told me, he was not yet ready to tackle such a demanding course. Upon returning to Israel, he began studying physics but failed all his courses. Instead of going to the lectures, he found himself sitting on the grass in the sunshine. His academic adviser suggested that he change his course of study, but David resisted the idea. It was at this point that he heard about the vipassana center in Israel and decided to participate in a course.

When I asked David why he chose to take a vipassana course, he told me that he had been seeking something that would produce a change. Earlier that year he had twice seen a psychologist, but he was not satisfied with the treatment. Vipassana courses thus were associated in his mind as venues for internal work. And indeed, during the first meditation course David experienced a strong self-liberating experience that became the reference point in his self-transformation narrative:

> On the seventh day, I was so concentrated that my mind was like a knife — so sharp. I was feeling all these sensations. In the evening meditation, I suddenly saw a very frightening face in front of me. This face disappeared, the meditation was over, and I went to sleep. Lying on the bed I see this face again in front of me and realize I cannot sleep. I stepped out of the room, walked around, entered the meditation hall, and just sat and meditated. As I meditated I saw the face again and realized it is Lior, the soldier who was just beside me in the incident. He was injured very seriously — he was shot in the leg, and then a grenade detonated between his legs and filled him with 150 pieces [of shrapnel] and he was pouring blood everywhere. And I was his commander, I . . . He looked at me all crying, shouting, "David, I was hit, I am going to die." . . . And that face is the face I saw. And as I saw it I had shivering all over my body, one shiver and then another and another. And I was just sitting there shivering all over, I don't know for how long. And then tears started falling — lots of shivering, I don't know for how long I was there — maybe for two hours. I really felt that I was dismantling the combat shock and the injury without any insights. It was a very, very strong physical experience of liberation.

This account exemplifies how embodied experiences in meditation can gain biographical meaning. David experienced a strong and unusual sensual experience that he connected to his biography. For him, the present experience was a reenactment of the past. But his past was now encountered in the secure, silent sphere of the meditation center. Much like those who reenact past experiences in the secure clinic of a mental health professional, David believed that by observing the sensations that were rising in the body without moving or reacting, by "zooming in" to the experience, he was "dismantling" the emotional impact of the combat shock. While David did not use the word *therapy*, his description points to an interpretation of this experience as a healing process, or, in his words, "liberating."

The interpretation of an experience as therapeutic requires a specific relationship toward one's past and future, one that is accessible in a society and culture in which notions such as PTSD have become mainstream. A monk would have probably given a different interpretation to such an experience, and as illustrated in the next sections, so would the more advanced meditators.

David's tale is rather extreme, but other stories presented similar elements. Some informants spoke of leaving behind heavy emotional baggage. Others told of having their eyes opened to the possibility of calmness (versus previous anxiety), or happiness (versus previous sadness or depression). Still others said that they felt that the first meditation course was like a whole process of psychotherapy squeezed into ten days. There were those who experienced this change already in the meditation center, and there were others, like Tom, with whom I began this chapter, who found in vipassana the salvation he had sought for months after the first meditation course. In all these stories, the after-meditation self is marked as a better version of the old one, a self freed from the shackles of sadness, trauma, and stress. Such experiences leave their mark as momentary liberating moments but also produce a new relation with the self and generate motivation to continue practicing.

The Reversibility of Selves: Progress, Regression, Maintenance

Initially my informants recounted the first life-course orientation described above, in which meditation enters a life that is already in transition or in search and is used as a tool for departure from an undesirable past toward a better future. Over time and further interviews, however, a more complex life-course orientation emerged in which the past is not so solidly gone. The rupture, which is characterized as an irreversible transformation, is revealed as reversible, and meditation becomes a part of an attempt to sustain a self that is slippery and fragile, a self that requires constant care.

Tony, age thirty-three, an Israeli financial adviser, recounted how already in his first vipassana retreat he encountered this sense of fragility:

> It was like a rollercoaster of up and down. I was not familiar with the feeling of equanimity and peace before, and I felt it for the first time. And I felt, wow—this was what I was looking for all my life! But then suddenly I felt this anxiety and sadness and asked myself, "Why are you here?" I remember that when I was feeling this high of calmness and this good feeling, I told myself, "Remember this feeling."

It typically takes meditators a bit of time—some days or weeks postcourse—to realize what Tony understood already in the sessions: that the sense of "wow, this is what I have been seeking for so long" or of "finding myself" or of "strong liberation" is transient. Lori, who wrote the following email to her friend after her first meditation course, described aptly such reversibility of self:

> It's now six days since I came home from vipassana—and they've been amazing—truly some of the best in my life. But now I'm feeling that I'm starting to come back to the old patterns of my existence, slowly. . . . I haven't been meditating, and I really want to start soon, cause I think it may actually hold the key to a more peaceful, truthful, happy life. I've experienced what it's like to actually be in peace, free from anxiety, or anger. Maybe some people feel like this often, but for me it's a little overwhelming. . . . and very emotional. I *have/had* so much anger in me—I don't know why, and it's been messing up my life. It's great to be free of anger. I hope it'll last. [emphasis added]

Lori's experience is familiar to meditators—after only six days, she felt she was returning to her old self. Her new self, which in her description is devoid of anger, turned into an ideal that can be reached only through continual meditation. She illustrates this emotional oscillation in her creative choice of a mixed grammatical tense when writing *have/had* in regard to her anger, as if she has not made up her mind yet whether having anger is a feature of the past or the present.

Like a folk sociologist, Lori encountered the social nature of identity and with it the multiplicity of selves. When in meditation, one aims to focus on the inner lining of experience and reduce direct engagement with others. When exiting meditation and returning to everyday life, one is recast as a person that others can relate to and thus finds oneself pulled back to fill in that social role, to fulfill the outer lining of "who I am" outlined by others.

In this life-course orientation, meditators made sense of meditation as a self-maintenance tool that can continually monitor a fluctuating interiority. Take Ifat, who lamented that only two days after the meditation course, she found herself screaming at her mother. Ifat was drawn to respond with the "natural" complementary "past" self, as this is the line of action that was most conveniently at hand. According to her, the maintenance required to remain focused on the inner lining, and with it the new self, was too great a demand. Thus she stopped meditating, despite the sense of liberation she had experienced in the vipassana course. As she explained when we spoke, "meditation requires a lot of effort—you really need to be serious for it to stick."

When practitioners become aware of a diminution of effect from their last meditation retreat, they reactivate it by returning to a social circle that fosters the practice of meditation and with it the desired emotional state. Such a social circle is a collective entity that is not immediately present in their every-day life outside of meditation. It provides a social anchor that helps them sustain the new self somewhat independently of their immediate, not-meditating family and friends. Many practitioners try to return to a meditation course once a year in order to "recharge the batteries." They join a group sitting, use a recording or meditation instructions, or download a meditation application — all these are tools that create an intersubjective collective space through which the new self can be maintained.

When people return to vipassana to "recharge" or to revive the kind of self they have experienced in their first course, they do so with expectations of certain outcomes, outcomes that are anchored in this-worldly hopes and possibilities. The warnings of vipassana teachers not to get attached to the sense of liberation, as from a Buddhist point of view this is as ephemeral as any other sensation, hardly deter students — even experienced ones — from raising such expectations. For example, anticipating an upcoming twenty-day meditation retreat, Peter told me:

> I know I am not supposed to have them, but of course I do [laughs]. I have this expectation that after the course I will be more focused, my mind will be clear, I'll come back light and fresh and will do all the things I need to do so easily and fast. And I also know that there is a chance this will not happen and that I might be disappointed.

Indeed, meditators' expectations are not always met. At some points in their meditation-related biographies, my informants sensed that meditation retreats and practice enabled them to maintain a desired self, or even to progress toward a more ideal self, and thus they could explain quite easily why they meditated. At other times, however, disappointment or even letdown might be the result. The following extreme instance of such a letdown can teach us about less extreme cases as well.

Ben is a young Israeli in his late twenties. When I met him, he meditated daily and was about to take his tenth meditation course. In addition, he volunteered in the vipassana organization in Israel. It was during a trip to India that he had taken his first meditation course. Here is an excerpt from our first interview:

BEN: I had a good friend who told me about vipassana — she wanted to do it. She spoke about it for a long time, but I didn't really connect to it. I did not even ask her what it is. But then my cousin took a course, and I met other people who did a course, and read about it in a book. . . . I was in

India and Nepal for seven months and I did the course there. . . . It was very strong. I felt I could do anything. I felt this is going to be difficult but good—challenging. I was very serious. I think it was the most serious course I took. But it was also the easiest. I felt fine the whole time. I did not want to run away and did not have any moments of crisis. I did count the days as always, but it was not because I was dying for it to end. I had all kinds of experiences in the course. But I remember that only after the course I felt that I [had gone] through something very powerful. That something had changed. I walked around and talked to people, and I remember feeling amazing.

MP: Did you start meditating daily right after that course?

BEN: Yes, but it was not easy. I think this is why I returned to a second course, because the quality of my practice was deteriorating. The second course was different. At the end of the course I felt anger toward people. I went to the meditation teacher and asked him, "What is going on? I felt so good after the first course, and now?" And he just answered, "You have to accept it. Accept whatever comes; you cannot control it." And I remember that after leaving the course my feeling improved, and after a while it improved even more, and by the time I got back to Israel I felt wonderful, and the whole first year was euphoric. I felt I could do anything. I was so strong, full of confidence, especially around people. I was in control. My friends and family were in shock. I returned calm, strong, and confident—a completely different person.

Ben's account of disappointment upon realizing that his newly crafted self was not as stable as he had hoped was a rather common one. But in his case the disappointment was mild, as shortly after that second course he returned to the "amazing" and "euphoric" feeling of his new self. In order to maintain this new self, Ben started to meditate daily. In his words, when he returned to Israel after two meditation retreats he was "a completely different person." In an interview, Ben's mother confirmed his observations. He indeed had returned a different person. The "old" Ben, she said, had been quite shy and had low self-confidence. The "new" Ben interacted with calmness and confidence. In fact, after seeing him she was persuaded to take a vipassana course herself.

Yet as Ben told me, after his third vipassana course he experienced another self-change. The euphoric feeling completely disappeared. He felt insecure and uncomfortable when interacting with other people. Not only did he lose the new self he acquired after his first courses, but he felt his situation is even worse when compared to his "old" premeditation self:

I had such a belief in vipassana as a way of life and thought that I am going to get stronger and stronger, and now this. . . . Ever since that course my situation became worse. I mean, I continued meditating, and took six courses since then. . . . But today I can hardly meditate with others. I have this problem of swallowing saliva—I cannot control it, it is a nightmare, and I constantly think that others can hear me. And this anxiety, this social anxiety, became stronger. My situation now is worse in comparison to how I was before I took my first vipassana course.

Initially Ben adopted an orientation of progress, of ongoing self-improvement. If he practiced meditation, he figured, his life would get better. But a long period of what Ben defined as "regression" placed this assumption into serious question. And this view received validation after he was diagnosed by a psychologist as suffering from social anxiety. How might he make sense of this emotional drop? How might he make it cohere with a trajectory of self-transformation and self-improvement?

Ben had two choices. Either he was mistaken about meditation and the orientation toward a better future had to be abandoned, or he could somehow incorporate his experience of descent into the trajectory of progress. He chose the second option. This choice is far from idiosyncratic. In fact, integrating downfalls into a trajectory of progress is a common strategy in both Western and Eastern cultures. Think about Thomas Edison's phrase "I failed my way to success" or the well-known Japanese maxim "Failure teaches success." If failure is interpreted as a lesson on the way to success and emotional downfall as an important detour on the way to enlightenment, the failure and the downfall are no longer outliers on the linear trajectory of progress. Instead, they constitute signs of that progress.

In order to re-create a trajectory of progress, Ben adopted an interpretation offered by meditation teachers that goes as follows: During meditation practice, deep unconscious psychological sediments may rise to the surface. If one continues to observe the sensations and thoughts calmly, they will eventually be eradicated. Many practitioners find this interpretation, which is based on elements from Buddhist philosophy that were translated into Western psychological terms, rather plausible. When understood as psychological sediment that rises to the surface, the appearance of social anxiety is no longer a regression; it is a process of cleansing—liberating oneself from something that was always there to begin with. The power of such an explanation is that it turns every emotional downfall into a part of the training and a temporary station on the way to a better state. It enables people to retain a belief in a trajectory of progress even in the context of descent.

Attaching such meaning to his experiences enabled Ben to integrate his fall into an orientation toward a better future. However, though he attempted to return to such future orientation, he was still deeply anchored in the past. As he told me:

> I must admit, whenever I remember that feeling after my first two courses it is difficult not to desire that state again. It felt so perfect. I was completely in control over every word I said. Today I find myself babbling with people, just throwing words out. And at that time, the silence, every word meant something. I know I am not supposed to expect that this will return, and that comparing is probably not a good idea, but it is difficult not to. I guess that somewhere inside I believe that if I continue meditating, this feeling will eventually return.

It is around such moments, moments that mix doubt and hope, moments of confusion regarding whether meditation still solves the specific problem at hand, that practitioners tend to drop the practice or reduce its intensity. Since most people have little social investment in meditation practice, dropping out is quite easy, especially in the absence of satisfaction or expected here-and-now benefits from the practice, benefits that attracted them to meditation in the first place.

Since Ben did not find a solution to his social anxiety in meditation, I thought he would drop the practice. Yet when I met him for the third interview, he was meditating every day for two hours and planning to take a long meditation course of twenty days. He also took upon himself serious volunteer work in the vipassana trust in Israel. Eventually he adopted a new orientation to meditation, one that characterizes the few who are "taken" by the practice. In this orientation, the motivation to practice is no longer anchored in specific "benefits" or "improvements." Instead meditation becomes a way of life.

Meditation as a Way of Life

In the bulk of biographical stories I collected, people meditate because it "works." This means that vipassana meets needs and provides solutions, holding out promise for a better, more desired self or a return to the desired self that was encountered through meditation. This is what drove most of my informants, a motivation that, as discussed in chapter 2, fits the culture of self-improvement and subjective well-being that prevails in contemporary Western society. Yet for a small minority, those who are eventually "captured" by the practice, meditation was no longer a tool to achieve a better life: it had become a way of life.

A way of life is a part of who I am, a part of my spiritual career, one that I plan to stick with for the duration. When meditators find themselves in this life-course orientation, they speak of a continual wish to "deepen" the practice, "deep" used as an embodied metaphor for diving more deeply inward and thus representing seriousness of practice. However, I found that turning meditation into a way of life is not just a question of internal orientation. It means reorganizing or shaping many "external" social relationships—friends, partners, family, and even work—so that these relationships can support a vipassana-practice-centered life.

There is no strict boundary between what I call the "light" and the "serious" categories of meditation practice. Some people practice meditation seriously already after a few retreats, and some have taken a dozen retreats and are still practicing only sporadically. Still, if a boundary is to be chosen, the station I chose to mark the entrance to what I refer to as the "serious" category of meditation as a way of life is taking a long retreat, referred to as a "long course" by my informants. This is because applying to a course longer than ten days requires a high level of commitment to the practice. The commitment is both chosen and required by the teaching school. Sitting in a long course is very difficult, and only those truly interested in deepening their practice usually apply to such a course. Meditation teachers and the registration committee serve as gatekeepers who validate the seriousness of the student and approve his or her registration. Seriousness is measured by time and effort devoted to the practice. The formal institutional guidelines in the Goenka vipassana school, for example, ask that before you sign up for a twenty-day course, you participate in five ten-day courses, volunteer in at least one ten-day course, and practice meditation daily for a year.

Peter's experience illustrates the orientation he adopted after taking a long course. I introduced Peter in chapter 4 when he described his strong sense of liberation after his first meditation course in France. I quoted him again in the previous section when he admitted to me, in one of our conversations, that he has high expectations from his next meditation retreat. That would be his first twenty-day course, and Peter was still making sense of meditation as something that "works," hoping that the retreat would reproduce the self he remembered from previous meditation retreats. The twenty-day course changed that orientation; the following excerpt is taken from our interview after he returned from it:

> I tried to watch TV and it was *Special Victims Unit* in *Law and Order* in which some sixteen-year-old girl in Queens dies and it turns out she was in porn movies and HIV positive and she infected like the entire population in Queens,

and then there was this show about children who were locked in a basement, and I just felt, "This is just terrible, this is so sad, so bad." I felt horrible emotionally and physically. And I just said, "This is not getting easier!" Since in the twenty-day course you get a chance to understand the enormousness of the task, in which you have to stay with dissatisfaction and bad sensations in every waking hour—and you can't switch it off, there is an effort required to stay with physical sensations—and this is why it is such an enormous task, since anything else you can turn off from time to time. And that really scared me. And there is this thought about your sense of *dukkha* [the Buddhist tenet of suffering/dissatisfaction]—and I felt, "Why do I want to know more about *dukkha*? I have enough of that; does that mean that everything in my life is going to taste like sand, is going to have a bitter aftertaste?" And this is the emotional state with which I came back.

Juxtaposing the transcriptions of the interviews with Peter clarified the enormous difference between our first and last conversations. In the first, Peter recounted the conclusion of his first ten-day meditation retreat and his ideas of putting vipassana to use in daily life—discovering how vipassana offers a solution to his social anxiety and how it can make his life easier. In the final interview, Peter described the end of his first twenty-day retreat, focusing on sadness and despair and thinking that vipassana might not make his life easier after all.

The latter account reminded me of accounts I heard from people who were extremely disappointed from their first meditation retreat. These individuals did not pursue the practice of vipassana. Perhaps if Peter had completed his first meditation retreat with the bitter aftertaste he felt later, he would have never returned for more. But such an experience at the advanced level of meditation is a different story. When I spoke to people about their first twenty-day retreat, neither liberation nor happiness was on their minds. Instead they described feeling overwhelmed or afraid of the return to normal life. And yet these experiences did not deter them from continuing to meditate and returning for longer retreats. Even Peter, who spoke in a highly negative tone of his experience after the course, continued to meditate.

All the serious meditators I met were originally attracted to meditation because it offered them a solution, a tool to improve their daily life. Without making a deliberate decision, however, they were slowly taken by the practice, becoming committed regardless of expectations and outcomes. Such a "gradual conversion" process includes a change in the way they now view their initial experiences in meditation.[10] As thirty-six-year-old Josh, a serious American meditator who took two twenty-day courses, told me: "Initially, the type of benefits I encountered . . . I would now call by-products, but initially they were very . . . I was very grateful to them and they were very profound and noticeable." As one turns meditation into a career path, the positive experiences are no longer the anchor of the practice, and negative experiences are accepted as important parts of the trajectory.

"Light" meditators sometimes notice this difference when observing serious practitioners. Doron took his first two courses in India in 1995, and another course in Israel. He then married, had three children, and did not practice for nearly ten years. His divorce led him back to meditation practice. After participating in several courses, he decided to strengthen his practice by volunteering in the Israeli vipassana trust. During his biweekly shift at the vipassana apartment in Tel Aviv, he met serious meditators who managed the activity of the vipassana trust in Israel. When we met for an interview, one of the first questions he asked me was "Do you think that people who take long courses are happier?" He added that the people he met at the business meeting of the vipassana trust did not seem particularly happy. He was wondering about this, as all he wanted in life was "to be happy, or at least to decrease my suffering." His disappointment from the lack of happiness of "long course" meditators teaches us about the gap between "light" and "serious" practitioners. Doron was right. For serious meditators, happiness, or at least happiness in the way Doron and many others in our culture define it, loses its salience.

Moreover, at the level of long retreats, Buddhist notions and cosmology begin to take center stage. Taught intensively during such courses, they penetrate the embodied experience of practitioners. While in shorter retreats the meditation teachings mainly address the Buddhist principle of impermanence—that is, noticing how the body is in constant change, in long retreats—all three tenets, impermanence, suffering (or, better, dissatisfaction), and not-self, become the focus of the practice. Specifically, participants in long retreats are taught to experience these three aspects of ultimate reality on the level of the body through the observation of sensations.[11] Tali, a thirty-three-year-old Israeli doctoral student, noted that in a long meditation course she felt impermanence in a much deeper way than she had in short courses: "In the long course, I could feel *anicca* [impermanence]. How everything changes. How my moods, emotions, sensations change all the time. I was really with *anicca*. I don't think that in a short course I ever felt it so clearly. It is something you can only experience in a long course."

These experiences of instability may lead meditators to a feeling of emptiness or "not-self," which is one of the most important characterizations of the Buddhist ultimate truth. Josh, for example, who took a thirty-day meditation course, described the following, which he experienced in deep meditation:

Then it came to me: What here is solid? What here is lasting? What is going to stay when this body falls away? And I don't have an answer; the only answer that comes up is again something that I can't really try to explain, it would be silly to try and explain, . . . and you know, at a certain point I say, "Jesus, everything is hollow here—what the hell is going on?"

Such experiences are common in long retreats, where participants face intensive dissatisfaction, emotional ups and downs, and psychological and even physical instability. As another long retreat meditator put it: "I had this strong realization that this mind is not mine, and this body is not mine. They don't belong do me. And it was very surprising because the feeling that these thoughts are mine is so deeply grounded."

These encounters with loss or disappearance of self-identity can be extremely troubling, as captured in the words "What the hell is going on?" Having knowledge and understanding of Buddhist concepts is critical in order to explain such experiences and accept them as a part of the training. In one case I encountered a "light" meditator who had an experience of flow, which in the category of advanced meditators frequently received the interpretation of not-self. As she put it, her body completely disappeared, and she was immersed in subtle sensations. But instead of this feeling leading to a realization of the Buddhist ultimate truth, she panicked. In an effort to regain her hold on reality, she moved. Moving, as described in chapter 4, brings the world back as attention shifts to the outer lining of experience. She got her "ordinary self" back. Such an account exemplifies how the same embodied experience can lead to radically different interpretations when encountered by meditators in different stages.

The notion of nirvana, or *nibbana* in Pali, also becomes more central for advanced meditators. How practitioners treat this concept varies, from psychological liberation to spiritual purification to religious purification. For many serious meditators, nirvana gradually becomes the end goal of the practice, even if according to vipassana teachers it is considered an experience that is probably achievable only in the next cycles of life. Belief in the migration of life from one cycle to another also becomes more common. Not everyone who takes long courses believes in past lives or future lives. Some play with these interpretations—not completely believing in them but also not opposing them. When Dana, an Israeli meditator, experienced a strange pain in her stomach during a twenty-day retreat, she had a feeling it might be a past life experience. She could not explain why: "It is just that that sensation was completely new. I have never felt it before. So I started wondering whether it came from a past life of mine." When I asked her if she believed in past lives, she said that she does not really know: "I guess that I think that if people that I respect and trust, such as meditation teachers, or Goenka, know that it exists, then I am inclined to believe in it."

Even though in this orientation salvation is postponed beyond this life course, alongside meditation as a way of life serious meditators hold a future orientation regarding healing. Allan, for example, experienced a strong pain in his shoulder on the twelfth day of a thirty-day retreat. Like David, whom we met earlier in this chapter and who connected an experience in the meditation retreat to his injury in battle, Allan connected this pain to a past—albeit not this-worldly—traumatic event. He was convinced that it came from an experience he had had in a past life. While he was meditating in his private meditation cell, he suddenly felt as if there were someone behind him holding a sword. A moment later he felt a burning pain in his shoulder. This strong pain stayed with him for seven days. As he told me,

> It was as if I was really hit with a sword in my shoulder—my whole right side was useless. . . . I didn't sleep for three days. . . . I tried to meditate but I was in so much pain. . . . One day we were going to a group meditation sitting and I was in so much pain I didn't want to go into my cell. I found a tree and I leaned on it on my left arm and just stood there—I stood outside until everyone came out and went into their sleeping quarters and I followed them. . . . And during day 19, the amazing pain, this wound started to come alive, it started to vibrate and move, moving away from the shoulder, and by the evening it just disappeared and went away. On day 20 it was all gone. It was amazing. And when I said I saw this man behind me with the sword—I never had pain in my shoulder in my life, and never again after the course. So the way I interpreted it is that this was a past-life experience that came out of me during this meditation course, was lodged in my shoulder, and now it is gone.

Here Allan produces an autobiography that extends into past lives. Unlike David, who used vipassana to dismantle his combat shock, Alan did not remember this event before the meditation retreat; it was not a memory that he sought therapy to deal with. Yet Allan's evident excitement (the event was "amazing") and the significance he granted to the statement "Now it is gone" illustrate a conviction that vipassana "works" in the sense of purifying oneself from past-life negative experiences that are "lodged" in the body.

When entering the life-course orientation of meditation as a way of life, the meditators I interviewed actively created a social circle with which to share their deep interest in meditation. In this orientation toward meditation, many practitioners become deeply involved in volunteer work in the meditation center or in managing the vipassana trust in their area. They frequently meet other long-course meditators. They will know at least one or two people in a long course, and usually more than two. Interestingly, even in this orientation, fellow meditators are not necessary friends in the sense of getting together outside the meditation contexts. But they are certainly no longer strangers.

In the "lighter" category of meditation, it was common to meet meditators whose life partners do not meditate. In the more "serious" category, I found that practitioners tend to seek a partner who also meditates. Long courses eat up workplace-related vacation days, and it is the rare nonmeditating partner that would put up with family vacations minus the meditator. In addition, when meditation becomes so important in one's life, it is difficult not to share it with one's partner. In fact, there are hardly any long-course practitioners who are married to nonmeditators. Those who wish to take long courses but have partners that do not meditate may find themselves parting with their partners. Such parting, or divorce, was not encouraged by the head teacher S. N. Goenka, who in his teachings stressed the importance of the household in this vipassana tradition. Specifically, he advised refraining from progressing too far in meditation when one's partner would be left behind. Goenka's teachings echo traditional norms in India, his home country, but Western practitioners are less inclined to adopt these norms.

Advanced meditators sometimes reconstruct their social relations so that they support their practice, perhaps moving close to a meditation center. This has led to the emergence of small communities of meditators. The biggest meditation community in the United States is located in the environs of the Massachusetts center. The community was established by people who took their first courses in the 1960s, 1970s, and 1980s and are now meditation teachers or serious volunteers in the meditation center. Others joined later. In this community I met whole families that meditate, including children. I also met families in which the parents meditated and the children expressed aversion to meditation. Many of the meditation teachers who lived in this community had older children who had been born before they became meditation teachers.

These communities did not seem to be attempting to produce alternative social structures or institutions (compare the commune structure of the 1960s). For example, properties were all privately owned by individual families, and the children I met attended mainstream schools. In addition, the social connections between the people in such communities are not necessary strong. An individual who resides in one of these areas commented that people sometimes come to live next to the meditation center thinking that this is a commune in which everyone is friends, but this is not the case. "Friendship," she said, "is based on something personal, something you find in the other person. So there are groups of friends here, and some may complain that these are 'cliques,' but this is how it is."

In Chicago, where a meditation center was established in 2005, and in Israel, where a new center was established in 2012, communities began emerging as well.[12] These communities are composed of younger people than those in the Massachusetts center, but the social relations are similar. Those who move to live close to the center are extremely serious meditators who see vipassana as their way of life. They are deeply engaged in volunteer work in the center, and some are meditation teachers. In Israel, where almost all teachers of meditation were appointed in the past ten years, it was common to meet couples who began their meditation path together in the 1990s and today are both teachers. These teachers are relatively young, around age forty, and the majority do not have children.

Only a very small fraction of the long-course practitioners will end up being meditation teachers. As I was told, the senior meditation teachers who are in contact with serious and committed volunteers decide on those who seem to them suitable for teaching. This selection process is based more on social skills and communicative abilities than on meditation seniority. Other factors include the ability to support oneself (as all meditation teachers are volunteers), the flexibility of one's occupation or income (some teachers live on a pension or on their inheritance), and family status (with a preference for teachers that are either married to another advanced meditator or single). Only once did I meet a meditation teacher whose husband did not meditate. From what I observed, in the case of married meditation teachers there seems to be a preference for appointing both partners as teachers so they can travel and teach together.

Those who are offered and accept teaching positions go through a period of training and apprenticeship. This means that not everyone who hopes to become a teacher will eventually become one. Of course no authoritative body presides over teaching vipassana—anyone can decide to teach, and outside of the organized teaching schools we find teachers who do not belong to a specific lineage of teachers. However, I found that when reaching the level of serious meditator, practitioners express commitment not only to the practice but also to a specific meditation school, adopting the Eastern tradition in which a senior teacher appoints the new teachers and announces them as part of his lineage.

We are witnessing a reconfiguration of existing relationships, or the shaping of new ones, that supports or suits vipassana practice. Surrounding oneself with others who meditate as friends and neighbors. Choosing partners that support the practice or divorcing those who do not. Choosing not to have children, or to have a single child — a very uncommon choice in Israeli society at large. Sometimes even switching jobs to permit enough free time for volunteering and taking courses. For some, especially teachers, their whole life is now centered around meditation as they travel from one meditation center to another and teach courses.

*

Our tour of various biographies of vipassana practitioners revealed stories of self-transformation that focus on the role of vipassana in orienting one's life course and organizing the autobiographical self. As we saw, vipassana was not regarded as a mere hobby but as an anchor for answering questions regarding "who I am." As such, vipassana shares a space with similar practices to which people turn during periods of rupture or transition, including psychotherapy, spirituality, and different bodily related practices such as running and dieting.[13] In all these cases people are searching for practices that can help them reorient themselves in life, using them to connect and make sense of past, present and future.

The entry points into meditation practice described in this chapter illustrate the importance of the way meditation is perceived by its potential audience — as a cure or solution to moments of rupture; as a tool in the search for subjective well-being, happiness, and meaning. This pragmatic framing prompts those seeking such tools to give meditation a try. Yet not all of them will find meditation positive or useful. The case of vipassana illustrates that for meditation to become attractive, the embodied experiences encountered in the practice should fit with specific needs and goals of individuals at a certain point in their life course. Thus for the same people meditation might offer salvation at a certain point in life, only to become useless at another point in their biography. For the same person, meditation can first be about self-improvement or therapy, later to become a religious tool toward enlightenment.

When making sense of their practice, meditators cannot rely on tradition, on social groups, or on religious belief. Although their social circles may acknowledge the benefits of meditation, the practice brings little prestige or external recognition, and for most meditators dropping out is an easy step that does not require breaking up families or disappointing friends. In this context, personal experiences become central to the biographies of vipassana practitioners. When meditators search for answers regarding why they meditate, they find them in personal experiences of transformation. This is why positive experiences of change were key to their life narratives. This is also why the discovery of the reversibility of selves can be disappointing, as they

realize that whatever they found in meditation is fragile and slippery and requires constant maintenance. This is also why once meditation stops "working" or requires too much effort for maintenance, people tend to drop out and
stop practicing.

The promise of therapeutic or self-improvement justifies meditation practice, as it is anchored in more general cultural support. Only when practitioners enter the serious meditators category does the importance of this promise
decline, and they then search for ways to anchor themselves in a social structure that will keep them in despite moments of doubt. In a somewhat paradoxical turn, those who commit themselves to meditation, who turn meditation into a way of life, end up purposefully recruiting the pressures of social
structures, reconfiguring their social circles so as to create social commitments and produce a social structure that contains them. In this sense, while
for all my informants commitment to the practice is first motivated by personal experiences, for this small group of serious meditators their commitment is gradually externalized as social circles are recruited to strengthen and
support it.

Pragmatic and instrumental orientations are not limited to meditators but
are key to the mid-high secular strata in contemporary postindustrial culture. In a world in which religion, family life, and professional identity are
defined as personal choices, questions like "how does this practice help me?"
and "how does it organize my life for the better?" become central. This does
not mean that social commitments no longer play an important role, but in
a culture that sanctifies personal choice these commitments may no longer
serve as convincing justifications. When people's social identities and social
participation cannot be taken for granted, when dropping out is unhindered
by social sanction, people turn their work, family, and religion into missions
that revolve around themselves as individuals rather than around tradition,
God, or an afterlife.

7

Bodies, Selves, and the Social World

Interiority has stepped into the spotlight. Today it is not only philosophers, mental health professionals, and religious virtuosi who are looking inward. Gazing within has become a global preoccupation, supplying new experiences to an ever-expanding market of audiences.

As part of this burgeoning interest in interiority, the body has become the subject of intense curiosity. Specialized practices of inward looking have spread beyond the psychotherapeutic world to incorporate body-based introspection techniques. The extraordinary popularization of vipassana has taken place in the context of the contemporary turn to the body in the hope of discovering solutions to this-worldly concerns.

This growing interest in the body is also evident in sociological thought. Since the 1980s, sociological attention has centered on the body and its importance for the production and maintenance of the social world. Reacting to profoundly cognitive and rational models of human action, sociologists introduced embodiment as a practical, habitual, subconscious base for action.[1] The "self," by contrast, is understood in sociological theory as a reflexive, conscious and abstract thought process based on "internal conversations."[2] From this perspective, social life is essentially dualistic, moving along two parallel tracks—the practical and the conceptual, the disattended and the attended, the habitual and the reflective.[3]

In this chapter I challenge this view by demonstrating that conscious attendance to the background embodiment of the self is an integral part of our everyday life. I show that the process described in this book in the context of meditation, as is set out in the next section, is a mere tip of the iceberg, an extreme case of more mundane processes in which we explicitly attend to the background, the invisible dimension.[4] Drawing on a variety of case studies, including, among others, alternative therapies, dieting, exercising, ballet dancing, self-cutting, fasting, praying, and even smoking, I establish that vipassana meditation and other socially recognized turn-to-the-body practices are collectively honored, institutionalized occasions for doing in an explicit and elaborated way what is a natural part of life.

When studying embodied practices, sociologists tend to focus on their symbolic power—how bodily movement, appearance, and taste serve as cultural capital, indicating social standing, distinction, inclusion, and exclusion.[5] Yet alongside their central role in projecting a competent self to others, these practices invite practitioners to focus on the inner lining and thus permit breaks in the continual attendance to the social gaze. When approaching embodied practices as subjecting people to social structures or as producing "docile bodies,"[6] studies disregard the possibility these practices afford of transcending social situatedness and social dependency.

The inner and the outer, the embodiment and the projection of self, are not two distinct processes: rather, to borrow Merleau-Ponty's apt image, they are two sides of the same leaf.[7] The social world supplies communities, routines, and rituals, some of which are considered religious, some secular, through which practitioners turn inward to their bodies without stepping out of society. Through such practices we discover how to be both social and corporeal, how to relieve anxiety regarding what others see or think: an embodied transcendence that permits a smooth movement between social relations.

The Microsocial World of Vipassana Meditation

I argue that the shift to the inner lining of experience is specifically social in nature, involving a new mode of interaction with others. Thus meditation is not merely a psychological act that takes place within individual minds. The turn inward is anchored in specific social relations that enable this flip. In this sense, subjectivity and intersubjectivity are so entwined that they need not be studied as distinct phenomena.

This inquiry is quite paradoxical: I am asking how individuals go about discovering the most private aspects of themselves precisely through being with others. In this way meditation becomes a space where people realize a truth about the human condition, the phenomenology of intertwining with the world. They discover their "being in the world" as they feel themselves through the world—through the touch of the air both inside (breathing) and outside (skin), the pressure on a leg that rests on the cushion, the feel of the ground when walking, the food in the mouth when eating, the cough that others hear, the anger that arises in relation to another's behavior, the anxiety that emerges when one meets certain others, the self-satisfaction of success-fully telling a joke.[8] In their attempt to observe the inner lining, people be-come folk phenomenologists, observing, resisting, or readjusting the "natural attitude" of social relations.[9]

THE FLIP AND THE PARADOX

Vipassana meditation moves attention away from action and toward bodily sensations that usually do not require attention—breathing, tingling of hands, sensations at the elbow or the ends of the toes. The meditator sets her atten-tion inward, away from the social world.

Consisting of crucial elements of behavior in daily life, the embodiment of the self usually remains at the periphery of attention. Within Goffman's metaphor of "attentional tracks," these operations belong to the "disattended" one—that is, the track at the background of social interaction.[10] The notion of "disattended" can be misleading, however, as these tracks are not ignored by participants. Rather they are attended to in a tacit way, serving as background bases from which we act in the world.

In the meditation center, as in everyday life, individuals are faced with the problem of choosing the right attentional track, selecting between the background and the foreground of action.[11] When people begin to meditate, they are attracted to an awareness of others. In this conventional track, the embodiment of the self remains tacit as individuals observe and respond to others, attending to the self as viewed by others. Soon they discover that vipas-sana aims to train practitioners to turn this "conventional track" into a back-ground one, to push back the self as seen by others, to push back the tendency to perceive interactionally.

The temptation to remain in the mundane or conventional track takes place at many levels of meditation. When I attempt to feel my elbow, I find myself visualizing my elbow as if I can step outside of my body and observe it. When I feel itchiness, I want to scratch the area, or when a fly lands on my lips, I want to move and drive it away—I want to shift from the inner lining (the sensation) to the expression, response, and adjustment in the world. When I move in meditation, I am tempted to shift my attention to my neigh-bor and his perception of me and control my movement. When I am annoyed by the sound of my roommate's clock, I am tempted to see myself as seen (or better, not seen) by my roommate, to which I respond by feeling anger for his lack of consideration (see more examples in chapters 3 and 5).

In meditation one notices the power of this temptation and strives to over-come it. Thus in meditation, orientation to the social world becomes a barrier to overcome. Practitioners may give too much attention to their projection of self, wondering how others see them. Or they may find their mind wandering to the social world that awaits them after meditation. As they progress in meditation, they find that they need to tilt the balance between these two tracks. If in everyday life we act from the body to the world, as the inner lining remains in the background of attention, meditation practice involves an inversion of this direction of attention with the inner lining taking center stage.[12]

Yet even when the background embodiment of the self takes a front seat and becomes explicit, the second track, that of the happening in the social world (either in proximity or in the more distanced social world), does not disappear—it is pushed to the background, periodically resurfacing to the center of attention. Thus when people are meditating with others, while most attention is set on tracing the inner lining of bodily experience, a peripheral part of practitioners' awareness is set on others and adjusts their bodies to other bodies. Tacitly, meditators adjust and synchronize with others' bodily stillness, silence, and emotional equanimity.

In other words, training in flipping the direction of attention takes place in a communal world that helps us overcome the natural tendency to focus on how others see us. In meditation I close my eyes, I do not speak, I am even told to try to ignore others. But I cannot really ignore others or forget about others. The best I can do is push the awareness to the way others see me to the background and thus tacitly track others without focused attention.

This tacit awareness of others enables me to "forget" about the worries and needs of the social world and about the "me" that I am in daily life. Others here serve as a negation of the disturbances of "regular" social interaction. They treat me as "invisible" by not responding to me, and I do the same for them. Their lack of response, their verbal and bodily silence, relieves me of the need to respond. They fill the space of the social world and enable me to dive inward.

This somewhat strange mode of interaction differs from the usual "focused interaction" or "interaction ritual" described by microsociologists.[13] Even though in the meditation hall people are engaged in the same activity, the actual content they are observing is accessible only to the individual practitioner. There is no joint object of attention to which all bodies are oriented. There is no joint meaning that people are producing together in action. There is only a shell, a thin layer of joint understanding that holds this structure together, a simple unanimous conversation of bodily gestures. It is a mode of interaction in which we help one another to ignore one another.

Through the participation in a community of strangers who together disattend to one another, who together sit quietly without moving even when a phone rings, even when someone cries loudly in the meditation hall, I learn to subdue my attention to my projection of self to the world. Through moving around in the meditation center without talking and responding to others, even when my roommate annoys me or when meditators are eating dinner together, I learn to subdue the expectations from social relations, to sub-do sociality.

In solitary individual meditation, practitioners find ways to reproduce this social anchor from which they turn inward. They do so by using meditation instructions through CDs or mobile applications, they use the same cushion as in the meditation center, or the same cover. They sit for the same period of one hour. Still, solitary meditation is reported as "less deep" than group meditation, indicating that the group has an important role in helping the meditator to let go of or bracket the outer world and go inward. Practitioners of vipassana thus find that they need to return to collective solitude, either in weekly group sittings or in meditation retreats, in order to maintain their meditation practice.

This brings us to the core of the issue: the reason it is helpful to be with others when meditating is that most people find it difficult, if not impossible, not to perceive interactionally. The presence of other meditators helps negate interaction with others in other times and places—to relax anxieties regarding how others perceive me, to relax anticipations regarding what I am going to do later in the day, to relax my response to the sound of conversation or to the ringing of the phone. Other meditators fill that necessary, inexorable slot of social interaction.

EXTENDING MEDITATION TO DAILY LIFE

Encountering the inner lining, the background embodiment of the self, reveals a certain truth about the way we act in the world. This truth can become significant and be generalized into everyday life. It can also remain meaningless, a hindrance to action in the world. In their efforts to explain their practice to themselves and others, practitioners seek significations that help them make sense of what they have experienced in meditation.

In the Buddhist world, meditation experiences are made sense of in light of Buddhist philosophy and belief, using ideas and terms such as ultimate reality or the concepts of suffering, impermanence, and not-self. In addition, Buddhist monks have strict rules regarding what it means to be a social person in conventional reality when interacting with others.[14] In the Buddhist context, navigation between the two realities, or the two modes of attention (and interaction), is structured by the monastic order and by Buddhist society at large.

My informants, in contrast, had no rules regarding the integration of meditation into their ordinary relationships. When entering daily life, they reencountered the challenge of navigating between two realities or two attentional tracks. During meditation, my projection of self to others, the "me" in the social world, is pushed to the background as I focus on the particulars that lie at the base of my embodiment. However, once meditation is over, either in a group or in an individual setting, I am once again someone who means something for others, and those others anticipate that I will respond to their expectations. As I step out of the meditation center and return to my relationships, I find no agreement regarding mutual disattendance in the real social world. On the contrary, others attend to me and expect me to attend to their perceptions of me, to respond, align, and divert attention to the self I am projecting.

Practitioners attempted to connect the inner lining discovered in meditation with their postmeditation life, to make sense of meditation as active social beings with a biography and place in the world. They produced these connections in varied ways. Some thought of meditation as a therapeutic tool, supplying moments of liberation from a traumatic past. Others found that through making contact with their mortal existence, they could temporarily escape the burden and stress of everyday life and return "refreshed" and "recharged." Some reported that the diversion of attention to sensations enables them to feel "comfortable in their own skin," reducing the attention they give to what others think of them. And still others used vipassana to control and monitor their behavior and emotions in daily life by becoming more focused, managing anger, or curtailing depression and anxiety.

In all these uses and interpretations, meditators practice reducing attendance to social expectations and judgments. Time and again they bracket the natural social attitude and slow down their responses. They step back from the "social game." This is what Peter did in the example introduced in chapter 4 when he observed and attempted to slow his heartbeat. He reduced his social anxiety, disattending to the "me" that he sensed was reflected in the eyes of others. This is also what Joanna did in chapter 5 when she observed her sensations of anger. She stepped back from arguments with her father by disattending to his invitations for a fight.

In all these examples the natural embodiment in the world is disturbed, and thus a space opens up for new meaning-making, a space for reflexivity and change.[15] This produces the possibility that meditation can become part of something broader, something that goes beyond the situated practice. As elaborated in chapter 2, the "unconventional" reality discovered in meditation received broader meanings dependent on the historical, social, and cultural context. Vipassana thus could become part of religious salvation, political resistance, exoticism, or the counterculture. The new perspective on self and social world can be integrated into a movement for social change. Yet most of my informants perceived in this bodily based transformation an opportunity to change their lives, their relationships, and their selves. They saw in meditation a tool to influence "this-worldly" microrelations.

EMBODIED TRANSCENDENCE

Taking together the different uses and interpretations of vipassana, we see that the common thread is that meditation offered my informants an experience of embodied transcendence. As Jack Katz writes: "What having a body most fundamentally means for a person is that he or she lives an ongoing continuity beyond the social situations passed through in everyday life."[16] When shifting attention to the inner lining of experience, when pushing awareness of the social self to the background, meditators find an affirmation of existence that is not dependent on relations with others.

The turn to the background embodiment of the self is used to transcend the shocks and splits to the self as people move through social relations. This is why many of my informants turned to meditation in moments of fracture: Tom experienced difficulties and alienation at work; Rachel recently went through a divorce and the death of her mother; Tanya, a recent immigrant, felt useless and lonely after her daughters left the house; David could no longer fulfill his dream of a military career. When social life was found to be disappointing and could no longer serve as an anchor to the self, in the search for "what is next?" all of them found the body to be comforting, reducing dependency on the social world.

The same goes for the more mundane splits of the self that people encounter in everyday life. In chapter 4 we saw how people use vipassana to smooth the transition between social relations and events. For example, I used awareness of the inner lining to be fully with my son and control the seeping of my work worries into my family life; Shai, the psychologist, used it to block his family troubles from seeping into his work time when listening to patients; Shira, a teacher for children with special needs, used it to handle the separation between her "caring" self at work and her personal life. Ron and Oren used it to handle the stress when entering or anticipating new social situations, which for Ron was provoked when applying to graduate programs, for Oren, by dating.

All of us are always moving between social situations—a meeting at work, playing with the children, a lecture at the university, sitting on the train, a job interview, a car accident, a romantic date. For some people, maybe a growing number of people in contemporary postindustrial society, such shifts from one situation to another, from one social relation to another, from one projection of self to another, are highly stressful.[17] The body offers an anchor that transcends such situations, a corporeal reality that is behind social life.

The kind of transcendence found in meditation is reflected in the "sensory" or "corporeal" grounding that vipassana practitioners spoke of and the freedom they experienced when meditation proved to be a practice through which they "found themselves." Such identity finding differs strikingly from the regular use of the notion of self in sociological writing. Since George Herbert Mead, *the self* has referred to how one is seen by others.[18] But Merleau-Ponty wrote of an experience of identity that precedes the self: "At the root of all our experiences and all our reflections, we find, then, a being which immediately recognizes itself . . . not by observation and as a given fact, nor by inference from any idea of itself, but through direct contact with that experience."[19]

When the inner lining becomes central in the daily life of my informants, a trade-off is revealed as the place of significant others in maintaining and sharing their intimate spheres declines. As Don put it aptly in chapter 4, in moments of difficulty he no longer "runs" to his friends but can run to "himself." This is why when trying to connect meditation to their intimate relationships, my informants experienced tension. The reduced attention to the social world, and with it to the projection of self, can be extremely frustrating for significant others who do not participate in the world of meditation.

As in the ethnomethodological experiments conducted by Harold Garfinkel's students, family members and friends may find it confusing that their loved one no longer responds to the self that they portray to her.[20] Borrowing Adam Kendon's notion, the "working consensus" of interaction is lost.[21] They may find their family member to be less interactive or "no longer a social guy" (see chapter 5). They then communicate their frustration to their family member, who herself becomes reflexive to the expectations and norms of daily life.

The focus on sensations can be used to control and change daily interactions, but since the structure of meditative awareness is based on the above-described inversion of the direction of attention, this control requires reducing the attention we give to the perception that others have about us. It asks us to relax the human tendency to respond to others' attempts to influence us, thus leaving unfulfilled their expectations for reciprocity and mutual attendance. This means that instead of turning to others to reassure the self, one turns inward, to oneself. Such independence from the gaze of others can be quite jarring to the meditator's significant others. Their centrality to her life, their intimate and superior role as mirroring to her who she is, meets with a maddening challenge.

As attention is diverted to that part of ourselves that others do not have access to, that normally hidden part on which we rely to perform in daily life, practitioners of meditation try to overcome the fragility of the self that is produced in interaction with others. In their turn to the inner lining, they resist certain elements in their social relations, elements that their intimate others may have taken for granted as natural and important.

Extending the Analytic Frame

The journey through the life-world of vipassana practitioners sheds light on a process in which the background embodiment of the self is turned explicit. This process is not unique to meditation practice. In fact, to use Kendon's terms, we can find in everyday life "gradients of explicitness"[22] in which certain elements of the embodied background shift to the foreground. In this sense, the hierarchy between the inner and the outer is reversible, and the inner can become a focus of attention.

While explicit attention to the inner lining can take place in the flow of everyday life, such as when I miss a step or when I bite my tongue, in most cases these are small moments in a more general effort to conceal and push these bodily elements to the background. Alongside this joint effort to ignore the background embodiment of the self, however, daily life presents us with socially institutionalized practices that allow us and even prompt us to shift attention to the inner lining.

In these practices we find a process of self-awareness that is not based on "internal conversations" or discursive/conceptual thinking. Instead the turn to the self takes place through a somatic, embodied channel.[23] At the same time, this embodied channel is not subconscious, habitual, or hidden from attention. The mode of self-awareness revealed in these practices resonates with Dewey's notion of "qualitative thought" in aesthetic experience, Csordas's "somatic mode of attention" in regard to religious healing, or Katz's "sensual/aesthetic" self-consciousness in emotional processes.[24] In all the practices introduced below we find a convergence of body and thought, soma and attention, sense and self.

In what follows I portray some extreme practices of attending to the inner lining of the self, after which I disclose analytically similar processes in daily practices which do not formally include an exploration of the self.[25]

The practices introduced below are homologous to meditation. The inner lining at the core of these practices takes different forms, as there are many levels to the invisible dimension—from breathing to movement to sensations to vocal sound. Uniting them is a socially organized and recognized practice that supports individuals in their (collective) effort to focus on the inner lining and, by way of this focus, break away from the self as seen by others.

EMBODIED THERAPIES

In addition to meditation, different bodily based practices have fed a growing hunger for therapeutic culture in Western societies. These include yoga, tai chi, qigong, biofeedback, the Alexander technique, rebirthing, Rolfing, and other alternative therapies that connect body and mind.

In yoga, tai chi, and qigong, attention is turned to the inner lining of the body as it moves throughout the day. One attends to how the center of the body moves and affects the peripheral parts. Rhythm of movement and breathing, and with it rhythmic coordination, becomes the object of focused awareness. Rhythm is a central dimension of the background embodiment of the self, as we tend to tacitly synchronize with others, to match our breathing, walking pace, speech patterns, and even menstrual cycle. In these practices the rhythmic coordination is moved to the foreground, becoming the "mainline" shared focus, or frame, of the activity.[26]

As in meditation, individuals do these practices in silence, keep a fixed and normative space between themselves, and try to refrain from comparing themselves to others. And as in the case of meditation, these practices help people to push to the background the self as viewed by others and focus on the typically tacit dimensions of their being. Such awareness does not stay limited to the situated practice, as meditators incorporate these practices within their daily life, turning them into an anchor of selfhood and a source of empowerment and personal development.[27]

Biofeedback is a bodily based technique that is explicitly defined as therapy-related and offered today in mainstream medical and psychological treatments. It is based on making explicit different background operations of the body, such as skin conduction, pulse, breathing, and heat. For example, in temperature-based biofeedback one learns to identify his own skin temperature and attempt to control it in order to reduce anxiety, negative thoughts, and alertness (all correlated with lower peripheral temperature) and increase feelings of calmness and security through an increase of skin temperature.

Likewise, the Alexander technique has practitioners "zoom in" to their posture and movement to correct habitual patterns of movements.[28] The Grinberg technique, for its part, highlights bodily reactions to fear and pain, aiming to adjust avoidance patterns and increase awareness of these sensations. Other alternative techniques, such as osteopathy, shiatzu, reflexology, Rolfing, and reiki, use touch to divert patients' attention to the hidden dimension of muscle and skeleton integration. In these spheres the emotionally neutralized touch of the therapist encourages the patient to focus on being touched, and through the touch of the other feel herself.

Leaving aside the issue of whether or not these techniques "work," we can say that they all provide an institutionalized social space in which one is encouraged, with the help of the touch of the therapist (shiatzu), an external machine (biofeedback), or the group (qigong), to turn attention to one's beneath-the-surface bodily dimensions. In all these cases the turn to the intimate part of the self requires help from the outside, a social institutionalized sphere.

In his work on emotions, Katz suggests that people use the turn to the body invoked by emotions to reconstruct identities in moments of falling out of the social embrace.[29] The embodied therapeutic practices surveyed above provide communal, ritualized ways of responding to the same falls from the social world. Embodied therapies are often experienced as soothing, relaxing, and tranquilizing, calming down the "emotional storm" (e.g., stress, anxiety, depression) and thus substituting one turn to the body (emotions) with another (the therapeutic practice). They provide a practical, culturally accepted corporeal resource for the reconstruction of self-identity.

BODILY CULTIVATION: WORKING OUT AND DIETING

Moving to the more "mundane" world, I continue with practices that focus on the care of the body as a form of self-cultivation.[30] Many of these practices have become enormously popular in recent years: gym workouts, running, Pilates, and swimming, alongside the flourishing of numerous diets and eating recommendations, from gluten-free to "Paleo" to juicing to weekly fasting.

In all of these practices background embodiment is brought to the foreground as a subject of attention around which the self revolves. The specific inner lining that is revealed varies from one practice to another. It might be breathing, heart rate, muscle tension, posture, rhythm, hunger, sugar rush, or another kind of bodily awareness. When swimming, for example, I attend to the unique way my body feels in water or to the rhythm of breathing, as being in the water offers a disruption of the natural and taken-for-granted being and breathing. When exercising in the gym, I attend to my heart rate or to muscle tension. When juicing or fasting, I attend to hunger, to feelings of lightness, to a sense of being energized.

Much like meditation, workouts, running, and dieting offer an alternative awareness of how I entwine with the world around me. People may find that they can continue stretching even when in pain, that they can continue running even though their body is tired, or that they can be without food for longer periods. Thus the taken-for-granted attitude toward pain, tiredness, or hunger is imbued with another meaning. In dieting, for example, a whole dimension of being, previously covert, becomes central in daily life as people begin to attend to their habits of eating—trying to eat smaller portions, more frequently, or more slowly. Not drinking coffee before the meal, or not drinking water while eating, or separating fruits from other foods. Not eating in the morning, or not eating after 7:00 p.m. Not eating meat or eating mainly meat. They track how certain foods (such as sugar) affect their bodies and minds. They attend to the particulars of the food and bodily indigestion, of the bodily food cycle in the course of a day.

A community of practitioners helps one concentrate on the inner lining of experience. As in meditation, other runners or Pilates class members fill in the need to track the outer lining, the social world. By synchronizing with the movements of others, I can put to rest my need to engage with and attend to others. Likewise, dieting practices are supported by social institutions and communities. It almost doesn't matter which diet you choose: what matters is that there are strict rules about what to eat and not to eat and when. These rules are frequently shared by a group of people, some of whom may meet in proximity (in dieting workshops and support groups) or online, and some may be silent members of a virtual community reading online what is "recommended" and the logic that drives that recommendation. Thus as in meditation and running, there are ritualistic rules and structures that enable the inversion of attention, that keep one in a social world while diverting attention inward.

Some people choose solitary exercising, such as running alone, while others cannot sustain the practice without external help. As in meditation, it is common for people to start in groups and then develop their own solitary practice. But even then the social community is there for support, and people like to revisit social spheres. Runners and bicyclists, for example, enjoy practicing for a marathon or any other collective event that gives social structure and meaning to their practice. In addition, even in solitary practice practitioners frequently rely on different objects that invite the social environment or community, even if this community is not nearby. They have their special shoes, their routine run, their series of exercises. They rely on ritualistic aids to perform the flip when alone. These ritualistic aids create a social frame, an interaction order into which one enters.

This is how the cultivation of the body becomes an honored, socially recognized space that gives a glimpse into the usually covert dimension of self. And this glimpse can be, and frequently is, extended into daily life. People who exercise or diet find that they become more aware of their bodies in general. Many find their body cultivation empowering. Some even find it therapeutic. It provides a private space that is beyond the reach of society, even when it is society that is doing the structuring. It is an anchor for selfhood that is not based on the gaze of others. It reveals that behind the stress, anxiety, and judgments of daily life there is a body that transcends social situations, a mortal corporeality. And this care of the body is frequently connected to long-term biographies, since eating the right foods and exercising are not just about the situated practice; they are perceived in terms of one's global health.

Thus bodily cultivation is much more than a way of indexing to others the belonging to a specific socioeconomic class by adhering to the ideal image of the slim and fit body.[31] Practitioners find in bodily cultivation a kind of refuge, a pause from social life (although exercised in and through an established social institution) where their daily relationships are pushed to the background and a more "intimate" experience of the self is maintained. Unsurprisingly, then, people turn to these practices in moments of life-course transition or ruptures, such as when middle-aged men turn to exercising and dieting.[32] These practices have become institutionalized and highly regarded solutions to stress, loss of life meaning, and a search for self.

Such withdrawal to an intimate experience of the self can turn into a kind of religion. As these practices become central to self-identities, significant others who do not share the practice sometimes start to object. Their family member, who they believed they know intimately, appears to be maintaining a separate "private" life. Is their love no longer "enough" to sustain the significant other's faith in life? As Dena put it aptly in chapter 5, he or she may suddenly seem "self-contained." The practitioners, for their part, experience the turn quite differently: from their perspective, these practices enable them to stay in the world—of which their loved ones are an important part—rather than flee from it.

PREPARATIONS FOR PUBLIC APPEARANCES

While meditation, biofeedback, physical training, and dieting are all centered on a deliberate turn inward in order to cultivate, heal, or transform the self, I now move to a set of practices that, at least formally, are oriented toward the social world as preparation for performances in public. Here the paradox becomes even more acute: while public performances are centered on the projection of self to others, I argue that the preparations for these performances carry a similar logic to that of meditation, a concentrated turn to the inner lining that enables one to reduce attention to the self as viewed by others when returning to the social world.

Think about exercising musical scales, practicing a ballet dance, or even repeating aloud the same lecture in front of the wall before an important job talk. In these situations you divert full attention to the body (including movement, rhythm, and voice), pushing the presence of others and the social world to the background. Ultimately, however, one seeks to reintegrate with other musicians or dancers or social life in general. Thus one homes in on the bodily execution of behavior with the intention of flipping back and forgetting about this bodily execution once on stage.

The image of jazz improvisation can help us here. In the first stages of study, the sight of the hands, a usually taken-for-granted part of ourselves, becomes central as one practices notes, scales, and chords. In his phenomenological account of learning to play jazz piano, David Sudnow describes struggling with the alignment of his fingers on the keyboard, cultivating sensitivity to pressure and posture as he practices "sinking into the chord."[33] At later stages and with growing competence, the sight of the hands is no longer needed, but sensitivity to place and pressure remains at the attentional foreground.

These are long moments of solitary practice in which hidden dimensions of musical reality are exposed — including the posture, pressure, alignment of the body, particulars of notes and scales, hearing the sounds (in contrast to listening to music as a fan), zooming in to the music, searching for routes of improvisation (in the case of jazz) — and are at the foreground of attention, while the full meaning and experience of the music, and with it the prospected audience, are pushed to the background and turn tacit. In these solitary moments one gains insight into the gap between what one knows as a performer and what others see as audience, to the background of musical life.

At the same time, as the performer prepares to mount the stage, he must balance different tracks of attention — too much attention to the body, like too much attention to the audience or to the way the music "sounds," will disrupt the performance. Thus, as in meditation, one walks a fine line between the dimensions of social life that is required for achieving a "good" performance.

The ballet dancers in Sybil Kleiner's study referred to this challenge as "finding that zone" or "getting yourself in the zone." An overload of self-

consciousness is "obsessive" and prevents them from finding the right entwining with the music.[34] Their life-world includes constant shifts between
watching themselves in the mirror for seven hours a day discovering the most
nuanced details such as "When I breathe in, I breathe in more through my left
lung than my right lung," or paying attention to the aesthetics when placing
the hand at the exact right place—an inch above or below—and public performances where all the work behind the scenes becomes completely invisible
and they "forget" about themselves.[35] In fact it is exactly this alternation between the training in pushing back anxiety and self-judgment that takes place
behind the stage and the self-forgetting on the stage (as one intertwines per-
fectly with the music and the world) that makes dancing such a deep experience that some even refer to it as "spiritual."

These periods of training, of diverting attention to the inner lining, create disturbances in the mundane embodiment of daily life, since we usually
ignore the sight of our hands or the nuances of our breath. Such disturbances
can invite different interpretations and generalizations that go beyond the
situated practice. In her study of the Japanese tea ceremony, Kristin Surak
shows how the embodiment acquired in the training process leads to new
or revived identifications with being Japanese. Training for the tea ceremony
includes diverting attention to the most taken-for-granted movements and
postures—sitting, bowing, moving from standing to sitting while wearing a
kimono. Tea ceremony students learn how not "to disturb the air around."[36]
They learn the minute of holding and cleaning the teapot and the timing of
movement and breathing. When practicing the tea ceremony, students focus
attention on the rhythm of intertwining with the world, a rhythm that in
daily life is unavailable for observation. As Surak demonstrates, these myriad
details end up invoking the spirit of a transcendent identity—that of being
Japanese.

In this sense it is through close encounters with the background operations of the art—be it music, ballet, or tea ceremony—that practitioners come
to appreciate the transcendent elements in it, elements that for others may not
be accessible. The aesthetics of the dance, the Japanese attitude, the improvisation in jazz: all emerge from endless moments of practice that are melded
to produce a performance in which the alignment of self and world is perfect.

PRIVATE WAYS OF KEEPING
THE INNER LINING ALIVE

Many of the practices I have discussed involve some level of keeping the inner
lining alive. Meditators, for instance, observe their breath during interaction,

dieters perceive hunger pangs and satiation during the course of the day, and runners feel their sore muscles. One set of practices take this privacy to the extreme and are considered deviant behaviors or even self-destructive. Self-cutting, taking drugs, and consuming pornography may serve as examples. In these practices there is a private turn to the body in ways that are deemed unacceptable and deviant, even though they are socially produced and learned. In all these practices there is a level of secrecy, of hiding certain bodily elements and experiences from public while keeping these elements internally alive as reminders of autonomy, empowerment, and control.

Let's consider self-harm and bodily manipulation techniques. In the following words of a self-cutter, we read how the invisible dimension is turned into an object of attention: "The blood always provided a certain comfort. . . . It took my mind away from the world for a while. Seeing the blood would be like reality coming back for a while, and I would often cry [and then] remain totally silent, numbed and still. I cannot remember even thinking about what had made me cut after I had done so, it seemed further away somehow. I'd be there, bleeding, and that would be it."[37]

Here the body provides a moment of transcendence from social situations, and with it a feeling of grounding and empowerment. The search for corporeal existence that pushes back dependency on the social world is signified by the words "away from the world" and "I'd be there, bleeding, and that would be it." As in meditation, for the self-harmer the body provides an escape from social judgments, from dependency on others in the production of self. It affords her an anchor that others cannot take away.

Still, this escape is not asocial. First, the motivation behind self-cutting is to be able to integrate back into the social world, to enable one to continue social life.[38] In addition, the practice of self-cutting is ritualistic: it is learned from others, either friends or the internet, it requires a gradual training and learning for it to "work" and become attractive, it is executed in very specific places on the body with a specific knife, it is an ordered and organized practice, and this order enables the inversion of attention. Thus while sitting numbly and observing the blood, the self-cutter is in an alternative social order, one that is recognized by other deviant participants.[39]

When stepping out of the situated practice and returning to the normative social world, the self-cutter flips back to social engagement—but now he or she must hide a secret. The wound must be treated so that it won't bleed or become infected. The sleeve or the trousers must hide the place. The knife must be disinfected and put away. When walking in the world, the self-cutter is now aware of the new wound, the inner lining that must be kept hidden. So the flip back to social engagement is not complete—part of the awareness is still set on the internal, keeping it alive.

Like self-cutting, so too disordered eating. In this case the embodied experience of hunger serves as an alternative anchor for selfhood: "I remember that in the early days I was really hungry at night, but I felt so awake..... I felt so good about it. I felt I could do anything."[40] Constant hunger keeps the inner lining alive, while at the same time the need to hide creates a solitary space within the social world. Eating disorders are also accompanied by ritualistic patterns of when, where, and what to eat, creating an alternative social order that supports the inversion of attention.

Such awareness to the background embodiment of the self, and with it the background of social life, characterizes the experience of the deviant. Howard Becker's work on becoming a marijuana smoker illustrates well the very paradox of meditation practice—the need in a social world to attend to the inner lining "properly."[41] Marijuana, Becker claims, may have a certain physiological influence, but the social circle is crucial to produce and appreciate this influence. So marijuana smoking, like other substance use, requires social circles in which people train in attending to the embodiment of drug use.[42]

In addition, smokers must move from a circle where the turn inward is accustomed and shared to a social world where this activity is viewed as deviant and immoral. As David Matza writes regarding marijuana smokers "High no longer, he re-enters the world acting as if the hand he held a short time ago did not include marijuana. He acts this way even if no one asks him. For a brief period, perhaps only episodically, the subject is 'on.'"[43] Working on being opaque, as Matza puts it, means balancing the two tracks of attention, being aware of the inner lining while at the same time being highly aware of what others see, thus trying to prevent exposure.

Active balancing of the two tracks is increased when deviant activity seeps into normative daily life, such as when a user is high in the company of non-users.[44] When among users, marijuana smokers create spaces of togetherness that accept the influence of the drug and with it the drifting in and out of social engagement. Outside of these circles, others have specific expectations regarding proper behavior. In these moments the user is challenged by keeping up an awareness of the two tracks of reality in a way that allows him or her to properly and "normally" engage in conversation or activity, even though he is always attracted to the sensual experience produced by the drug. These moments can be threatening, but they also carry a seductive dimension: by being high in the normative social world, I keep the inner lining alive, I keep something private to myself.

Such playing with whether you can get away with hiding what is going on in your body may also characterize contemporary viewing of highly accessible pornography. Think about youth who watch pornography together or alone in daily life—when eating breakfast, during breaks at school, or even, as shown in the movie *Don Jon*, while sitting in a classroom.[45] Consider, too, such viewing as a private way of keeping the inner lining alive. These behaviors, which are frequently referred to as "addictions," are seductive not only due to the pleasure of pornography but because they invite and encourage an inversion in the order of attention, producing a separate, private realm.

EVERYDAY PRACTICES FOR ATTENDING TO THE EMBODIMENT OF THE SELF

Even in the flow of daily life, involving no commitment to a special lifestyle or adoption of an inward-looking practice, there are practices that enable and encourage us to divert focused attention to the background embodiment of the self. Glimpses of the background dimension of social reality are not a privilege of meditators, sociologists, deviants, or skilled performers—they are a central part of what it means to be human.

In everyday life we find various strips of interaction in which people engage in the same activity and produce we-relationships while tilting the focus of attention toward aspects of the inner lining. In smoking, coffee breaks, shared meals, or sexual intercourse, for example, people use the other, or the shared object of attention (the smoke, the heat of the coffee, the touch), to bring to the fore the usually tacit background embodiment of the self in a shared and celebrated way. And these shared practices produce breaks and pauses in the ongoing engagement with how others see us. Amidst the doubt that accompanies the projection of self to others, these practices open up spaces for a refresh, a charging of the batteries. Such practices are the mirror image, the background supporting antistructure, of daily social life.

We can clearly see the celebration of attending to the inner lining with the help of another in sexual relations. It provides a social space for managing the "circle of the touched and the touching," since in sex one uses the touch of the other in order to feel oneself.[46] Sex does not only provide an intimacy with another; it provides intimacy with the self, a "means of revealing and touching otherwise hidden features of one's identity."[47] This is how sexual interaction can offer a meaningful anchor for self-constitution.[48]

As in the case of meditation, sexual interaction requires that one balance attending to the other and attending to the self. Such a juggling act of touching and being touched, seeing and being seen, is deceptively difficult. It is thus not surprising that people need to "learn" how to enjoy sex with another person.[49] Just as in meditation or ballet dancing, you need to relax attendance to the way the other is viewing you, as such awareness is an obstacle to attending to the body.

When the right balance is struck in sexual interaction, one can, with the help of the other, focus on the inner lining and "forget" or push back the self as seen by others. This is what makes sex, like meditation, a space to refresh and charge up. It is also what enables "making up" or conflict resolution, as it offers a space where both partners can disattend their conflicted argument, disattend their social roles and expectations of each other.

Like running and dieting, sex can be used as a resource for embodied transcendence in periods of transition and rupture, when people lose their place in the world. Research has shown that infidelity increases after the birth of a couple's first child, when the parents are taking on a new identity and experience changes and ruptures in their relationships.[50] Likewise it has been found that American men use sex as a source of empowerment when their masculine identity is threatened, such as when unemployed or in financial difficulties.[51] Such empowerment, I suggest, not only is symbolic in the sense of "conquering" more women (a symbol of masculinity in our culture) but provides a space of transcendence in moments of identity search, a bodily anchor in periods of fracture.

Smoking is another social institution that incites a turn to the background embodiment of the self while in the presence of others. While nicotine may have a physiological influence on humans, it can be regarded as attractive in certain social circles and completely useless and even harmful in others. Like marijuana smoking, tobacco smoking is learned in a group, and most smokers seem to begin their smoking careers as "social smokers." As Randal Collins argues, "No one could have a stable experience of tobacco or of coffee or tea, if they were not introduced to it through social rituals."[52] In these groups, individuals learn not only to perform smoking in the right way but also to appreciate and control the influence of smoking, to play with the rhythm of inhaling and exhaling, to shift from attending inward to speaking with others and back again. From this social world, solitary smoking emerges, both evoking and replacing the community.

Smoking in a group is not necessarily an activity that is formally focused on the inner lining. Smoking interaction can instead be focused on the conversation, while the smoking itself remains at the background, an "out of frame" activity, as Goffman puts it.[53] But the unique corporality of smoking encourages a shift, or inversion of attention, even when the formal activity is talking. The respiratory system blurs the distinction between in and out, a closed space inside the body that is invisible but nonetheless is reachable by the air that goes in and out.[54] Thus "drawing in smoke and then exhaling it makes that connection between inside and outside visible."[55] When smoking together, we inhale each other's smoke even when in conversation. In this way the usually tacit dimensions of rhythmic coordination of breathing and talking enter the foreground. In fact, some smokers specifically state that a "habitual" cigarette, one that does not include awareness of internal processes, is not enjoyable, hinting at the possibility that the pleasure in smoking lies in a "right" balance between attention to the social world and attention to the body.[56]

Interviews with contemporary smokers in the United States and Britain reveal that smoking is interpreted by practitioners as a "time out," as a way of coping, a "stress reliever," or as "partner" or "friend" in need that replaces dependency on others.[57] These descriptions are reminiscent of the instrumental descriptions of meditation, running, and dieting, turning the situated practice of smoking into something that has a relevance to daily life as a whole, into "smoking-for."[58] The accessibility of cigarette smoking, generated by the cigarette industry to enhance mass use, turns it into a simple, always-within-reach possibility, a "moment of self-caring which, unlike a cup of tea or coffee, needed no preparation," as one smoker put it.[59]

Like the other practices described above, smoking offers an embodied transcendence of social situations. It is not surprising that smoking is used as a way to step into the day (morning cigarette) or out of the day (night cigarette), as an occasion to interrupt work and, in general, as a way in and out of daily activities. As a study on the daily contexts of smoking suggests, smoking can be treated "as a connective practice that maintained people's unproblematic flow from one occasion to another."[60] This power of connecting and producing the flow in life helps to explain why pregnant women find it so hard to quit smoking even under immense social pressure, as smoking provides needed assurance and corporeal stability in this period of intense change.[61]

Recent tobacco regulations produced new social institutions and spheres for a communal turn to the inner lining. These regulations turn smoking into a compartmentalized activity, isolating the practice from the regular flow of life. It produces fascinating spaces, not yet studied, of collective solitude where strangers gather together in places like small transparent rooms in airports, each attending to his own bodily sensations while inhaling the smoke exhaled by others.[62]

To extend the frame even further, we might consider coffee breaks, afternoon tea, or ordered and synchronized joint food consumption. These are highly institutionalized social practices that involve tilting some attendance toward the inner lining. All are "connecting" behaviors in the sense that they offer embodied transcendence that help to organize the flow and movement from one daily occasion to the other, breaks in which one can attend to the embodiment of the self and then return to the work of social life and social relations. Again, like cigarettes, coffee and meals can be highly social, remaining a tacit background to the main event of socializing. Yet at the same time they allow for legitimated and accepted moments of social withdrawal, in the sense of reduced awareness of others. Eating interrupts conversation, and in some cultures people are expected to eat in silence. The heat of coffee and tea attracts one's attention to internal processes, thus distracting at least some attention from the interaction.

We might also consider mundane self-care practices such as daily solitary showers and careful flossing of the teeth every evening, or even practices that are part of the beauty culture such as skilled application of makeup in the morning, or fixing the hair, or even hair removal.[63] These are practices that are "officially" oriented to the projection of the self to the public but have a tacit background dimension of solitary or joint action in which one attends to bodily movement and sensations. Thus if we look at the other side of the coin of beauty-related practices that are frequently critiqued as representing conformity to patriarchic power relations, we find communal and honored self-care that provides women control over a dimension unavailable to the male gaze, keeping the inner self private and protected, hidden behind the mask that they themselves actively prepared.[64]

These practices reveal periodical turns to the background embodiment of the self, after which one refocuses on the world and engaged interaction. In all these examples, social life is lived in loops, shifting periodically from more explicit attendance to the inner lining to pushing it to the periphery of attention, from attending to the social world and to the self as viewed by others to distancing from this self, pausing from engaged social life.

Religious Practice and Embodied Transcendence

The bodily based transcendence of the aforementioned practices can become attached to the mystical, the immortal or divine. We can think of religion as working on two dimensions or two tracks. The one is the theological, belief-based track, the transcendence or salvation that religions focus on thematically. Yet this track is brought to life through religious practices, such as meditation, which elicit this transcendence corporeally. This is why many of the above practices have elaborated religious or spiritual versions—fasting, pilgrimage, self-mutilation, dancing, singing. In this sense religious embodied practices draw their strength not from a rejection of profane corporeality but from the grounding of the thematic theological world in the most corporeal, intimate embodiment of the self.[65]

Take fasting. A common religious practice, fasting is built into the ritual schedule of many religions. Generally it is analyzed through the prism of moral asceticism and self-deprivation, the actual experience of fasting left aside. In his ethnography of Muslim conversion, Daniel Winchester offers a glimpse of how fasting can be used to make contact with the tacit dimension. He uses expressions such as "I 'feel' my stomach gurgling and rumbling: I 'sense' the tiredness of my limbs: I 'taste' the dryness in my mouth." Fasting, he writes, leads to an inversion of attention as "the visceral body ceases to recede from consciousness and becomes a focal point of one's everyday experience."[66] In this sense fasting pulls us out of everyday engagement. It ruptures the regular experience of self in the world. It reminds us of our corporality, of bare existence.

Fasting, however, is not about a complete withdrawal from society. Religious fasting is quite communal. Traditionally, Jews spend most of Yom Kippur in the synagogue, praying collectively. During Ramadan, Muslims are expected to engage in normal daily activities. Meditators' attempts to attend to the breath while interacting, then, can be likened to tasting dryness in the mouth that is produced by fasting: it takes place while one engages with the world. In this sense fasting exposes the challenge of attending simultaneously to the two tracks, tilting the direction of attention toward the inner lining. And this tilting is often accomplished with the help of others who are aware of one's fasting, who together disattend to certain expectations and behaviors, who celebrate together the inward shift.

Prayer, too, is an embodied act. In Christianity, prayer is frequently carried out in uncomfortable positions such as kneeling. In Judaism it is done in synchronized movement back and forth, and many times includes strangers who join the *minyan* (quorum of ten). In Islam, prayer requires a full bodily operation that is synchronized with the posture of all other Muslims in the area five times a day.

An ethnography of postulants in a Mexican Catholic convent reveals the centrality of awareness to the inner lining in the process of becoming a nun. As Rebecca Lester writes, the postulants are asked to train in "kneeling for hours in prayer and to become extraordinary sensitive to the sensations this discipline produces such as exhaustion, nausea, resentment, physical pain."[67] Such emphasis on bodily sensations takes the mind away from the social world the postulants are asked to forget, away from the "self" they left behind. The diversion of awareness to the body is a tactical measure to disconnect the young postulants from ordinary social life and attach them to the world of spiritual introspection.

The transcendence offered by bodily centered practices affords an embodied bridge through which one can discover dedication to God, the divine, or anything that is beyond everyday social life. Valentine Daniel's account of a Hindu pilgrimage may be helpful here.[68] Daniel describes his own awareness of the growing pain of the journey, "caused by blisters under one's toenails and those on one's heels . . . the pain arising from strained calf muscles and tendons . . . the headache caused by the heat of the noon sun." In his view this bodily awareness leads to a new phenomenology of the world and of oneself, crucial to the development of self-knowledge that is part of pilgrimage. In other words, the process of connecting to the sacred, which is the purpose of pilgrimage, is achieved not through zooming out to abstract symbols or theology but zooming in to the details of feeling oneself feeling the world.

These religious practices are institutionalized, honored, and socially recognized ways to turn inward to the background embodiment of the self. They strategically involve a universally accessible, collective focus on the tacit or background body, a focus that carries relevance and represents daily uses of the body in social life. Collective rituals such as praying, singing, and dancing are examples of religious rituals that synchronize with others while pushing back acknowledged and focused interaction. Special dietary rules, smoking, drug and alcohol consumption, and pilgrimages can all be encountered in religious contexts, and all carry the same structure of the flip in the direction of attention offering trips to transcendence.

The proliferation of secularized versions of religious practices, such as nonreligious versions of meditation, fasting, pilgrimage, and the different uses of bodily transcendence in contemporary embodied therapies suggest that it might be time to reconsider the accepted distinction between "religious" and "secular." In the secularization of these practices, religion was not lost but adapted. No longer holding a monopoly on these practices, religion finds itself in competition with a growing number of body-oriented practices for communal, ritualized access to embodied transcendence. From this perspective, the culture of health that promotes dieting and exercising, the growing popularity of New Age or alternative therapy–related techniques, and even the culture of beauty work all supply alternatives to religion, offering a "this-worldly" salvation from the problem of being human.

*

This book opened with the puzzles that brought me to study vipassana as an extreme and exceptional turn inward that seemed to counter both everyday life and the accepted sociological understanding of the relation between body, self, and sociality. It is ending with a vision of vipassana as providing a new perspective on social life outside of meditation: how human beings negotiate the fact that they are simultaneously corporeal and social, and the social institutions and strategies employed to balance these two dimensions of our being.

These institutions and strategies are not opposed to daily social life. Quite the contrary: the same practices that are formally oriented to project a self to others, to improve one's social standing, appearance, and coping, to produce solidarity and social identities, have a hidden side that permits breaks from the social gaze of others. In the flow of everyday life, people incorporate activities in which they consciously attend to the inner lining, to the invisible part of their being, to the "solitary" and "private" dimension, without the need to step out of social life, without being isolated or excluded from the social fabric. This turn to the body is then used to return to engaged interaction transformed, refreshed, empowered—thereby molding social relations and identities.

It is through these engineered gaps in engaged interaction, through cracks in the mirror of the self as viewed by others, through the fact that we all have bodies that are always accessible, that people manage and negotiate the tensions engendered by social life, bridging the corporeal and the social, the private and the public, the solitary and the collective.

Methodological Appendix:
Ethnography of Experience

On the last day of a vipassana meditation retreat, I sat at a table with several volunteers. An advanced student came by, and I mentioned that I had written a paper on my research that might interest her. She did want to read it, she said, but then added, "Words cannot catch it. They only circle around it, they cannot really touch it." Her hand inscribed circles in the air as she observed my response.

I did not argue. This was not the first time I had heard this sentiment. "You cannot explain it" and "It cannot be put into words" were common comments; "it" cannot be described, cannot be put in a category, cannot be assigned a title. Vipassana practitioners referred to meditation experiences as ineffable— "you have to experience it in order to understand it." In fact, in line with Buddhist thought, language was frequently suspected as leading to a misrepresentation of experience, thus mirroring Peirce's claim regarding experiences of firstness: "Only, remember that every description of it must be false to it."[1]

An ethnographer's stock in trade is words and observations. That is the paradox in penning an ethnography of the inner lining of experience. By definition, this inner lining is invisible, the part of our being that is hidden from others. When I observe others, I observe the outer lining of experience, the expressive part of their body. When I speak with others about their bodily experiences, they must make their experiences visible in order to share these with me. This is why the subjects of this study will always consider that the common "external" methods of inquiry have circumlocuted their encounter with vipassana.

Setting out to study meditation from a microsocial perspective, I found myself in constant oscillation, moving between attempts to capture my informants' experience from their point of view to shedding light on layers that were unacknowledged or even resisted. This book set out to challenge strict oppositions between external and internal, the social and the individual, the private and the public. My goal was to grasp dimensions of meditation that practitioners themselves tend to ignore or underestimate. I aimed to show that there are important relations and connections between the inner lining of experience and the outer, between the background embodiment of the self and the self that is reflected back from others. By observing people, speaking to them and to their family members, and tracking my own experiences (in words), I tried to track the dialectic movement between these two sides of the leaf, between the inner and outer dimensions of experience.

This focus on the social world that surrounds vipassana enabled me to confront an important methodological obstacle—that of causal explanations. Practitioners of vipassana take vipassana to be a causal force in their life, one that leads to specific transformations. It is thus not surprising that most studies of meditation focus on the "benefits" of meditation practice. However, these "benefits" or transformations are not necessarily observable by an external viewer, and, as I found when I started interviewing family members, they may be variously interpreted. As an ethnographer I record and describe these attributions of change as an important part of vipassana practice. However, since I do not have access to "before" and "after" data, I do not know whether the lives of the subjects of this study would have been different had they not meditated.

Meditation in this study is not an independent variable that produces certain "objective" and measurable changes in individuals. Instead I see vipassana as a mode of attention, a mode that my subjects of study use to reposition themselves in the social world.[2] Rather than asking about vipassana outcomes or benefits (as is common in scientific studies on the impact of meditation), I explore how people use meditation practice to purposefully restructure their self and their social life. Thus although this book is about experiences of self-transformation, I do not regard self-transformation as "objective" changes in character and behavior. Self-transformation, in my view, is an ongoing process of experimentation in relating and attending to oneself, a process that takes place through and with others.

In what follows I lay out the different venues I used to conduct what I call an experience-focused microsociological ethnography. These venues are based on Csordas's recommendation of doing an ethnography *from* the body rather than an ethnography *of* the body.[3] The *from* and *of* are crucial here, as they represent the difference between studying the body as a subject and studying the body as an object. I track my efforts to use my own body and the bodies of my informants as sources of information. In the process I strive to shed light on the limitations of each methodological venue I used and how I think these venues complement one another.

Using My Own Body: Autoethnography

My own participation in meditation retreats and my ongoing meditation practice forms the backbone of this research. The autoethnographic part of this fieldwork can be traced back to 2002, three years before I began the study. At that time I was twenty-six years old and living in Israel. I participated in a vipassana meditation course with no idea that vipassana had anything to do with Buddhism. I had long wanted to practice meditation, and a friend recommended vipassana. I had practiced yoga in the past as well as tai chi. Thus I moved in circles where meditation was highly regarded.

Like many of my informants, I chose to participate in a meditation course during a period of life transition. In between romantic relationships, I was planning to cross the ocean to begin a demanding doctoral program. I did not record or track the meditation course. I was pleased that I had participated but had no plans to return for a second ordeal. I remember being amazed at my ability to concentrate on one point below my nose and observe my breath. I found this a calming practice and still appreciate it today.

Six months after the course, I left Israel to begin coursework at the University of Chicago. Alone in a foreign city, overwhelmed by a new language and a mountain of books, I was drawn back to meditation. My daily practice was solitary, as I did not take another course or know anyone else who was meditating. A year later I moved in with a good friend and felt less and less need for meditation practice—which became more and more sporadic.

During a visit to Israel in 2005, I was surprised to discover that vipassana meditation had exploded in popularity. Suddenly everyone I met had either taken a course or knew someone who had. The word *vipassana* had even entered the media: one Israeli politician, referring to another's silence, castigated him for "doing vipassana." It seems that vipassana had become fashionable for middle-class Israelis between the ages of twenty-five and thirty-five. When I returned to the US, I found that a vipassana center had just been established not far from Chicago and that vipassana meditation group sittings were available on campus. As a sociologist, I found this phenomenon intriguing. My experience with vipassana had left me with the impression that this was an extreme practice limited to a small audience searching for alternative modes of consciousness. How, I wondered, could such an experience be relevant to a larger "normative" audience?

Already in my first vipassana course, I sensed a certain resonance between phenomenological and constructivist approaches in sociology and my experience in meditation. In addition, as I zeroed in on the sociology of the self, I started seeing interesting paradoxes between the private experience of meditation and the collective phenomenon of the search of self. I was drawn to these connections between private and public, inner and outer, especially when situating the body as a bridge between the two. It occurred to me that the unique emphasis placed by Goenka's teaching school on the body as the central object of mindfulness offered the perfect field to study, flesh out, and also challenge sociological and phenomenological theoretical ideas regarding the self.

It was a tripartite decision, then, to embark on this study: a personal experience of meditation intersected with the rising popularity of vipassana practice and a theoretical interest in a theory of the self. Once my curiosity was piqued, the first thing I did was to take another meditation course, this time with my ethnographic imagination working. I then sought permission to conduct my study, contacting vipassana teachers in both Israel and the United States. Since I had already taken a vipassana meditation course, I was considered an "old student" and was granted permission to do my research providing I did not interfere with the ongoing work at the center.

The autoethnographic venue of this study includes two parts. First, between 2005 and 2009 I participated as a student (see next section for the volunteering part of this study) in five long meditation retreats (three of ten days' duration, one of seven days' duration, and two of three days' duration) and three one-day retreats as a student. In addition, in 2011 I returned to another three-day meditation retreat. In these retreats I went back and forth between observing my own experiences and observing those of others. Thus the experience in these retreats was somewhat different from that of my informants, who specifically learn to disattend to others. In other words, I had a social interest that occupied my mind. However, my observation of others was limited, as I did not want to interrupt the meditation course. For the sake of the autoethnographical part of this study, I decided to devote my time to meditation. Since writing is prohibited during meditation retreats, I made mental notes or scribbled words that I hoped would help my recall. I wrote everything down as soon as possible after the retreats. Although I was able to record my observations in writing only after the events, I found that I remembered many details. Hence while the quotations are not verbatim, I trust that the situations and incidents described faithfully represent actual occurrences. The exception in this regard was a special seven-day course in which reading and writing was permitted; there I was able to take written notes without disturbing others.

The second autoethnographic part of this study consisted of my attempt to practice meditation daily for a year, turning myself into a subject of sociological inquiry. This included joining collective meditation sittings once a week. I followed my own experiences in a detailed personal diary, where I described my feelings, thoughts, and experiences as connected to meditation practice. In the beginning I did not know what to write. Meditation sessions can be decidedly dull, and sometimes the main experience was fighting the desire to sleep. Moreover, recording my experiences countered the spirit of meditation. Instead of observing the impermanence of experience, I anchored it in language and pinned it to a page. This was a mode of self-reflection that differed markedly from that which is exercised in meditation and which probably had its own impact on me. As I began to grasp the importance of the microsocial world of meditation, I started tracking my responses to others while meditating. I followed the different ways I dwelled in their minds and in their bodies. I saw how my body reacted to the breathing of my neighbor and how my hand moved without my intention. This illuminating tracking of my own production of intersubjectivity served as a base for tracking others.

I also tracked my own use of vipassana in regard to relations with others, especially in intimate relations with family and friends. I continued to track such episodes sporadically as my life became more complicated—I became a wife and a mother, took my first tenure-track job, and faced the fractures and tensions that most upper-middle-class working mothers encounter. In this period, which ended with the publication of this book, I rarely meditated on the cushion. Nonetheless, I did attend regularly to my breath and sensations, especially at stressful moments.

When studying practices that include self-cultivation or embodied knowledge, there is extra wisdom in using one's own body as a tool in fieldwork. To borrow a notion from Loïc Wacquant, it permits "initiation into an embodied craft."[4] The word *initiation* is crucial here: the ethnographer is unlikely to reach a professional level in the studied craft. Certainly I remained a novice. I never participated in a meditation retreat that lasted longer than ten days. I never meditated in an isolated meditation cell. Still, the novitiate state is probably the most important point in transition to a new embodiment, the most eye-opening point in the process.

Importantly, one need not adopt a particular set of beliefs in order to carry out an autoethnography. Much can be learned from tracking the ways embodied practices attune the body and change its relation to the world while retaining a measure of skepticism or doubt.[5] Given this, the worldview of the ethnographer and her subjects of study can diverge. In my case, for example, while some advanced meditators attached to their experiences a connection to a previous life, as an ethnographer who embodied their world, I can understand this interpretation without personally subscribing to reincarnation.

The fact that I myself meditated turned out to be both a help and a hindrance in the ethnographic process. Embodying the world of meditation was illuminating, but it engendered problems. Doing justice to my informants' experiences as well as my own was a difficult juggling act. Had I not meditated, the writing would have been eased by a certain sense of distance. I finally achieved this distance four years after my final meditation course. At that point I felt able to observe my field notes regarding my own experiences as an external observer, turning them into data not unlike the data I extracted from others. This researcher-meditator oscillation accounts for the somewhat split identity I present in the book. Sometimes I am a "true believer," portraying the part of "me" that was completely engrossed in vipassana practice; at other times I am a skeptic, aiming to shed light on things hidden from the meditators' gaze.

Observing the Bodies of Others

My second source of data was the observation of others while in meditation retreats and in group sittings. The bulk of participant observation was conducted in the vipassana meditation center in Israel and at the vipassana meditation center in Illinois. In addition, I visited the meditation center in Massachusetts for four days. The participant observation was not continuous, and the longest I stayed at the meditation center was ten days. During my stay at meditation centers I either participated in courses or volunteered behind the scenes. In the research period I spent a total of ninety days in meditation centers while meditation retreats were taking place, about half of which were in the capacity of student and about half as a volunteer. I also paid day-long visits to the centers in periods between meditation retreats, for meetings, interviews, and daily volunteering.

In addition, I conducted participant observations in meditation group sittings. I visited the meditation apartment in Tel Aviv once a week and joined other meditation groups around Israel. While in Chicago, I joined the weekly meditation sitting group and even organized an informal group sitting for a period of two months. It was in these group sittings that I made contacts for my research and observed social interactions (although the social interactions were quite minimal, as discussed in chapter 3).

When I entered the field, I did not foresee the prominence that observation of others in the meditation center would take as a source of data. As I have written elsewhere, I aimed to find people who would talk to me and to observe "normal" verbal interactions between meditators.[6] What went on between people at the meditation center seemed impoverished in comparison to interactions described in other ethnographies I read. My observations included hours upon hours of nonmovement. I wanted to know what goes on in people's minds while meditating, and for that I wanted to talk to them or hear them recount their experiences to others.

During a drive to the Illinois center with two others who were planning to participate in a meditation course, one of them—an experienced practitioner—remarked: "I like this meditation school because it is very individual—you have to walk your own path. But this is also what is so difficult about it: you are on your own." Suddenly I was hit with the paradoxical nature of meditation, the radical balance between being together and being apart. I had caught an inkling of the mode of "being together" afforded by meditation retreats and why practitioners feel "on their own" while being surrounded by others.

The best way to observe the movements and expressions of bodies is via videography.[7] Filming permits observation of the influence of one body on another, the dynamic between talking and moving, emotional expressions and bodily gestures. Oftentimes during my fieldwork I found myself wishing that I could film the meditation sittings. But I could only observe and listen. Luckily, meditation practice entails few movements. With no words to pay attention to, I was free to follow bodies and note details that I might have normally missed. Still, filming would have exposed a more nuanced dynamic than the one I was able to extract.

As noted above, it was tricky to take field notes while in the meditation center. I had to make mental notes of the movements of bodies and their mutual influences (coughing, moving, laughter, and so on) and record after the fact what I had seen. I took most of my notes while volunteering, as I could observe others and detail these observations between meditation sessions and meals.

Yet words were still part of the observation process. I observed verbal interactions between teachers and students (in the breaks when students can ask questions or in weekly meditation sessions) as well as interactions between participants on the last day of the meditation retreats—a day when participants are allowed to speak. Here I could observe how meditators verbalize and make sense of their experiences.

I gleaned important information while observing the everyday social interaction of informants, how they use vipassana in their everyday life. Unfortunately I had limited access to the everyday life of practitioners outside the meditation center. I followed some of my key informants in their daily life, but these were sporadic observations. In general, my access to informants' daily lives was limited to the stories they and their significant others chose to tell. This leads us to the third methodological venue—interviews.

Talking to Others about Their Experiences

There are two drawbacks to the use of observation to study experience. First, observations are limited to specific public or semi-public spaces. With this method informants' private moments remain private—and such moments are a big part of the life experience of people in contemporary society. Second, observations do not offer the point of view of the owner of the body, the one that has a past and a future and a subjective biography that he brings into the social situation. Both of these perspectives are crucial to a project that aims to capture interiority without reducing it to whatever is visible in public space.

Let us return to the methodological paradox that arises when study of nonverbal semiotics and embodied experiences is dependent on discursive accounts. While I followed the subjects of this study using participant observation, more than half of the data regarding emotions, embodiment, and self-reflexivity was extracted from practitioners' reports regarding past events, information provided in interviews or obtained in informal conversations, or accounts recorded in personal diaries. Much of the data in the book was produced through meta-reflexive events (the interviews) that were predominantly discursive and informed by second-order interpretations. I attempted to take this issue into account in my interpretation of the data.

My data—the words and descriptions I relied on—were delivered through different venues. First, although practitioners of vipassana generally do not share their experiences in a public sphere, I collected stories and impressions during my stays in the meditation center, especially when talking to volunteers and participants on the last day of the courses. Some descriptions were provided in informal conversations in which I took part as either a participant or an observer, such as conversations of students with meditation teachers. The drives to and from the meditation center with others turned out to be rich venues of data.

Second, alongside these informal conversations, between 2005 and 2008 I conducted in-depth interviews with sixty meditators, twenty in North America and forty in Israel. The interviews were based on a snowball sample, and they were all recorded. I used these interviews as ethnographic material, tracking and recording different aspects of the meetings. This enabled me to supplement the verbal transcription of the interview with data regarding the surroundings, interaction, self-presentation, emotional expressions, and behavior. I tried to interview meditators with different levels of expertise and seriousness of practice. This gave me access to different experiences from different stations on the road to becoming a serious meditator. I used an interview guide during the interviews themselves, but I kept the interview as open as possible, and only at the end of the open conversation did I return to the interview guide to make sure we discussed all the topics.

Such formal interviews have their drawbacks. These are artificial spaces in which the "self" becomes a subject of inquiry in ways that may not reflect daily sociality. Interviews encourage turning the preobjective into objective information that can be discussed. They also include a dimension of the projection of self to the interviewer that might not be representative of the everyday self. That said, I found formal interviews to be an important source for stories and experiences that I could not reach through informal conversations, mainly because informal conversations tend to take place in public spaces while the interviews were almost always conducted at the homes of my informants, in their intimate space. While meditators spoke explicitly about the limits of words to capture experience, the interviews were rather rich with elaborated descriptions. My informants, I found, were quite skilled in symbolic reflexive thought and verbal descriptions. This is true despite the fact that in many cases I was the first person with whom they had shared their meditation experiences.[8]

To embody the world of others is like learning their language—it is a tool for communication and we-relations. We are all familiar with the bond that is created with others who have gone through what we believe is an experience similar to our own. Completing a ten-day meditation course together—which can be likened to running a marathon together—is an important channel for connecting, even if people do not exchange a word during the event. My first interviewees were my roommates from a meditation retreat in which I participated. Although I did not actually share a retreat with most of my interviewees, the fact that I had participated in such an experience was important for them. In interviews with people who had not met me in a prior meditation context, among the first questions I was asked were whether I had experience in meditation and whether I had participated in a ten-day retreat. Upon hearing my affirmative answer, they responded with something along the lines of "So you would know what I mean." It is as if the problem of only "circling around it" was relaxed once they knew I also experienced "it." From their perspective, their interlocutor (me) was aware of the gap between words and experience and knew something about the experience itself from direct contact.

The sound of silence was one of the most profound noises I shared with my informants. I met many of them while participating in meditation retreats. About a fifth of my interviews started with a joint meditation session. This was not always easy for me, as in the interviews that began with a meditation sitting, I was always the most novice meditator. I knew that in these events I was quite self-conscious in the symbolic sense and that I had to work hard to not disturb the other meditator through movement or sound. Moving from silently being together into a conversation always required a short phase of accommodation, usually accompanied by a cup of tea, but when we moved into the conversation I found that small talk was not required, as if the ice had already been broken through the shared meditation sitting.

Finding the right balance between such we-relations and being a stranger can be complicated. On the one hand, a degree of trust is required for interviewees to share with me intimate moments and emotional events. But at the same time being too comfortable, or feeling I already knew what they were talking about, could also be problematic: as an investigator, I wanted them to explain, elaborate, and articulate what they felt. I frequently found myself asking my informants to explain and provide examples. This was because I tried to approach the conversation from a naive position, not allowing my interviewees to assume a joint understanding that was beneath the words. Notwithstanding my efforts, however, I know that such assumptions were made. One wonders what the interviews would have sounded like if they had been conducted by someone completely unfamiliar with meditation practice.

In general, interviews can be used in two distinct ways. The first is to capture the manner of speech, the discourse, the concepts, with which people present themselves and their experiences. In this case the researcher is not interested in the events themselves but only in the common interpretive frames, and thus is not disturbed by any gap that may exist between what people say and what has actually happened. The second way is to take these descriptions as indexing "real" events, meaning what the informants recall taking place, those events that left a mark on them or that they view as exemplary of their experience.

In my analysis I refer to the descriptions offered to me in interviews as events that "actually happened," taking into account that their exact description may be inaccurate. When I write "actually happened" I do not mean an objective past that exists separately from the subjective memory and experience of informants. I mean that for them, these accounts represent their phenomenological reality. To understand this reality, I tried to get as much information as possible about meditators' daily life. I always insisted on concrete examples, either from a meditation course or from last week or last month, and sometimes returned repeatedly to a described event.

At the same time I was interested in the conceptualizing and framing of these experiences. However, since interviews can be biased by norms of talk defined within a group, it is important to mention that norms regarding "speaking about meditation" do not exist among vipassana meditators, simply because they do not have formal or informal spaces for talking about meditation experiences with other meditators. Thus conceptions and framing did not reflect internal group norms of the meditators but instead reflected the more general culture in which the informant was embedded, such as the therapeutic framework or Buddhist philosophy.

Since I relied on descriptions of "real" events, I had to factor in the fact that memory has its limits. Stories tend to change, especially if people tell them over and over again. I relied on the fact that for many of my informants, this was the first time they had told this story. That means that their story likely did not go through processes of extensive revisions and meaning-making that usually happen when a narrative is being told and retold. Again, it also meant that in terms of a "group culture," there was no shared communal discourse or genre being transmitted from one meditator to another as a way to present these experiences. That said, I was aware of the limits of such descriptions of past events and treat these descriptions as subjective data, representing the point of view of my informants, as moments that they remember and interpret as meaningful.

Recurrent Interviews and Significant Others

The final data source I used was a follow-up with twelve informants for a period of three years (with seven the follow-up continued through a total of eight years), which included interviews with their significant others (family or friends). I chose these informants based on three criteria: first, I interviewed them fairly early in my research and thus could follow them for a longer period; second, these individuals had agreed to be followed, which probably meant that for some reason they enjoyed the connection with me as an interviewer; and last, these were people who continued to meditate, or at least did something connected to meditation, in the first year. Three of the twelve stopped meditating after two years, but I kept in touch with them nonetheless, checking to see whether meditation reentered their lives.

When studying the cultivation of embodied skills or crafts, following people over time is informative. The ethnographer can track transformations in embodied experience—change in bodily skill, in movement, in emotionality, as well as modifications of the interpretations given to experience. Meditation is an interesting case in this regard; although it is an embodied skill, it is almost impossible to capture progress through external evaluations, especially when one has limited access to everyday interactions. Thus while I observed their bodies, the main transformation I was able to capture was through their own reports. This follow-up included both informal conversations and meetings, and three to five formal, open-ended interviews. These provided a fuller perspective on everyday life and social experience.

I also decided to interview the meditators' family members or friends. I chose one significant other for each informant, except for two cases in which I interviewed two significant others (two parents together; sister and father). It is rare to find ethnographic studies that incorporate the perspective of significant others who are not a part of the studied social institution or sphere. In interviewing informants' significant others, I sought to hear about everyday life interactions from another point of view.

One way to use the reports of significant others is to confirm claims that informants make regarding their behavior and experience in everyday social life. These figures contributed to what ethnographers refer to as "triangulations" in qualitative research. They enabled me to track how people in the close surroundings of the vipassana practitioner perceive the other person, and how this perception relates to the practitioner's own experience. The second important data in these reports is how those who do not meditate experience the change (if such a change occurred) in social life and social interaction, and how they evaluate such a change in relation to the kind of sociality they expect or see as a norm. Last, such reports give the ethnographer a glimpse into the intimate life of practitioners outside of the meditation context. So even though I did not observe this sphere of the meditators' lives, I received an account of it from another point of view.

Final Note about Locations and Choice of Vipassana School

This fieldwork focused on one vipassana teaching school—vipassana meditation as taught by S. N. Goenka. This teaching school is one among several that have become popular in the non-Buddhist world. I chose it because in both Israel and Illinois, this was the vipassana school that had permanent meditation centers (in these locations other schools occasionally offered courses in temporary facilities). In addition, entry into the field was eased thanks to my prior experience with this meditation school. Finally, this school offered an ideal case study in regard to the embodiment of the self, as the version of vipassana it teaches puts more emphasis on the body and bodily sensations than do other vipassana schools.

The choice of this vipassana school may limit the generalization of my findings to other meditation venues. First, this school is relatively conservative in terms of incorporating changes, and as discussed in the second chapter, its meditation retreats are strict in terms of silence and disconnection from the outside world. This means that the social world that is introduced throughout this book is a relatively extreme example of the social world of vipassana meditation. That said, I suggest that the choice of an "extreme" case helps me to shed light on processes that are present also in the less extreme cases in a reduced "volume" or in more covert ways. Second, this school's emphasis on bodily sensations is unique when compared to other vipassana schools teaching a more "open" mindfulness that includes paying equal attention to bodily sensations and thoughts. Nonetheless, based on my experience in other vipassana traditions, including mindfulness as taught in MBSR courses, I would say that there is more overlap than difference. All the vipassana schools maintain the logic of "detached observation of the body and mind phenomenon."

This fieldwork was conducted in two locations—Israel and the United States. These regions were chosen based on my own biography—an Israeli living in Chicago. When I began my research, I was planning to add a comparative view between Israel and the United States. Since the teaching school I chose had a standardized teaching method, I was interested to see what happens to this standardization when it encounters different audiences. I soon discovered that the two locations attract a highly similar audience, that is, the middle to higher-educated class. I met doctoral students, lawyers, social workers, psychologists, financial advisers, teachers, and physicians. The religious identification of my subjects in Israel and the United States was also quite similar. With the exception of one Israeli who grew up in a religious Jewish family (he left orthodoxy in adulthood), all the Israelis I interviewed were raised in families identified as "secular Jewish." In the United States people came from more diverse backgrounds: from Christianity to Judaism to Hinduism. With the exception of one woman who self-identified as a believing Christian and another who was an observant Hindu, they now considered themselves secular. Their motivations, goals, interests, and practices were not unique to the location, and if I were to conceal the language and specific cultural and social identifications, it would probably have been impossible to differentiate between the Israeli and American interviews.

*

To conclude, I return to the "it" that cannot be described in words. Katz and Csordas distinguish between two types of phenomenological ethnographies.[9] The first is ethnography that is oriented toward capturing lived experience from the point of view of the "natives." The second is a skeptical and critical ethnography that aims to deconstruct and decipher this lived experience. While these approaches may seem contradictory, they can also complement each other.

In this book I sought to capture "it" by using different venues and methods. I tried to see the world from the eyes of the people I studied and present their lived experience. At the same time I attempted to shed light on processes that they considered unimportant or that received little attention, processes they took for granted and did not question. This is why I insisted on both the first-person perspective (my autoethnography and the stories collected from informants) and a third-person perspective (observations and speaking with significant others). When writing, I found myself moving between these approaches, at certain moments trying to reconstitute an experience and at others questioning (though not criticizing) the viewpoint that was offered to me.

Bodily based practices can be approached as symbols, as lifestyles, as messages about status and cultural capital. In this book I chose a different route: to study the way these practices relate to being in the world, and with it the relation between self and other, self and the social world. This is a specific focus that oriented both my epistemological choice—the venues in which I collected the data—and my analytic choice, the theoretical perspective of phenomenology and microsociology through which I analyzed the endless pages of notes that I collected in fieldwork. I used meditation as an entry point into something that I see as "existing" beyond meditation and thus beyond the specific field I studied. To study vipassana was to study the background embodiment of the self, and with it the relation between one's own body and the bodies of others.

Notes

Chapter One

1. For such critical perspectives see, for example, Rieff 1966; Lasch 1980; Cushman 1996; Madsen 2014.

2. Mead 1934:142. When using the word *linguistic* here, Mead refers to "language-like" mediums, meaning symbolic representations that are part of what he calls "significant gestures." For the centrality of language as the main medium through which individuals relate to themselves, see also Vygotsky 1962; Ricoeur 1981.

3. Foucault 1997.

4. Illouz 2007:178.

5. For recent writings on embodied meaning and knowledge see for example O'Connor 2005; Ignatow 2007; Shalin 2007; Wacquant 2015; Lizardo 2017.

6. For habitus see Bourdieu 1977.

7. Using Polanyi's (1966) spatial metaphor, the body is the "from" from which I act "to" the world. The "from," according to Polanyi, is the tacit dimension of action and knowledge.

8. Merleau-Ponty 1968:9. In the *Visible and the Invisible*, Merleau-Ponty offers the example of the right hand touching the left hand, and the tension in perceiving both touching and being touched simultaneously. He names this "circle of the touched and the touching" (1968:143) the "intertwining/chiasm."

9. Weber 1946.

10. All names of practitioners are pseudonyms.

11. Interviews with Israelis were conducted in Hebrew, and chosen quotes were translated into English by the author.

12. In the same year, Wendy Cadge's (2005) pioneering ethnography on Theravada Buddhism was published; it offered a starting point to embark on this study.

13. *Mindfulness, vipassana*, and *insight meditations* all denote the same Buddhist practice—the open, nonjudgmental awareness of body and mind phenomena. All these meditations are based on the same sutta—*MahaSatipatthana Sutta*, translated as "the great discourse on mindfulness" or "the great discourse on awareness."

14. Gombrich 1983; Jordt 2007.

15. I use the notion "meditation school" to refer to a teaching tradition that follows a specific lineage of teachers.

16. Clarke et al. 2018.

17. See Goffman 1974 for the notion "attention track."

18. Leder (1990) discusses how in routinized action we tend to "forget" about our bodies, arguing that the body receives focused attention only in "dysfunctional" states.

19. Cooley (1902) 1998; Mead 1934; Goffman 1959; Wiley 1994; Weigert and Gecas 2003.

20. I am drawing on and extending Katz's notion that the turn to the body offers a sensual/aesthetic transcendence of social situations. See Katz 1996, 1999.

21. Sociologists and social psychologists have written extensively about the experience of rupture and the problem of identity in modern Western society. See, for example, Simmel 2011, Gergen 1991, Berger et al. 1973, Giddens 1991, Bauman 2000.

22. Bourdieu (1977, 1984) argues that the body holds an internal set of dispositions, a "structuring structure" that is prereflective. The vast sociological literature that builds on Bourdieu's work continues the focus on the dispositional, nonreflective role of the body.

Chapter Two

1. Weber 1958b. This secularization thesis was later revised into a theory of individualization and privatization of religion. See for example Bellah et al. (1985) 2007.

2. For recent studies of religion in public institutions see Bender et al. 2012.

3. *Theravada* means "the teachings of the elders" in Pali.

4. Rahula 1959; Collins 1982.

5. Gombrich 1983; Jordt 2007.

6. Jordt 2007; Cook 2010.

7. Jordt 2007. For a parallel historical move that connects meditation with nationalism in Japan, see Sharf 1993.

8. Weber 1958a.

9. See also Spiro 1970, who differentiates between two "Buddhisms"—Nibanic Buddhism, practiced by the monks as a way to achieve enlightenment (which included meditation practice), and Kammatic Buddhism, practiced by laypeople as a way to attain merit for future lives through giving donations and performing rituals.

10. Literacy, or direct access to the sacred texts, is a common strategy for maintaining power relations in religious social life. In the case of Christianity and Buddhism, the laity's lack of access to texts upheld the seniority of the priests or monks. In contrast, in Judaism literacy and knowledge of religious texts were common among most men throughout history but was still used as a tool for preserving patriarchy through the denial of access to religious texts for Jewish women.

11. Braun 2013.

12. Ibid.

13. For example, Sharf (1995) claims that the emphasis on experience in Buddhist practice is a modern phenomenon, while Jordt (2007) argues that it has been characteristic of Buddhist reformations throughout history.

14. Jordt 2007; Carrithers 1983. See also Sharf 2015 for a similar argument regarding mindfulness-based practices in medieval China.

15. Thapar 1982:291.

16. Gombrich and Obeyesekere 1988.

17. Queen and King 1996.

18. For the central role played by U Ba Khin in Burma's mass meditation movement, see Houtman 1997.

19. Rahmani and Pagis 2015.

20. Jordt 2007.

21. Jordt 2007:23.

22. U Thwin was knighted by the British for his donations during the colonial British administration (Jordt 2007:27).

23. Spiro 1970; Jordt 2007.

24. Elias (1939) 1982.

25. Gombrich and Obeyesekere 1988:237.

26. Houtman 1990.

27. Cook 2010.

28. Jordt 2007:92; *sasana* means the teaching of the Buddha in Pali.

29. Campbell 2015.

30. Tweed 1992.

31. Tweed 1992:65.

32. Campbell 2015:156.

33. Katz unpublished manuscript describing 1900 Hollywood.

34. Tweed 1992:54.

35. Suzuki spoke at the Theosophical Society in San Francisco in 1903. In 1920 he introduced Zen meditation to English-speaking audiences. See Algeo 2007.

36. Tweed 1992:50.

37. Federman 2015.

38. For the full story of these monks, see Federman 2015.

39. Ibid.

40. Bender 2010. See also Heelas 1996.

41. Heelas 1996.

42. Sigalow 2019.

43. Navon's meditation diary written in 1961 was recently published in Israel (2017).

44. For a social analysis of the decline of Buddhism in India, see Collins 2000:182.

45. See Tweed 2000 for the notion of "cradle Buddhists." For a review of the common distinction between two groups of Buddhists in the US, see Numrich 2003.

46. Cadge 2005.

47. In contrast, in Buddhist temples in the US, household-related rituals are an important part of services alongside meditation classes. See Cadge 2005.

48. Cadge 2005.

49. See Kucinskas 2018 regarding the influence of the reputation of TM on the meditation field at large. Interestingly, sociologists contributed to this negative reputation. See, for example, Bainbridge and Stark 1980, which defines TM as a cult.

50. For a similar process regarding yoga practice, see Jain 2015.

51. Article by Joel Stein, *Time*, October 27, 2003.

52. Kucinskas 2014.

53. Even though meditation is also practiced by a large group of Asians, and studies show that more women than men are involved in meditation practice, white men remain the majority among leaders and teachers. Kucinskas (2018) reports that two thirds of the 101 meditation-related leaders she interviewed in the US were men, 85% were white, 96% had a college degree or higher, and many of them held prestigious jobs. See also Cadge 2004.

54. Davidson et al. 1976.

55. Kabat-Zinn's (2005) program—Mindfulness Based Stress Reduction (MBSR)—follows Zen and vipassana principles of being aware of the present and includes the body scan technique taught by S. N. Goenka.

56. Goleman 2006; Varela et al. 1991.

57. Fleischman's life trajectory is quite similar to those of the other diffusion agents discussed above. Born in 1945, Fleischman studied India intensively at the University of Chicago. In 1970, during medical training at Yale, he visited India in order to study Ayurveda (Indian medicine). After completing his MD, he returned to learn meditation with S. N. Goenka. In 1993 he was honored by the American Psychiatric Association with the Oskar Pfister Award for significant contributions to the field of religion and psychiatry. In 1998 he was asked by Goenka to start teaching vipassana and became a meditation teacher.

58. Cadge 2005.

59. Kucinskas 2014:7.

60. Kucinskas 2018. Johnston (1980) illustrates how TM (Transcendental Meditation) used a similar tactic in the 1970s, and in fact entered many secular institutions until it was suspected of being a cult and its popularity declined.

61. It is important to state that warrior-monks are not a new phenomenon in Buddhist history. Moreover, Buddhist societies cannot necessarily be characterized as nonviolent, as can be seen in the current violence against Muslims in Myanmar, instigated by Buddhist monks.

62. Kucinskas 2018.

63. Shwed 2015.

64. See, for example, Damasio 1999; LeDoux 1996.

65. In Israel, for example, a center called Conscious was recently founded in a private academic institution—the IDC. This center is headed by a neurobiologist and offers mindfulness-based meditation courses that are referred to as "brain training."

66. Strang and Meyer 1993:493.

67. See, for example, the article by vipassana meditation teacher Sharon Salzberg on Oprah Winfrey's website: http://www.oprah.com/spirit/Getting-Started-with-Meditation_1.

68. These new technologies are sometimes criticized as being "Mcmindfulness": meditation turned into a standardized commodity. See for example Purser and Loy 2013; Hyland 2015.

69. See Wilson 2013.

70. For a similar "institutional takeover" in the field of alternative medicine, see Fadlon 2005. As Ferree (2003) has argued, the strategy of reframing a cultural object in order for it to "fit" a new audience may hinder the possibility to elicit social change.

71. For a discussion of these dilemmas within the contemplative movement, see Kucinskas 2018. For the question whether it is important that mindfulness is "Buddhist," see Sharf 2015.

72. Bender 2010.

73. Zen meditation is anchored in Japanese tradition and thus has more affinity with Japanese and Chinese martial arts such as aikido and tai chi. Vipassana, for its part, originated in India and is practiced in Southeast Asia, and thus is more closely related to yoga practice.

74. For Pew survey see Masci and Hackett 2018. For NHIS survey see Clarke et al. 2018. For previous surveys see Barnes et al. 2008; Olano et al. 2015; Cramer et al. 2016.

75. Cadge 2005.

76. For example, vipassana meditation teachers that follow the teachings of the Thai teacher Sirimangalow (a student of the Burmese teacher Mahasi Sayadaw) request that new students

join a fourteen-day silent meditation course and ask them to refrain from eating after noon and sleeping more than six hours a day.

77. Zen and Tibetan meditation can be taught in weekly classes, but extended meditation retreats are considered crucial for the practice. Mindfulness meditation is taught in weekly classes, but the teachers recommend joining vipassana or Zen retreats, and they themselves have experience in such retreats.

78. Cadge 2005.

79. See also books that introduce Goenka's teaching such as Hart 1987 and Hetherington 2011.

80. S. N. Goenka founded the Vipassana Research Institute (VRI), which produces impressive research projects such as digitally encoding the entire Pali canon in its original script, including commentaries and translations to other languages.

81. https://www.dhamma.org/en-US/index, accessed May 8, 2017.

82. This direct anchoring in a mythical past is common to contemporary spiritual circles; see Bender 2010.

83. E.g., Maltby et al. 1999; Masters and Spielmans 2007.

84. Pickert 2014; Wilson 2015.

Chapter Three

1. For example, Brown and Ryan 2003; Kabat-Zinn 2005; Segal et al. 2002.

2. Learning meditation from a book is possible, but such training does not seem to fit a mass audience, and many people prefer to take a class or a course.

3. I am drawing on Csordas's (1993:138) notion "somatic mode of attention," defined as "culturally elaborated ways of attending to and with one's body in surroundings that include the embodied presence of others." See also Csordas 1994.

4. For a similar description of the nonsharing of meditation experiences, see Cook's (2010) ethnography in a Buddhist monastery in Thailand.

5. In the teaching school I studied, there is a norm to separate men and women, as is customary in meditation centers in Southeast Asia.

6. Schutz 1967:142.

7. Schutz 1973:64.

8. In Zen meditation, in contrast, it is common for students to sit in a circle facing one another or in one line all facing the wall. See Preston 1988.

9. Goffman 1981:103.

10. Schutz (1967) and Collins (2004) stress the centrality of a shared object of attention for the production of intersubjectivity. And yet, as we see from the case of the meditation hall, intersubjectivity can also arise from sharing an activity without sharing an object of attention. Elsewhere I term this kind of intersubjectivity "structural intersubjectivity" (Pagis 2010b).

11. For the contagious nature of emotions, see Hatfield, Cacioppo, and Rapson 1994; Collins 2004; Summers-Effler 2010.

12. Collins 2004 analyzed these energies as part of the more general "emotional energy" that people seek in social situations.

13. Katz 1999.

14. Polanyi 1966.

15. Cooley (1902) 1998; Goffman 1967.

Chapter Four

1. According to Pragmatist thought, meaning emerges through action in the world — that is, the meaning of an object or a practice relates to the context in which it is used. Following this perspective, studying the significance given to vipassana involves tracking the social situations and contexts in which meditators chose to use the meditative mode of attention.

2. I am relying here on Polanyi's (1966) notion of "the tacit dimension" and on Merleau-Ponty's (1968) writings on "the invisible" and "inner lining," all referring to the same idea that for everyday action we rely on an embodied background that is concealed from the eyes of others and often also from ourselves.

3. The observation of breath is called *anapana* meditation and is an essential part of vipassana teaching in all schools.

4. This technique, sometimes referred to as "body scan," is central in the teachings of Goenka. While awareness of the body is key in all vipassana techniques, other schools use a more open awareness to body and mind without a systematic bodily scan. In MBSR programs, body scans are taught alongside more open awareness.

5. Some of my field notes were taken during meditation courses, and some were reconstructed after the meditation course, as one of the instructions in meditation retreats is to avoid writing. See methodological appendix.

6. Mead 1934:169.

7. Merleau-Ponty 1968:9.

8. In Gestalt visual examples, such as the duck-rabbit illusion, we cannot see the two figures at the same time. When one figure is pushed to the front, elements from the other figure turn into the background (see Koffka 1935). While Gestalt sees the background-figure as oppositions, a more accurate description would be a gradient in which elements that are pushed to the background gradually fade and remain on the periphery. The fact that we can easily switch back and reverse the direction of attention shows that some awareness of the background's potential to become meaningful again is kept even when it is not the focus of our attention. See Gurwitsch 1964. For sociological applications, see Tavory 2010.

9. Polanyi 1966:19.

10. This shift is discussed by Collins (1982) in his book on the Buddhist notion of not-self. Monks may experience "ultimate" truth of not-self while meditating, but they are asked to return to everyday "conventional" reality that requires tacit assumptions regarding the existence of selves.

11. Rahula 1956; Collins 1994.

12. Turner 1974.

13. Fleischman 2005:17.

14. For the notion "ontological security" as related to late modernity, see Giddens 1991.

15. For a neuroscientific study that illustrates emotional management through mindfulness practice, see Farb et al. 2010.

16. For a recent critique of the growing moral demand to "be in the present," see Whippman 2016.

17. E.g., Damasio 1999; Lowenstein and Lerner 2003.

18. See Goleman 2006. To recall chapter 2, Goleman participated in vipassana retreats, has written on meditation practice, and serves on the board of the Mind and Life Institute.

19. McGrane 1994:194.

20. Katz 1999.

21. See also Berger 2011 on Zen driving.

22. Goffman 1959:235.

23. E.g., Illouz 2007; Madsen 2014; Pagis 2016; Nehring et al. 2016.

24. For the idea of cultures of self (*moi* in French), see Mauss 1985. For Buddhism analyzed from this perspective, see Carrithers 1985.

25. Illouz 2007.

26. Pagis 2009.

Chapter Five

1. Weber 1946:325.

2. Weber distinguished between world rejection and otherworldliness (also referred to as "world fleeing"). World rejection can take place through an active attempt to change the "natural" social order instead of fleeing from it.

3. Weber 1946:330.

4. Bellah (1999:277) translated Weber's notion *Liebesakosmismus* (which was usually translated as acosmic or acosmistic love) into "world-denying love."

5. In the words of the Buddha: "Full of hindrances is household life, a path for the dust of passion. Free as the air is the life of him who has renounced all worldly things. How difficult is it for the man who dwells at home to live the higher life in all its fullness, in all its purity, in all its bright perfection! Let me then cut off my hair and beard, let me clothe myself in the orange-colored robes, and let me go forth from the household life into the homeless state" (Dialogues of the Buddha, pt. 1, 78).

6. See for example the lives of forest monks in Sri Lanka in Carrithers 1983.

7. Wasserman 2016.

8. Gombrich and Obeyesekere 1988.

9. Troeltsch (1922) 1960 in Dumont 1985:98.

10. Houtman 1990; Jordt 2007; Cook 2010.

11. Goffman 1971.

12. Katz 1999:335.

13. Collins 2004.

14. For a sociological understanding of equanimity see Pagis 2015.

15. Students are also encouraged to keep the five Buddhist precepts: to avoid lying, stealing, killing, sexual misconduct, and intoxicants.

16. As Goffman (1959:235) wrote on the presentation of self in everyday life: "Behind many masks and many characters, each performer tends to wear a single look, a naked unsocialized look, a look of concentration, a look of one who is privately engaged in a difficult, treacherous task."

17. Irvine 1999.

18. Klinenberg 2012.

19. For different cultural perspectives on arguments and the expression of anger, see Schiffrin 1984; Simchai and Shoshana 2018.

20. For the Protestant origin of the ideals of self-help and personal responsibility in American culture, see Moskowitz 2001.

21. See for example Race 2014; Chambers and Ulbrick 2016.

22. Rosenberg 2015. Non-Violent Communication was developed in the 80s by the Jewish American clinical psychologist Marshal Rosenberg. The 2015 edition of his book includes a fore-

word by Deepak Chopra, a well-known American (originally from India) self-help writer/guru and advocate of alternative medicine, who bases his teachings on Buddhist and Hindu thought. This is one example among many of the emergence of such hybrid connections.

23. For example, according to nonviolent communication, when my daughter shouts at me or curses me, I should depart from what such cursing indicates about me as a parent, withhold from the "mundane" emotional responses that such cursing invokes, and treat her with empathy.

24. Putnam 2001.

25. Wuthnow 2002.

26. Klinenberg 2012; Levin 2004.

Chapter Six

1. To track these biographies, I use narrated memories of practitioners I either interviewed once or followed with a series of interviews over a period of three years. This methodology has its limitations; see the methodological appendix.

2. Kornfield 2001 and 2003. Jack Kornfield studied with different meditation teachers in Thailand, India, and Burma. His meditation teaching follows the tradition of Mahasi Sayadaw from Burma (see chapter 2). He was one of the founders of the Insight Meditation Society in Massachusetts and the Spirit Rock meditation center in California.

3. Hanh 2006.

4. Leach 1961.

5. As noted in chapter 2, in this school, vipassana meditation is considered the "boot camp" of meditation. As such, it attracts "seekers" searching for self-transformation.

6. The descriptions of self-transformation offered by vipassana practitioners echo what William James ([1902] 1985) called "mystical experiences." However, they are almost completely devoid of mystical or religious content and instead are assigned psychological and therapeutic meaning that is decidedly secular in nature. Only in the virtuosi category of meditation practice do practitioners interpret their "enlightening" experiences using mystical and religious content.

7. For the social logic behind the integrating of moments of personal discovery into a biographical narrative, see Degloma 2014. See also Riesebrodt 2010 for the common structure of conversion narratives.

8. Brooks 2007.

9. Noy 2007.

10. In his work on evangelical Protestantism among men in Caracas, Venezuela, Smilde (2007) illustrates how the initial turn to religion is motivated by a pragmatic search for life improvement, such as overcoming substance abuse or avoiding crime and violence. As with meditation, for some this pragmatic turn leads to a gradual conversion process that ends in adoption of the full belief system and practice.

11. See Pagis 2010a.

12. In Israel, the meditation center in Hazeva where I conducted research was a rented space and thus temporary. Only in 2012 did the Israeli vipassana trust buy land in the north of the country in order to establish a permanent center.

13. See chapter 7 for a discussion of bodily based practices to which people turn in periods of transition.

Chapter Seven

1. This perspective on embodiment characterizes the notion of "habitus" introduced by Bourdieu (1977 and 1984), i.e., a subconscious, bodily ingrained set of dispositions, a "structuring structure" (1984:170) that is out of reach of direct reflection. A similar perspective can be found in Foucault's (1979) highly influential analysis of the emergence of the modern "disciplinary power" which produces "docile bodies." Foucault's later (1986) work on Greek antiquity offers a more complex account of the relation between self and body when discussing the place of "concerns of the body" in the care of the self.

2. Mead 1934; Whiley 1994; Archer 2003.

3. This dual perspective is both shared by interactionists—as can be seen in G. H. Mead's (1934) claim that the body is "habitual" and thus not a "self," or Blumer's (1936) definition of 'non-symbolic interaction"—and by sociologists of culture who draw on Bourdieu's (1977) theorization of the habitus (for example, Vaisey 2009). For ethnographic studies that attempt to bridge this duality in different ways, see for example Wacquant 2004; Crossley 2004; Leschziner and Green 2013; Winchester 2016.

4. Merleau-Ponty 1968.

5. E.g., Bourdieu 1984; Shilling 1991; Vandebroeck 2016.

6. Foucault 1979.

7. Merleau-Ponty 1968.

8. See Merleau-Ponty 1968, especially his discussion on the intertwining/chiasm. For a sociological perspective on the chiasm see Katz 1996.

9. For natural attitude as referring to the taken-for-granted perception of reality, see Husserl 1982; Schutz 1973.

10. Goffman 1974.

11. Kendon 1990:244.

12. I am using here Polanyi's (1968) spatial metaphor of "from" and "to" as related to action and knowledge. According to Polanyi, we act from the proximate to the distal. For example, when I am using a pen, the proximate is the pressure of the pen against my fingers, while the distal is the text I am writing.

13. Goffman 1967; Blumer 1986; Collins 2004.

14. Collins (1982) called this duality of the Buddhist monk "selfless persons" in the sense that while the Buddhist monk experiences not-self on the level of ultimate truth, in conventional truth he is a social person with a role, location, and status in the community of believers.

15. Surak 2017.

16. Katz 1999:37. See also Katz 1988 for aesthetic/sensual transcendence related to crime and deviance.

17. For example, working parents, especially mothers, experience tensions when attempting to manage both the work and the family spheres. See Offer and Schneider 2011.

18. Mead 1934. In Mead's earlier writings (e.g., Mead 1903) we find references to the idea that "the self is directly accessible to reflection" (Joas 1985:87; see also Boyle 1985:73). As Joas writes, this emphasis seems to contradict Mead's known theory of the social genesis of the self. And yet if we take this direct accessibility to be a different kind of self-awareness, an embodied one, then this contradiction may be resolved.

19. Merleau-Ponty (1945) 2002:432.

20. Garfinkel 1967.

21. Kendon 1990:242.

22. Kendon 1990:260.

23. Pagis 2009.

24. Dewey 1969; Csordas 1993; Katz 1999:34.

25. See Glaeser 2006 for a processual perspective that utilizes an ethnographic case study to explain and analyze parallel situations and cases. See also Abbott 2004; Zerubavel 2007.

26. Goffman 1974.

27. See Brown and Leledaki 2010 for a discussion of Eastern moving practices in the West. For the Eastern practice of yoga, see Strauss 2005.

28. Tarr 2011.

29. Katz 1996. Katz uses the scheme of "fall/metamorphosis/narrative reconstruction" to explain the bodily based transcendence that lies in emotions which provides a resource for self-reconstruction. See also Katz 1999.

30. Drawing on Marcell Mauss (1973), Crossley (2004: 38) names these practices "reflexive body techniques," defining them as deliberate modifications done to the body in the service of projection of bodily self to others: "objectifying or thematizing and acting upon our embodied existence, generating a bodily 'me.'" Here I illustrate the other side of these modifications, which are officially oriented to the production of the social "me" but include a private, hidden dimension in which one gains a break, or relaxation, from the gaze of others.

31. For the study of sport and exercising from the perspective of lifestyle, social distinction, and inequality, see for example Bourdieu 1978; Wheaton 2004; Stempel 2005.

32. Ben-Ytzhak 2012.

33. Sudnow 1978:9.

34. Kleiner 2009:238.

35. Kleiner 2009:244.

36. Surak 2017:321.

37. Leaf and Schrock 2011:159.

38. Le Breton 2018.

39. Ibid. See also Chandler 2012.

40. Gooldin 2008:280.

41. Becker 1953.

42. See Gomart and Hennion 1999 for the ways drug users organize their social world so as to create optimal drug experiences.

43. Matza 1969:151.

44. Becker 1963 in Matza 1969:149.

45. Joseph Gordon-Levitt, dir., *Don Jon* (Voltage Pictures 2013).

46. Merleau-Ponty 1968:143.

47. Katz 1996:552.

48. In Collins's (2004) terms, sexual interactions provide emotional energy that produces solidarity between the partners. This solidarity, I suggest, is based on the realization of this mutual dependency, realization of what the other can offer me in terms of my own self-discovery.

49. Collins 2004:226.

50. Aron et al. 2010.

51. Munsch 2015.

52. Collins 2004:304.

53. Goffman 1974.

54. Katz 1999.

55. Macnaughton et al. 2012:462.

56. Laurier et al. 2000.

57. See for example Graham 1987; Laurier et al. 2000; Robinson and Holdsworth 2013.

58. Laurier et al. 2000:296.

59. Graham 1987 in Macnaughton et al. 2012:461.

60. Laurier et al. 2000:299.

61. Graham 1987.

62. For discussion of changes in social contexts of smoking following "smoke-free" regulations, see Hargreaves et al. 2010.

63. Brushing the teeth can be habitual; however, the health recommendation to brush for at least two minutes or to carefully floss the teeth push people to increase focused attention and reduce the habitual, unconscious character of the practice.

64. See Gimlin 2002 for ethnographical investigation of the social spheres of beauty work in American culture.

65. Recently interest in the sociological study of the mechanisms of religious experience has revived, with a focus on embodied practices, emotions, and aesthetics. See, for example, McGuire 2007; McRoberts 2004; Summers-Effler 2010; Tavory and Winchester 2012.

66. Winchester 2008:1768.

67. Lester 2005:178.

68. Daniel 1984:267. See also Haberman 1994.

Methodological Appendix

1. Peirce 1960:1:357.

2. For modes of attention see Csordas 1993.

3. Csordas 1990.

4. For studies that follow such initiation using their own bodies in the field, see Wacquant 2004; Sudnow 1978; O'Connor 2005.

5. See, for example, Klin-Oron's (2014) ethnography of channeling in which he reaches the state of hearing voices while at the same time remaining a complete nonbeliever in terms of the provenance of these voices. See also McRoberts 2004 for a discussion of the methodological problem of studying religious experience. As he writes, the ethnographer who does not share the same set of beliefs as his informants can still experience the aesthetics of religious practices and rituals.

6. Pagis 2010b.

7. Collins 2015.

8. All of the interviews were long, lasting between two and three hours.

9. Katz and Csordas 2003.

References

Abbott, Andrew. 2004. *Methods of Discovery: Heuristics for the Social Sciences.* New York: W. W. Norton.

Algeo, A. S. 2007. "Beatrice Lane Suzuki: An American Theosophist in Japan." *Quest* 95:13–17.

Archer, Margaret S. 2003. *Structure, Agency, and the Internal Conversation.* Cambridge: Cambridge University Press.

Aron, Arthur, Helen E. Fisher, and Irene Tsapelas. 2010. "Infidelity: When, Where, Why." In *The Dark Side of Close Relationships*, edited by Brian H. Spitzberg and William R. Cupach, 195–216. New York: Routledge.

Bainbridge, William S. and Rodney Stark. 1980. "Client and Audience Cults in America." *Sociological Analysis* 41:199–214.

Barnes, P. M., B. Bloom, and R. Nahin. 2008. "Complementary and Alternative Medicine Use among Adults and Children: United States, 2007." *CDC National Health Statistics Report*, no. 2.

Bauman, Zygmunt. 2000. *Liquid Modernity.* Cambridge, UK: Polity.

Becker, Howard S. 1953. "Becoming a Marihuana User." *American Journal of Sociology* 59, no. 3: 235–42.

Becker, Howard S. 1963. *Outsiders.* New York: Free Press.

Bellah, Robert. N. 1999. "Max Weber and World-Denying Love: A Look at the Historical Sociology of Religion." *Journal of the American Academy of Religion* 67, no. 2: 277–304.

Bellah, Robert N., Richard Madsen, William M. Sullivan, Ann Swidler, and Steven M. Tipton. (1985) 2007. *Habits of the Heart: Individualism and Commitment in American Life.* Berkeley: University of California Press.

Bender, Courtney. 2010. *The New Metaphysicals: Spirituality and the American Religious Imagination.* Chicago: University of Chicago Press.

Bender, Courtney, Peggy Levitt, David Shields, and Wendy Cage. 2012. *Religion on the Edge: De-centering and Re-centering the Sociology of Religion.* Oxford: Oxford University Press.

Ben-Ytzhak, Orit. 2012. "חוויות הדחק של גברים ישראלים בתקופת אמצע החיים" [Stress experiences among Israeli men during the midlife period]. MA thesis, Bar Ilan University.

Berger, K. T. 2011. *Zen Driving: Be a Buddha behind the Wheel of Your Automobile.* New York: Ballantine Books.

Berger, Peter, Brigette Berger, and Hansfried Kellner. 1973. *The Homeless Mind: Modernization and Consciousness.* New York: Random House.

Blumer, Herbert. 1936. "Social Attitudes and Nonsymbolic Interaction." *Journal of Educational Sociology* 9:515–23.

Blumer, Herbert. 1986. *Symbolic Interactionism: Perspective and Method.* Berkeley: University of California Press.

Bourdieu, Pierre. 1977. *Outline of a Theory of Practice.* Cambridge: Cambridge University Press.

Bourdieu, Pierre. 1978. "Sport and Social Class." *Information (International Social Science Council)* 17, no. 6: 819–40.

Bourdieu, Pierre. 1984. *Distinction: A Social Critique of the Judgment of Taste.* Cambridge, MA: Harvard University Press.

Boyle, Richard P. 1985. "The Dark Side of Mead: Neuropsychological Foundations for Immediate Experience and Mystical Consciousness." *Studies in Symbolic Interaction* 6:59–78.

Braun, Erik. 2013. *The Birth of Insight: Meditation, Modern Buddhism, and the Burmese Monk Ledi Sayadaw.* Chicago: University of Chicago Press.

Brooks, David. 2007. "The Odyssey Years." *New York Times,* October 9.

Brown, David, and Aspasia Leledaki. 2010. "Eastern Movement Forms as Body-Self Transforming Cultural Practices in the West: Towards a Sociological Perspective." *Cultural Sociology* 4:123–54.

Brown, Kirk Warren, and Richard M. Ryan. 2003. "The Benefits of Being Present: Mindfulness and Its Role in Psychological Well-Being." *Journal of Personality and Social Psychology* 84: 822–48.

Cadge, Wendy. 2004. "Gendered Religious Organizations: The Case of Theravada Buddhism in America." *Gender & Society* 18:777–93.

Cadge, Wendy. 2005. *Heartwood: The First Generation of Theravada Buddhism in America.* Chicago: University of Chicago Press.

Campbell, Colin. 2015. *Easternization of the West: A Thematic Account of Cultural Change in the Modern Era.* New York: Routledge.

Carrithers, Michael. 1983. *The Forest Monks of Sri Lanka: An Anthropological and Historical Study.* Delhi: Oxford University Press.

Carrithers, Michael. 1985. "An Alternative Social History of the Self." In *The Category of the Person: Anthropology, Philosophy, History,* edited by M. Carrithers, S. Collins, and S. Lukes, 234–56. Cambridge: Cambridge University Press.

Chambers, Richard, and Margie Ulbrick. 2016. *Mindful Relationships: Creating Genuine Connections with Ourselves and Others.* Dunedin, NZ: Exisle.

Chandler, Amy. 2012. "Self-Injury as Embodied Emotion Work: Managing Rationality, Emotions and Bodies." *Sociology* 46:442–57.

Clarke, T. C., P. M. Barnes, L. I. Black, B. J. Stussman, and R. L. Nahin. 2018. "Use of Yoga, Meditation, and Chiropractors among U.S. Adults Aged 18 and Over." NCHS Data Brief 325. Hyattsville, MD: National Center for Health Statistics.

Collins, Randall. 2000. *The Sociology of Philosophies: A Global Theory of Intellectual Change.* Cambridge, MA: Harvard University Press.

Collins, Randall. 2004. *Interaction Ritual Chains.* Princeton, NJ: Princeton University Press.

Collins, Randall. 2015. "Visual Micro-sociology and the Sociology of Flesh and Blood: Comment on Wacquant." *Qualitative Sociology* 38:13–17.

Collins, Steven. 1982. *Selfless Persons: Imagery and Thought in Theravada Buddhism.* Cambridge: Cambridge University Press.

Collins, Steven. 1994. "What Are Buddhists Doing When They Deny the Self?" In *Religion and Practical Reason: New Essays in the Comparative Philosophy of Religions*, edited by Frank E. Reynolds and David Tracy, 59–86. Albany: State University of New York Press.

Cook, Joanna. 2010. *Meditation in Modern Buddhism: Renunciation and Change in Thai Monastic Life*. Cambridge: Cambridge University Press.

Cooley, Charles H. (1902) 1998. *On Self and Social Organization*. Chicago: University of Chicago Press.

Cramer, H., H. Hall, M. Leach, J. Frawley, Y. Zhang, B. Leung, J. Adams, and R. Lauche. 2016. "Prevalence, Patterns, and Predictors of Meditation Use among US Adults: A Nationally Representative Survey." *Scientific Reports* 6:36760.

Crossley, Nick. 2004. "The Circuit Trainer's Habitus: Reflexive Body Techniques and the Sociality of the Workout." *Body & Society* 10, no. 1: 37–69.

Csordas, Thomas. J. 1990. "Embodiment as a Paradigm for Anthropology." *Ethos* 18:5–47.

Csordas, Thomas. 1993. "Somatic Modes of Attention." *Cultural Anthropology* 8:135–56.

Csordas, Thomas. 1994. *The Sacred Self: A Cultural Phenomenology of Charismatic Healers*. Berkeley: University of California Press.

Cushman, Philip. 1996. *Constructing the Self, Constructing America: A Cultural History of Psychotherapy*. Boston: Da Capo.

Damasio, Antonio. 1999. *The Feeling of What Happens: Body and Emotion in the Making of Consciousness*. San Diego: Harcourt.

Daniel, Valentine E. 1984. *Fluid Signs: Being a Person the Tamil Way*. Berkeley: University of California Press.

Davidson, R. J., D. J. Goleman, and G. E. Schwartz. 1976. "Attentional and Affective Concomitants of Meditation: A Cross-Sectional Study." *Journal of Abnormal Psychology* 85:235–38.

DeGloma, Thomas. 2014. *Seeing the Light: The Social Logic of Personal Discovery*. Chicago: University of Chicago Press.

Dewey, John. 1969. "Qualitative Thought." In *John Dewey: The Later Works: 1925–1953*, edited by Jo A. Boydston, 243–62. Carbondale: Southern Illinois University Press.

Dumont, Louis. 1985. "A Modified View of Our Origin: The Christian Beginnings of Modern Individualism." In *The Category of the Person: Anthropology, Philosophy, History*, edited by M. Carrithers, S. Collins, and S. Lukes, 93–122. Cambridge: Cambridge University Press.

Elias, Norbert. (1939) 1982. *The Civilizing Process*. Oxford: Blackwell.

Fadlon, Judith. 2005. *Negotiating the Holistic Turn: The Domestication of Alternative Medicine*. New York: SUNY Press.

Farb, Norman A. S., Adam K. Anderson, Helen Mayberg, Jim Bean, Deborah McKeon, and Zindel V. Segal. 2010. "Minding One's Emotions: Mindfulness Training Alters the Neural Expression of Sadness." *Emotion* 10:25–33.

Federman, Asaf. 2015. "Buddhist Meditation in Britain: 1853 and 1945." *Religion* 45:553–72.

Ferree, Myra Marx. 2003. "Resonance and Radicalism: Feminist Framing in the Abortion Debates of the United States and Germany." *American Journal of Sociology* 109:304–44.

Fleischman, Paul R. 2005. *Karma and Chaos: New and Collected Essays on Vipassana Meditation*. Onalaska, WA: Vipassana Research Publications.

Foucault, Michel. 1979. *Discipline and Punish*. New York: Vintage Books.

Foucault, Michel. 1986. *The Care of the Self*, vol. 3 of *The History of Sexuality*. New York: Pantheon.

Foucault, Michel. 1997. "Technologies of the Self." In *Ethics: Subjectivity and Truth*, edited by Paul Rabinow, 223–51. New York: New Press.

Garfinkel, Harold. 1967. *Studies in Ethnomethodology*. Englewood Cliffs, NJ: Prentice Hall.

Gergen, Kenneth J. 1991. *The Saturated Self: Dilemmas of Identity in Modern Life*. New York: Basic Books.

Giddens, Anthony. 1991. *Modernity and Self Identity: Self and Society in the Late Modern Age*. Stanford, CA: Stanford University Press.

Gimlin, Debra. 2002. *Body Work: Beauty and Self-Image in American Culture*. Berkeley: University of California Press.

Glaeser, Andreas. 2006. "An Ontology for the Ethnographic Analysis of Social Processes: Extending the Extended-Case Method." In *The Manchester School: Practice and Ethnographic Praxis in Anthropology*, edited by T. M. S. Evens and Don Handelman. Oxford: Berghahn Books.

Goffman, Erving. 1959. *The Presentation of the Self in Everyday Life*. New York: Doubleday Anchor Books.

Goffman, Erving. 1967. *Interaction Ritual: Essays on Face-to-Face Behavior*. New York: Pantheon Books.

Goffman, Erving. 1971. *Relations in Public*. New York: Basic Books.

Goffman, Erving. 1974. *Frame Analysis: An Essay on the Organization of Experience*. Cambridge, MA: Harvard University Press.

Goffman, Erving. 1981. *Forms of Talk*. Philadelphia: University of Pennsylvania Press.

Goleman, Daniel. 2006. *Emotional Intelligence*. New York: Bantam.

Gombrich, Richard. 1983. "From Monastery to Meditation Center: Lay Meditation in Contemporary Sri Lanka." In *Buddhist Studies Ancient and Modern*, edited by Philip Denwood and Alexander Piatigorsky. London: Curzon.

Gombrich, Richard, and Gananath Obeyesekere. 1988. *Buddhism Transformed: Religious Change in Sri Lanka*. Princeton, NJ: Princeton University Press.

Gomart, Emilie, and Antoine Hennion. 1999. "A Sociology of Attachment: Music Amateurs, Drug Users." *Sociological Review* 47:220–47.

Gooldin, Sigal. 2008. "Being Anorexic." *Medical Anthropology Quarterly* 22:274–96.

Graham, Hilary. 1987. "Women's Smoking and Family Health." *Social Science & Medicine* 25: 47–56.

Gurwitsch, Aron. 1964. *The Field of Consciousness*. Pittsburgh: Duquesne University Press.

Haberman, David L. 1994. *Journey through the Twelve Forests: An Encounter with Krishna*. New York: Oxford University Press.

Hanh, Thich Nhat. 1975. *The Miracle of Mindfulness*. Boston: Beacon.

Hargreaves, Katrina, et al. 2010. "The Social Context of Change in Tobacco Consumption following the Introduction of 'Smokefree' England Legislation: A Qualitative, Longitudinal Study." *Social Science & Medicine* 71:459–66.

Hart, William. 1987. *The Art of Living: Vipassana Meditation as Taught by S. N. Goenka*. San Francisco: Harper & Row.

Hatfield, Elaine, John T. Cacioppo, and Richard L. Rapson. 1994. *Emotional Contagion*. Cambridge: Cambridge University Press.

Heelas, Paul. 1996. *The New Age Movement: Religion, Culture and Society in the Age of Postmodernity*. Oxford: Blackwell.

Hetherington, Ian. 2011. *Realizing Change: Vipassana Meditation in Action*. Seattle: Vipassana Research Publications.

Houtman, Gustaaf. 1990. "Traditions of Buddhist Practice in Burma." PhD thesis, London University.

Houtman, Gustaaf. 1997. "Beyond the Cradle and past the Grave: The Biography of Burmese Meditation Master U Ba Khin." In *Sacred Biography in the Buddhist Traditions of South and Southeast Asia*, edited by Juliane Schober, 310–44. Honolulu: University of Hawai'i Press.

Husserl, Edmond. 1982. *Ideas Pertaining to a Pure Phenomenology and to a Phenomenological Philosophy: First Book, General Introduction to a Pure Phenomenology*. Boston: Kluwer Academic.

Hyland, Terry. 2015. "McMindfulness in the Workplace: Vocational Learning and the Commodification of the Present Moment." *Journal of Vocational Education & Training* 67:219–34.

Ignatow, Gabriel. 2007. "Theories of Embodied Knowledge: New Directions for Cultural and Cognitive Sociology?" *Journal for the Theory of Social Behaviour* 37, no. 2: 115–35.

Illouz, Eva. 2007. *Cold Intimacies: The Making of Emotional Capitalism*. Cambridge, UK: Polity.

Irvine, Leslie. 1999. *Codependent Forevermore: The Invention of Self in a Twelve Step Group*. Chicago: University of Chicago Press.

Jain, Andrea. 2015. *Selling Yoga: From Counterculture to Pop Culture*. New York: Oxford University Press.

James, William. (1902) 1985. *The Varieties of Religious Experience*. Cambridge, MA: Harvard University Press.

Joas, Hans. 1985. *G. H. Mead: A Contemporary Re-examination of His Thought*. Cambridge, UK: Polity.

Johnston, Hank. 1980. "The Marketed Social Movement: A Case Study of the Rapid Growth of TM." *The Pacific Sociological Review* 23, no. 3: 333–54.

Jordt, Ingrid. 2007. *Burma's Mass Lay Meditation Movement: Buddhism and the Cultural Construction of Power*. Athens: Ohio University Press.

Kabat-Zinn, Jon. 2005. *Coming to Our Senses: Healing Ourselves and the World through Mindfulness*. New York: Hyperion.

Katz, Jack. 1988. *Seductions of Crime: Moral and Sensual Attractions in Doing Evil*. New York: Basic Books.

Katz, Jack. 1996. "The Social Psychology of Adam and Eve." *Theory and Society* 25, no. 4: 545–82.

Katz, Jack. 1999. *How Emotions Work*. Chicago: University of Chicago Press.

Katz, Jack, and Thomas J. Csordas. 2003. "Phenomenological Ethnography in Sociology and Anthropology." *Ethnography* 4:275–88.

Kendon, Adam. 1990. *Conducting Interaction: Patterns of Behavior in Focused Encounters*. Cambridge: Cambridge University Press.

Kleiner, S. 2009. "Thinking with the Mind, Syncing with the Body: Ballet as Symbolic and Nonsymbolic Interaction." *Symbolic Interaction* 32:236–59.

Klinenberg, Eric. 2012. *Going Solo: The Extraordinary Rise and Surprising Appeal of Living Alone*. New York: Penguin.

Klin-Oron, Adam. 2014. "How I Learned to Channel: Epistemology, Phenomenology, and Practice in a New Age Course." *American Ethnologist* 41:635–47.

Koffka, K. 1935. *Gestalt Psychology*. New York: Harcourt, Brace & World.

Kornfield, Jack. 2001. *After the Ecstasy, the Laundry: How the Heart Grows Wise on the Spiritual Path*. New York: Bantam.

Kornfield, Jack. 2003. *A Path with Heart: A Guide through the Perils and Promises of Spiritual Life*. New York: Bantam.

Kucinskas, Jaime. 2014. "The Unobtrusive Tactics of Religious Movements." *Sociology of Religion* 75:537–50.

Kucinskas, Jaime. 2018. *The Mindful Elite: Mobilizing from the Inside Out*. Oxford: Oxford University Press.

Lasch, Christopher. 1980. *The Culture of Narcissism: American Life in an Age of Diminishing Expectations*. New York: Warner Books.

Laurier, Eric, Linda McKie, and Norma Goodwin. 2000. "Daily and Lifecourse Contexts of Smoking." *Sociology of Health & Illness* 22:289–309.

Leach, Edmund R. 1961. "Two Essays concerning the Symbolic Representation of Time." In *Rethinking Anthropology*, 124–36. London: Athlone.

Leaf, Margaret, and Douglas P. Schrock, D. 2011. "'What I Had to Do to Survive': Self-Injurers' Bodily Emotion Work." In *Embodied Resistance: Challenging the Norms, Breaking the Rules*, edited by Chris Bobel and Samantha Kwan, 156–66. Nashville: Vanderbilt University Press.

Le Breton, David. 2018. "Understanding Skin-Cutting in Adolescence: Sacrificing a Part to Save the Whole." *Body & Society* 24:33–54.

Leder, Drew. 1990. *The Absent Body*. Chicago: University of Chicago Press.

LeDoux, Joseph. 1996. *The Emotional Brain: The Mysterious Underpinnings of Emotional Life*. New York: Simon & Schuster.

Leschziner, Vanina, and Adam Green. 2013. "Thinking about Food and Sex: Deliberate Cognition in the Routine Practices of a Field." *Sociological Theory* 31:116–44.

Lester, Rebecca J. 2005. *Jesus in Our Wombs: Embodying Modernity in a Mexican Convent*. Berkeley: University of California Press.

Levin, Irene. 2004. "Living Apart Together: A New Family Form." *Current Sociology* 52:223–40.

Lizardo, Omar. 2017. "Improving Cultural Analysis: Considering Personal Culture in its Declarative and Nondeclarative Modes." *American Sociological Review* 82:88–115.

Lowenstein, G., and J. S. Lerner. 2003. "The Role of Affect in Decision Making." In *Handbook of Affective Science*, edited by R. Davidson, K. Scherer, and H. Goldsmith, 619–42. New York: Oxford University Press.

Macnaughton, Jane, Susana Carro-Ripalda, and Andrew Russell. 2012. "'Risking Enchantment': How Are We to View the Smoking Person?" *Critical Public Health* 22:455–69.

Madsen, Ole Jacob. 2014. *The Therapeutic Turn: How Psychology Altered Western Culture*. New York: Routledge.

Maltby, John, Christopher Alan Lewis, and Liza Day. 1999. "Religious Orientation and Psychological Well-being: The Role of the Frequency of Personal Prayer." *British Journal of Health Psychology* 4: 363–378.

Masci, David, and Conard Hackett. 2018. "Meditation Is Common across Many Religious Groups in the U.S." *FactTank* (Pew Research Center), January 2, 2018. http://pewrsr.ch/21HcoHC.

Masters, Kevin S., and Glen I. Spielmans. 2007. "Prayer and Health: Review, Meta-analysis, and Research Agenda." *Journal of Behavioral Medicine* 30: 329–338.

Matza, David, 1969. *Becoming Deviant*. Englewood Cliffs. NJ: Prentice Hall.

Mauss, Marcel. 1973. "Techniques of the Body." *Economy and Society* 2:70–88.

Mauss, Marcel. 1985. "A Category of the Human Mind." In *The Category of the Person: Anthropology, Philosophy, History*, edited by M. Carrithers, S. Collins, and S. Lukes, 1–25. Cambridge: Cambridge University Press.

McGrane, Bernard. 1994. *The Un-TV and the 10 Mph Car: Experiments in Personal Freedom and Everyday Life*. Fort Bragg, CA: Small Press.

McGuire, Meredith. 2007. "Embodied Practices: Negotiation and Resistance." In *Everyday Religion: Observing Modern Religious Lives*, edited by Nancy T. Ammerman, 187–200. Oxford: Oxford University Press.

McRoberts, Omar M. 2004. "Beyond Mysterium Tremendum: Thoughts toward an Aesthetic Study of Religious Experience." *Annals of the American Academy of Political and Social Science* 595:190–203.

Mead, George Herbert. 1903. "The Definition of the Psychical." *Decennial Publications of the University of Chicago*, 1st ser., 3:77–112.

Mead, George Herbert. 1934. *Mind Self and Society: From the Standpoint of a Social Behaviorist.* Chicago: The University of Chicago press.

Merleau-Ponty, Maurice. (ca. 1945) 2002. *Phenomenology of Perception.* London: Routledge.

Merleau-Ponty, Maurice. 1968. *The Visible and the Invisible.* Evanston, IL: Northwestern University Press.

Moskowitz, Eva S. 2001. *In Therapy We Trust: America's Obsession with Self-Fulfillment.* Baltimore: John Hopkins University.

Munsch, Christin L. 2015. "Her Support, His Support: Money, Masculinity, and Marital Infidelity." *American Sociological Review* 80:469–95.

Navon, Yzhak. 2017. יומן מדיטציה: מחוויותיו של הנשיא החמישי במנזר בודהיסטי בבורמה [Meditation Diary: The fifth president's experiences at a Buddhist monastery in Burma]. Tel Aviv: Hadkeren.

Nehring, D., E. Alvarado, E. C. Hendriks, and D. Kerrigan. 2016. *Transnational Popular Psychology and the Global Self-Help Industry.* London: Palgrave Macmillan.

Noy, Chaim. 2007. *Narrative Community: Voices of Israeli Backpackers.* Detroit: Wayne State University Press.

Numrich, Paul David. 2003. "Two Buddhisms Further Considered." *Contemporary Buddhism* 4:55–78.

O'Connor, Erin. 2005. "Embodied Knowledge: The Experience of Meaning and the Struggle towards Proficiency in Glassblowing." *Ethnography* 6:183–204.

Offer, Shira, and Barbara Schneider. 2011. "Revisiting the Gender Gap in Time-Use Patterns: Multitasking and Well-Being among Mothers and Fathers in Dual-Earner Families." *American Sociological Review* 76:809–33.

Olano, Henry A., Diana Kachan, Stacey L. Tannenbaum, Ashwin Mehta, Debra Annane, and David J. Lee. 2015. "Engagement in Mindfulness Practices by US Adults: Sociodemographic Barriers." *Journal of Alternative and Complementary Medicine* 21:100–102.

Pagis, Michal. 2009. "Embodied Self-Reflexivity." *Social Psychology Quarterly* 72:265–83.

Pagis, Michal. 2010a. "From Abstract Concepts to Experiential Knowledge: Embodying Enlightenment in a Meditation Center." *Qualitative Sociology* 33:469–89.

Pagis, Michal. 2010b. "Producing Intersubjectivity in Silence: An Ethnography of Meditation Practices." *Ethnography* 11:309–28.

Pagis, Michal. 2015. "Evoking Equanimity: Silent Interaction Rituals in Vipassana Meditation Retreats." *Qualitative Sociology* 38:39–56.

Pagis, Michal. 2016. "Fashioning Futures: Life-Coaching and the Self-Made Identity Paradox." *Sociological Forum* 31:1083–103.

Peirce, Charles S. 1960. *Collected Papers.* Cambridge, MA: Harvard University Press.

Pickert, Kate. 2014. "The Mindful Revolution." *Time*, February 3, 34–48.

Polanyi, Michael. 1966. *The Tacit Dimension.* London: Routledge.

Preston, David 1988. *The Social Organization of Zen Practice: Constructing Transcultural Reality.* Cambridge: Cambridge University Press.

Purser, Ron, and David Loy. 2013. "Beyond McMindfulness." *Huffington Post* 1, no. 7: 13.

Putnam, Robert D. 2001. *Bowling Alone: The Collapse and Revival of American Community.* New York: Simon & Schuster.

Queen, Christopher S., and Sallie B. King. 1996. *Engaged Buddhism: Buddhist Liberation Movements in Asia*. New York: SUNY Press.

Race, Kristin. 2014. *Mindful Parenting*. New York: St. Martin's.

Rahmani, Sara, and Michal Pagis. 2015. "Vipassana Meditation as Taught by S. N. Goenka." World Religions and Spirituality Project, dir. David Bromely, https://wrldrels.org/2016/10/08/vipassana-meditation/.

Rahula, Walpola. 1959. *What the Buddha Taught*. New York: Grove Place.

Ricoeur, Paul. 1981. *Hermeneutics and the Human Sciences: Essays on Language, Action, and Interpretation*. Cambridge: Cambridge University Press.

Rieff, Philip. 1966. *The Triumph of the Therapeutic*. Chicago: University of Chicago Press.

Riesebrodt, Martin. 2010. *The Promise of Salvation: A Theory of Religion*. Chicago: University of Chicago Press.

Robinson, Jude, and Clare Holdsworth. 2013. "'They Don't Live in My House Every Day': How Understanding Lives Can Aid Understandings of Smoking." *Contemporary Drug Problems* 40:47–70.

Rosenberg, Marshall. 2015. *Nonviolent Communication, a Language of Life: Life-Changing Tools for Healthy Relationships*. Encinitas, CA: PuddleDancer.

Schutz, Alfred. 1967. *The Phenomenology of the Social World*. Evanston, IL: Northwestern University Press.

Schutz, Alfred. 1973. *Structures of Lifeworld*. Evanston, IL: Northwestern University Press.

Schiffrin, Deborah. 1984. "Jewish Argument as Sociability." *Language in Society* 13:311–35.

Segal, Zindel V., J. Mark G. Williams, and John D. Teasdale. 2002. *Mindfulness-Based Cognitive Therapy for Depression: A New Approach to Preventing Relapse*. New York: Guilford.

Shalin, Dmitri N. 2007. "Signing in the Flesh: Notes of Pragmatist Hermeneutics." *Sociological Theory* 25:193–224.

Sharf, Robert H. 1993. "The Zen of Japanese Nationalism." *History of Religions* 33:1–43.

Sharf, Robert H. 1995. "Buddhist Modernism and the Rhetoric of Meditative Experience." *Numen* 42:229–83.

Sharf, Robert H. 2015. "Is Mindfulness Buddhist? (and Why It Matters)." *Transcultural Psychiatry* 52:470–84.

Shilling, Chris. 1991. "Educating the Body: Physical Capital and the Production of Social Inequalities." *Sociology* 25:653–72.

Shwed, Uri. 2016. "סיולים על מפת המדע: מבט סיינטומטרי על תרגום מושגים מדעיים" [Journeys on the map of knowledge: A scientometric view on the translation of scientific concepts]. In *Beyond the Consulting room: Psychological Discourse in Contemporary Culture*, edited by José Brunner and Galia Plotkin Amrami, 301–27. Tel Aviv: Resling.

Sigalow, Emily. 2019. *American JUBU: Jews, Buddhists, and Religious Change in the United States*. Princeton, NJ: Princeton University Press.

Simchai, Dalit, and Avihu Shoshana. 2018. "The Ethic of Spirituality and the Non-angry Subject." *Ethos* 46:115–33.

Simmel, Georg. 2011. *On Individuality and Social Forms*. Chicago: University of Chicago Press.

Smilde, David. 2013. *Reason to Believe: Cultural Agency in Latin American Evangelicalism*. Berkeley: University of California Press.

Spiro, Melford E. 1970. *Buddhism and Society: The Great Tradition and Its Burmese Vicissitudes*. New York: Harper & Row.

Stempel, Carl. 2005. "Adult Participation Sports as Cultural Capital: A Test of Bourdieu's Theory of the Field of Sports." *International Review for the Sociology of Sport* 40:411–32.

Strang, David, and John W. Meyer. 1993. "Institutional Conditions for Diffusion." *Theory and Society* 22:487–511.

Strauss, Sarah. 2005. *Positioning Yoga: Balancing Acts across Cultures.* London: Bloomsbury.

Sudnow, David. 1978. *Ways of the Hand: The Organization of Improvised Conduct.* Cambridge, MA: MIT Press.

Summers-Effler, Erika. 2010. *Laughing Saints and Righteous Heroes: Emotional Rhythms in Social Movement Groups.* Chicago: University of Chicago Press.

Surak, Kristin. 2017. "Rupture and Rhythm: A Phenomenology of National Experiences." *Sociological Theory* 35:312–33.

Tarr, Jennifer. 2011. "Educating with the Hands: Working on the Body/Self in Alexander Technique." *Sociology of Health & Illness* 33:252–65.

Tavory, Iddo. 2010. "Of Yarmulkes and Categories: Delegating Boundaries and the Phenomenology of Interactional Expectation." *Theory and Society* 39:49–68.

Tavory, Iddo, and Daniel Winchester. 2012. "Experiential Careers: The Routinization and Deroutinization of Religious Life." *Theory and Society* 41:351–73.

Thapar, Romila. 1982. "The Householder and the Renouncer in the Brahmanical and Buddhist Traditions." In *Way of Life: King, Householder, Renouncer; Essays in Honor of Louis Dumont,* edited by Madan T.N., 274–319. New Delhi: Vikas.

Troeltsch, Ernst. (1922) 1960. *The Social Teaching of the Christian Churches.* New York: Harper Torchbooks.

Turner, Victor. 1974. "Liminal to Liminoid, in Play, Flow, and Ritual: An Essay in Comparative Symbology." *Rice Institute Pamphlet—Rice University Studies* 60, no. 3: 43–92.

Tweed, Thomas A. 1992. *The American Encounter with Buddhism, 1844–1912: Victorian Culture and the Limits of Dissent.* Bloomington: Indiana University Press.

Tweed, Thomas A. 2002. "Who Is a Buddhist? Night-Stand Buddhists and Other Creatures," In *Westward Dharma: Buddhism beyond Asia,* edited by Charles S. Prebish and Martin Baumann, 17–33. Berkeley: University of California Press.

Vaisey, Stephen. 2009. "Motivation and Justification: A Dual-Process Model of Culture in Action." *American Journal of Sociology* 114:1675–715.

Vandebroeck, Dieter. 2016. *Distinctions in the Flesh: Social Class and the Embodiment of Inequality.* New York: Routledge.

Varela, F., E. Thompson, and E. Rosch. 1991. *The Embodied Mind: Cognitive Science and Human Experience.* Cambridge, MA: MIT Press.

Vygotsky, L. S. 1962. *Thought and Language.* Cambridge, MA: MIT Press.

Wacquant, Loic J. D. 2004. *Body & Soul: Notebooks of an Apprentice Boxer.* Oxford: Oxford University Press.

Wacquant, Loic J. D. 2015. "For a Sociology of Flesh and Blood." *Qualitative Sociology* 38:1–11.

Wasserman, Nava. 2015. זוגיות בחסידות גור :מימי לא קראתי לאשתי [I have never called my wife: Marital relations in Gur Hasidism]. Sde Boker: Ben Gurion University Press.

Weber, Max. 1946. "Religious Rejections of the World and Their Directions." In *From Max Weber: Essays in Sociology,* edited by H. H. Gerth and C. Wright Mills, 323–59. Oxford: Oxford University Press.

Weber, Max. 1958a. *The Religion of India: The Sociology of Hinduism and Buddhism.* Glencoe, IL: Free Press.

Weber, Max. 1958b. "Science as a Vocation." *Daedalus* 87, no. 1: 111–34.

Weigert, Andrew J., and Viktor Gecas. 2003. "Self." In *Handbook of Symbolic Interactionism,* edited by Larry T. Reynolds and Nancy J. Herman-Kinney, 267–88. Walnut Creek, CA: Alta-Mira.

Wheaton, Belinda. 2004. *Understanding Lifestyle Sport: Consumption, Identity and Difference.* New York: Routledge.

Whippman, Ruth. 2016. "Actually, Let's Not Be in the Moment." *New York Times*, November 26.

Wiley, Norbert. 1994. *The Semiotic Self.* Chicago: University of Chicago Press.

Wilson, Jeff. 2013. *Mindful America: Meditation and the Mutual Transformation of Buddhism and American Culture.* Oxford: Oxford University Press.

Winchester, Daniel. 2008. "Embodying the Faith: Religious Practice and the Making of a Muslim Moral Habitus." *Social Forces* 86:1753–80.

Winchester, Daniel. 2016. "A Hunger for God: Embodied Metaphor as Cultural Cognition in Action." *Social Forces* 95:585–606.

Wuthnow, Robert. 2002. *Loose Connections: Joining Together in America's Fragmented Communities.* Cambridge, MA: Harvard University Press.

Zerubavel, Eviatar. 2007. "Generally Speaking: The Logic and Mechanics of Social Pattern Analysis." *Sociological Forum* 22:131–45.

Index

The letter *f* following a page number denotes a table.